Bed & Breakfast
GETAWAYS *from*
CLEVELAND

Doris Larson

GRAY & COMPANY, PUBLISHERS
CLEVELAND

Gray & Company, Publishers
1588 E. 40th Street
Cleveland, Ohio 44103
(216) 431-2665
www.grayco.com

This guide was prepared on the basis of the author's best knowledge at the time of publication. However, because of constantly changing conditions beyond the author's control, the author disclaims any responsibility for the accuracy and completeness of the information in this guide. Users of this guide are cautioned not to place undue reliance upon the validity of the information contained herein and to use this guide at their own risk.

Maps of Canada © 1999 Government of Canada with permission from Natural Resources Canada.

Photographs courtesy of the bed and breakfasts or taken by the author except for the following:
p. 57, Inn at Honey Run, by Nate Vanetta
p. 60, Miller Haus, by Doyle Yoder
p. 91, Whispering Pines B&B, by Tim Ryan
p. 228, 229, Book Inn, by George Gardner
p. 239, 240, Inn at Willow Pond, Nancy Rotenberg

Printed in the United States of America

10 9 8 7 6 5 4 3 2 1

ISBN 1-886228-38-8

CONTENTS

Acknowledgments

I am grateful to the following people:

Editor Karen Fuller for gently nurturing this book;

Hannelore Hahn, founder of the International Women's Writing Guild, for providing a place for women writers to meet and the support of those IWWG friends around the world;

The members of my writing group for their unfailing support and cheer;

Herbert L. Hiller for his mentoring;

Edward Stinson and Alice McVetty Vars for sharing their expertise in antiques;

Kathleen McAteer for answering my many gardening questions;

My children, Karen Stinson and Carl Larson, and my granddaughters, Mary and Lydia Stinson, for their patience with my schedule and absences this past year;

And especially to my husband, Gerald, for giving me the space and time to write and for keeping the home fires burning.

INTRODUCTION

*"Old buildings are not ours. They belong partly
to those who built them and partly to the generations
of mankind who are to follow us."*

— JOHN RUSKIN

It all started with a book—a book on country inns I gave my husband one Christmas. We both read it and loved the idea of getting away to stay in a house with some history. A trip to New England gave us the first opportunity to explore these hostelries, and I was hooked. Later, traveling with children, we stayed at family-friendly motels, but I continued to seek out bed and breakfasts and country inns. On our trips, I would walk past a Victorian in a small town and stop to talk to the innkeeper, fascinated by the architecture and the history of the place.

A position as writer and reviewer for the Ohio Bed and Breakfast Association took me into many accommodations, and I came to realize that those who rescue old houses are saving America's architecture. While visiting a beautifully restored Queen Anne in a college town, I noticed a paved parking lot next to the bed and breakfast. It was a pleasant residential area, and I asked what used to be there. The answer: another elegant late Victorian house. I became aware of what was lost and appreciative of these preservationists-turned-innkeepers. There's a term VOV—vacant, open, and vandalized—that describes the condition in which many of these properties were found. As you read this guide to bed and breakfasts and inns, you'll learn the kinds of problems many innkeepers faced in renovating and restoring their properties.

As I traveled Ohio and nearby states in researching the book, I talked to guests as well as innkeepers. When asked why they chose to stay in a bed and breakfast or inn, their answers varied. I heard, "We stay because of the infinite variety of dwellings, the rural charm, the small-town feeling, the friendliness, the peace and quiet." Others told me that they grew up in the ranch houses, split-levels, and Colonials in the subdivisions that sprawled across our country and just want to go back to stay in a house like Grandma's. They like to go to sleep under a puffy duvet, tucked under the eaves, and wake to the delicious smells of breakfast being cooked by someone else. Pat Hardy, co-executive director of the Professional Association of Innkeepers International, says that thirty percent of inn guests say they would like to own a bed and breakfast.

Along the way, I discovered that the profile of inn-goers is changing. These accommodations are no longer solely destinations for romantic weekenders; midweek business travelers, women traveling solo, and family reunion groups are discovering the pleasures of staying in an inn. The innkeeper group is changing as well. I found younger innkeepers, including some raising families at their inn.

This book is based on personal visits with overnight stays whenever possible. I traveled on my own during the week and with my husband, Jerry, on weekends. None of the accommodations paid to be in the guide. My heartfelt thanks go to those innkeepers who patiently answered my questions, gave me the run of the place, and in the exchange became friends. I salute you—preservationists, urban pioneers, keepers of the inn—for saving America's treasures.

— Doris Larson

How to Use this Book

INN OR BED AND BREAKFAST? By formal definition, a B&B offers an overnight stay and breakfast, while a country inn has more guest rooms, includes breakfast, and serves dinner at least four or more nights a week. Of course, you will find some B&Bs that offer the amenities of an inn, and some places that are called inns, but actually operate more like B&Bs; the terms are almost interchangeable. The one thing I can say for sure is that it's great fun experimenting to find out which are really which. I've noted the inns and B&Bs in this book that are members of the Independent Innkeepers' Association (IIA), which means they meet certain standards of quality; for more information about the IIA, call (800) 344-5244.

CHOOSING YOUR GETAWAY: Each inn and bed and breakfast in this book has its own personality. Some hearken back to the stately Victorian age; some are like ranches or farms, appealing to outdoorsy types; still others offer a sophisticated destination in a modern, artsy environment.

How do you decide which one to visit? Consider, first of all, your mood. As you read the descriptions in this book, note the inns that strike your fancy. Some are perfect for a themed holiday getaway, some for outdoor adventure, others for strolling, shopping, and discovering quaint towns.

Think about destination. Do you want to visit someplace really close to home for a quick overnight stay, or do you need to put some serious miles between yourself and your own neighborhood? The inns in this book are grouped into chapters to help you find destinations close to Cleveland—Amish Country, The Western Reserve, The Heartland—and places farther away—Worth the Drive. Plus, I've organized some inns according to their specialty—Lake Erie Stays, College Town Stays, City Stays, and Theme Inns.

MORE HELP CHOOSING—THE IDEA INDEX: In addition to the standard name and location indexes, I've included an Idea Index at the back of this book. Looking for an inn that offers horseback riding or spa services? How about one with a golf course nearby, or one that is perfect for a secluded winter getaway? The Idea Index can help you choose an inn based on the type of experience you're looking for.

Keep in mind that children are not welcome at many inns. But there are plenty of places that welcome children and are perfect for a family getaway. Check the Idea Index for suggestions.

Here's another idea: Almost every bed and breakfast nowadays welcomes business travelers; many even offer corporate discounts. The Idea Index will guide you to the ones that provide conference and meeting rooms, but just about every inn in the book is equipped to offer excellent accommodations for business travelers. So next time you're on the road for business, add a little pleasure by staying at a bed and breakfast—call an inn near your destination and ask about corporate specials.

And once you've made a decision . . .

DETAILS, DETAILS, DETAILS-THE GRAY BOX: I've gathered all the information you'll need to know—rates and payment, types of meals served, and special considerations such as if the inn is handicapped accessible and if pets are allowed. You'll find this information in the gray boxes at the beginning of each inn's description.

The rates for the inns are listed in ranges to give you a general idea of what you can expect to pay for an overnight accommodation. I used the following scale:

$ = under $65
$$ = $65–$90
$$$ = $90–$125
$$$$ = $125+

WHAT TO EXPECT: When you make your reservation, be sure to ask about specials. There are a variety of two-night stays at some of the best inns— quite a deal.

Also, don't be afraid to talk with the innkeepers about the type of stay you'd prefer. Some guests like to sleep in and enjoy a private continental breakfast on the porch, and some get up bright and early to sit with other guests in the dining room, enjoying the aroma from the kitchen. Let the innkeepers know your style, and they'll be happy to accommodate you.

If you've never stayed at an inn before, you're in for a treat. At any bed and breakfast you choose, you'll be a welcome guest. Explore the house and grounds, make yourself comfortable in the common sitting rooms and talk with other guests, or take a book out to the porch and spend some quiet time alone. And when you're ready to venture out, ask the innkeepers for suggestions. I've discovered some of my favorite places this way.

Bed & Breakfast
Breakfast
GETAWAYS *from*
CLEVELAND

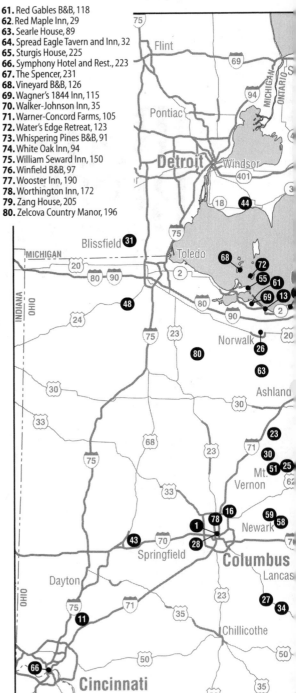

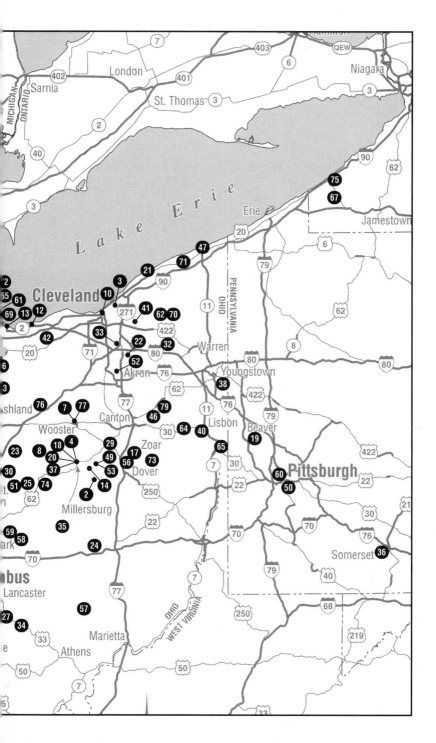

Chapter 1

NEARBY—THE WESTERN RESERVE

*In the villages and towns of the Western Reserve, reminders
of the New England of the early settlers—a village green,
white steepled churches, and simple houses of Greek Revival
or Federal design—can be found today.*

The need for streams and rivers to generate power dictated the location of mill towns in this area, and transplanted New Englanders were delighted to find sugar maple forests here. The green campuses of early seminaries and academies remain, and students in the twenty-first century walk the same well-worn paths. A hostelry from the canal era welcomes travelers with food and lodging as it did in the mid-1800s.

With the Western Reserve's reputation for snowy winters, cross-country skiing is popular during the cold months. In the summer, theater presentations and ice cream socials on the green await visitors. Festivals abound with events centering on crafts and antiques. Century Village in Burton and Hale Homestead near Bath provide a chance to tour early villages.

Home to the fourth-largest Amish population, this area offers the well-crafted products visitors search for—baskets, quilts, and furniture. May events include an Amish benefit auction in Middlefield and a Civil War encampment at Century Village. Stop at a farm stand or pick your own produce on the back roads.

In any season, it's a pleasure to come upon one of these communities that usually include simple white dwellings and a beautifully proportioned church grouped around a green or town square. For a closer look at the architectural details of the houses, take time for a self-guided walking tour.

When booking a stay in this area, take your pick from accommodations reviewed in this chapter—Greek Revival homes, an early tavern, a Victorian townhouse, a new inn designed in the Western Reserve style, a "Painted Lady" from the turn of the century, and an 1930s Tudor.

Fitzgerald's Irish Bed and Breakfast

Irish music fills the air and the guest rooms carry Irish names.

Debra and Tom Fitzgerald, Innkeepers
47 Mentor Ave..
Painesville, OH
(440) 639-0845
www.geocities.com/fitzgeraldsbnb

RATES & RESERVATIONS:
Season: Year round;
Rates: $$;
Specials: $10/night discount for
3 or more consecutive nights;
Reservations required;
Check, Visa, MC accepted

ACCOMMODATIONS: 3 rooms w/bath

AMENITIES: Internet, air cond.,
satellite TV

MEALS: Full breakfast on weekends,
expanded continental during the
week, snacks

SPECIAL CONSIDERATIONS:
Not fully handicapped accessible;
Parking available: Lot, on street

"Cead Mile Failte: One hundred thousand welcomes to our home and table," reads the blessing on the dining table placemats at Fitzgerald's Irish Bed and Breakfast in Painesville's historic district. Think Irish when you visit this bed and breakfast—owners/innkeepers Tom and Debra Fitzgerald have many touches of the Emerald Isle in their home. Irish music fills the air, and the guest rooms carry Irish names—Mayo, Dublin, and Old Bushmill's Distillery. Debra prepares a traditional Irish breakfast on weekends featuring fried eggs, bangers, rashers, fried tomatoes, and mushrooms. Tom loves to bake, and the brown bread served at breakfast is his contribution; Irish tea and Tom's shortbread cookies are served at tea time.

The Fitzgeralds, distance runners who participate in marathons, discovered this house while out on a Sunday run. They stopped just to take a look and ended up buying it eight weeks later. A small album of before-and-after pictures tells the story of this structure, which had stood unoccupied for five years. Overgrown with shrubbery, it was in need of a new furnace and electrical and plumbing systems. The Fitzgeralds spent a year and half bringing the house back, completely gutting the kitchen and their own quarters. Mustard-colored kitchen cabinets were replaced with mellow dark wood, and the countertops are now oatmeal-hued. A center island and many built-in features make it a gourmet cook's delight.

The architectural style of this house, built in 1937, appears to be a combination of French Revival (with a conical entrance tower and steeply pitched roof) and Tudor styling (with a half-timbered exterior). There's a wonderful Old World feel to the interior, with Oriental rugs against polished wood floors and dark beams contrasting with creamy plaster walls. On my first walk through the house, I discovered that the tower provides a delightful turret room at the top of the stairs. Take time to sit awhile in the rocking chair and survey the rooms spread out below. Royal Doulton character jugs line the mantel of the 11-foot flagstone fireplace, and an elegant chandelier is centered over a comfortable grouping of a sofa, wingback chairs, and occasional chairs. Tom's mother made the ecru lace curtains on the small-paned windows. When I visited, the Fitzgeralds had just returned from two weeks in Ireland and brought mementos back including a Bodhran, a traditional Irish drum. The dining room walls are enlivened by the couple's collection of Dean Morrissey's whimsical art. Guests are invited to use the library/TV room as well as a screened-in porch. I took my second cup of coffee out to the porch and found the well landscaped backyard a welcome refuge, with brick pathways and birds flitting between the feeders and bird bath.

I love the little unexpected twists and turns, sloping ceilings, and huge closets in a house of this era. Stairs lead from the living room to the turret landing. A few more steps take you to the Mayo Room, with its queen four-poster and an adjoining bath that the Fitzgeralds created out of a good-size closet. Step up to the Dublin Room on the next level, with its charming leaf-print wallpaper, a sleigh bed, and a view of the garden below. Winding stairs take you to the top of the house and Old Bushmill's Distillery Room. Debra said that although this is the smallest room, folks seem to like the coziness and especially enjoy waking up to the sound of rain on the slate roof.

During my overnight stay, I enjoyed the cozy retreat Fitzgerald's offered in the evening light as well as the sunlight-filled rooms it presented in the morning. And I left convinced that Debra and Tom have the passion for innkeeping required in this business.

THINGS TO DO: In Painesville, the Busy Day Gourmet and State Street Cafe are within walking distance of the bed and breakfast. For seafood, head out to Pickle Bill's on the Grand River, where you can have a casual meal or an upscale dining experience in Admiral Charlie's dining room. Picnic and swim at Headlands Beach—Ohio's longest natural beach, on Lake Erie. The recently restored James A. Garfield National Historic Site in Mentor allows a look back at a house from the period 1880–1904.

DIRECTIONS: SR 2 to SR 283 (Richmond St.); right on SR 283 (Richmond); right on US 20 (Mentor Ave..); on left

NEARBY ATTRACTIONS: Lake Erie beaches and lighthouse, Lake Erie College, James A. Garfield National Historic Site, Holden Arboretum, Lake Farmpark, Ohio wineries

Flannigan's Historic Guest House

Feel the airiness of high-ceilinged rooms and tall windows in this Greek Revival home.

Sharon Flannigan, Innkeeper
34 Aurora St.
Hudson, OH
(330) 342-0340
www.flanniganhouse.com

RATES & RESERVATIONS:
Season: Year round;
Rates: $$$;
Specials: 3 day, corporate and Academy discounts;
Reservations required;
Check, Visa, MC, cash accepted

ACCOMMODATIONS:
2 rooms w/bath; 1 suite w/bath

AMENITIES: Cable TV, phone in room, air cond.

MEALS: Continental breakfast

SPECIAL CONSIDERATIONS:
Cat living at inn;
Not fully handicapped accessible;
Parking available: Lot

Visitors to Hudson are lucky. They don't have to be content with just driving past the century homes lining the tree-shaded streets of this Western Reserve community; they can stay in one. Flannigan's Historic Guest House, a Greek Revival home known also as the Henry Holmes House, is two doors from the Hudson Library and Historical Society on Aurora Street. You can walk to Hudson's Main Street shops and restaurants from Flannigan's, and that's the best way to gain an appreciation of the architectural details of the homes, churches, and other early structures. On your walk, you'll pass a building at the corner of Aurora and Main that has been in continuous commercial use since it was established as Brewster's Store in 1839; (a bank occupies the space today).

Owner/innkeeper Sharon Flannigan loves to share her charming home and has hosted international visitors who come to the Encore School of Strings for six weeks each summer, prospective students and parents who visit the Western Reserve Academy, and corporate guests. Although she didn't plan to run a bed and breakfast when she purchased the property in 1991, she began to think of opening her house to guests when her daughter left for college.

Sharon says she has worked to preserve the integrity of this historic home while making the necessary renovations. And it seems she's not afraid to tackle some of the work herself. I noticed the scaffolding on one side of the house when I arrived and learned that Sharon does all the exterior work, from scraping and priming the surface to painting. Sharon's renovation saga includes the addition of two bathrooms to the second story, which entailed having the downstairs ceiling reinforced with steel beams. The staircase had to be jacked up seven inches and the chimney repointed, along with the expected repair of walls and ceilings throughout the house.

There's an airiness to the interior of this bed and breakfast due both to Sharon's sense of style and to the natural light that streams from the home's tall windows. Stepping into the parlor, guests are welcomed by an Italian marble fireplace, flowered fabrics, and 100-year-old oak floors that provide a comfortable ambiance. In preserving the character of the house, Sharon changed the flat woodwork and moldings from a 1950s addition to scrolled moldings. She serves breakfast in the dining room at tables set with china, crystal, linen, and flowers.

Guests have a choice of three rooms. Although varied in size, all are comfortable and beautifully decorated. Sharon not only paints and does repairs, she is also a seamstress—evident in her combinations of fabrics and colors. I loved the Studio Suite on the first floor, which opens to a patio through French doors. As I explored the patio, set up with an umbrella table, I found a second patio as well as wicker groupings in the yard

beyond. The Studio Suite is a soothing study in peach, blue, and rose against a white background. The bed is super-king size and can be switched to twin beds. A desk area, sofa, small refrigerator, and the extras Sharon provides in all the rooms— coffeemaker, iron, and ironing board— make it attractive to business travelers as well as prospective students and parents. There's another room that corporate guests request—the Business Suite on the second floor. It's a no-nonsense space done up in burgundy and gray with a queen bed, built-in desk, and bookshelves accented by a

border of the New York City skyline. A black and white bathroom with stall shower adjoins the room.

And for those who come for a romantic weekend or the solo traveler looking for luxury, there's the Rose Room with an enormous bathroom (converted from a former bedroom). A deep pedestal tub with a brass shower takes the place of honor on an oak platform encircled by lace curtains. A pedestal sink and old-fashioned vanity complete the room.

THINGS TO DO: There's a choice of restaurants within walking distance of Flannigan's. For an upscale, gourmet dining experience, stroll over to the Inn at Turner's Mill. If you're looking for lighter fare, you'll find good food and value at Mary and Ted's Restaurant on Main Street. A local favorite, hidden in a shopping mall, is the Red Tomato—a small, bistro-like place where the homemade sauces are so good some folks stop just to buy the sauce to take home.

Those who come to stay at Flannigan's Historic Guest House remember their walks in this lovely community, where the fire whistle announces that it is noon, the church bells peal at 5:00 p.m., and folks relax on the green on summer evenings listening to a band concert.

DIRECTIONS: WEST: I-80 to exit 180 for SR 8; south on SR 8; left (east) on SR 303; left (north) on SR 91; right on Aurora Rd.; on right
EAST: I-271 to exit 18 for SR 8; south on SR 8; left (east) on SR 303; left (north) on SR 91; right on Aurora Rd.; on right.

NEARBY ATTRACTIONS: Historic Hudson, Sea World, Six Flags, Amish country, Akron, Cleveland

Inn at Brandywine Falls

A perennial favorite nestled in the Cuyahoga Valley

George and Katie Hoy, Innkeepers
8230 Brandywine Rd.
Sagamore Hills, OH
(330) 467-1812
www.innatbrandywinefalls.com

RATES & RESERVATIONS:
Hours: 24 hours;
Season: Year round;
Rates: $$$–$$$$;
Reservations recommended;
Check, Visa, MC, Disc, Amex accepted

ACCOMMODATIONS:
3 rooms w/bath; 3 suites w/bath

AMENITIES: Hot tub, phone in room, Internet, air cond.

MEALS: Full breakfast

SPECIAL CONSIDERATIONS:
Handicapped accessible
Parking available: Lot

When I arrived at the Inn at Brandywine Falls, in the Cuyahoga Valley National Recreation Area, innkeeper George Hoy welcomed me and suggested a tour of the inn—then he handed me a tape player. After 10,500 guests in the last 11 years, George decided an audio tape could easily take visitors around this 1848 farmhouse. Tape player in hand, I started the tour, which not only took me through public rooms and guest rooms but also provided a mini-lecture from George on the architecture and interiors of the time.

The Hoys spent 14 months renovating the place. Before they started working on the interior, Katie Hoy carefully researched the Greek Revival period and stayed as true as possible to the era in decorating the house. An example of her attention to detail is the James Wallace Parlour. Once the setting in the Wallace home for family events such as funerals, it is now an elegant main-floor guest room with a tiger maple sleigh bed, a signed, 1840 cream and navy coverlet, and blue Axminster carpet. In keeping with the style of the day, George painted scenes on the roller shades. With white painted mantel and woodwork, simple blue swags at

the window, and a wing chair, this elegant room provides a peaceful retreat and is handicapped accessible. Guest rooms upstairs include the
Simon Perkins Room, with two quilt-covered, four-poster double beds,
and a low chest under the south windows for a view of Brandywine Falls.
Adeline's Retreat, named for James Wallace's wife, features a red and
cream stenciled floor, rag rugs, a coverlet from 1856, and a good selection of Ohio and travel books. There was something about the beds in
this inn that induced sleep, and I learned that merino wool mattress
pads and flannel or cotton sheets—depending upon the season—sure
can make a difference.

At the end of the hall, a suite known as Anna Hale's Garret offers a
sitting room and bedroom with two cannonball double beds. Sloping
ceilings, quilts in yellows and blues, teddy bears, and dolls make it a
charming spot for a couple or a family stay. Be sure to ask George about
the history of the window in this suite—it is one of many tales he loves
to tell.

A second project for the Hoys became an 18-month renovation of
the carriage barn just behind the house into two luxurious suites: the
Granary and the Loft. Each unit has a king-size bed in the loft, a bath
with double-size Jacuzzi, and a spacious sitting room on the lower level,
with greenhouse windows looking out to a hemlock grove. A microwave, refrigerator, wood-burning stove, collection of CDs, TV, and
breakfast delivered and set up right in the room make these suites delightful, rustic getaways.

You soon become aware during a stay at the Inn at Brandywine Falls
that this is also the Hoy's home. Family pictures line the walls and guests

are encouraged to gather in the kitchen to sit at the well-worn poplar table near the soapstone hearth. The steady tick-tock of the clock on the fireplace wall, the warmth of the fire, and the easy repartee of the Hoys as they share cooking duties soon relaxes even the most stressed guest. George bakes bread and Katie does the desserts. Their cookbook, *Inn Good Taste*, is more than a collection of recipes—it is also about the guests of this country inn and the stories shared around the breakfast table or by the fire.

It's almost a sure bet that you will leave this inn wiser about the architecture and history of the farmhouse and warmed by the engaging hosts. When it comes to innkeeping, the Hoys are pros.

THINGS TO DO: You can step out the door at the Inn at Brandywine Falls to hike the Brandywine Gorge Trail, which begins right outside the inn's gate. Name a season and you will find beauty in this valley—the splendor of the autumnal landscape, the beauty of the falls frozen in winter, the gentle arrival of spring, and the lushness of summer gardens in full bloom. A short drive will take you to the Boston Store, once the company store of the Boston Land and Manufacturing Company and now a museum devoted to the history of canal-boat building in this nineteenth-century village. Explore the shops and galleries in Peninsula and choose from the list of area restaurants the Hoys provide.

DIRECTIONS: I-271 to exit 18 for SR 8; south on SR 8; right (west) on Twinsburg Rd.; right on Brandywine Rd.; on left.

NEARBY ATTRACTIONS: Cuyahoga Valley National Park, Cleveland and Akron area attractions, museums, and parks

Inn at the Green

Lounge on a windowed porch that looks out over an English perennial garden.

Ginny and Steve Meloy, Innkeepers
500 S. Main St.
Poland, OH
(330) 757-4688
www.acountryvillage.com/innatgreen

RATES & RESERVATIONS:
Season: Year round;
Rates: $;
Reservations required;
Check, Disc, MC, Visa accepted

ACCOMMODATIONS: 4 rooms w/bath

AMENITIES: Cable TV,
phone in room, air cond., radio,
tape player, working fireplaces

MEALS: Expanded
continental breakfast

SPECIAL CONSIDERATIONS:
Not fully handicapped accessible;
Parking available: Lot

The Inn at the Green in Poland is a classic example of a historic dwelling saved by a couple interested in history and in starting their own bed and breakfast. Ginny and Steve Meloy lived down the street from this 1876 Victorian "Baltimore" townhouse, and on their walks through the neighborhood they became concerned about its deteriorating condition. Deserted for four years, it was overgrown with vines, and its steeply pitched mansard roof was falling in. After purchasing the house in 1985, the Meloys made major repairs, did extensive decorative work and welcomed the first guests the next spring. I wasn't surprised to learn that Steve Meloy serves as president of the Poland Preservation Society, charged with saving historic homes in Poland Village.

Standing at the south end of the Poland Village Green, the inn is surrounded by early-nineteenth-century homes. Architecture aficionados will revel in the Connecticut Western Reserve, Federal, and Greek Revival-style homes in this National Register Historic District. Poland's place in history is secure as it carries the distinction of being Township 1 in Range 1 of the Western Reserve. From its early years, the village was

known for its excellent education system: President William McKinley's father moved his family to Poland to take advantage of the fine schools. McKinley, who lived here from age 9 to age 24, attended public school and graduated from Lee's Poland Academy. Other luminaries who came to the village include Ida Mae Tarbell, the muckraker journalist, who spent a year teaching at the Poland Seminary, and William Holmes McGuffey, of McGuffey Reader fame, who taught in a one-room school here in 1820.

Entrance to the inn is through the Greeting Room, an intimate area furnished with Ohio antiques and P. Buckley Moss art. Guests enjoy an expanded continental breakfast in this room or on the adjoining windowed porch, furnished in white wicker, which looks out over the English perennial garden.

Rather than excessive Victorian decor, the Meloys opted for a light and bright look, keeping the interior wooden shutters open on the tall windows. The music room, anchored by a grand piano, showcases their collection of nineteenth- and early-twentieth-century American art, English antiques, and a fine selection of area history books. The decorative 12-foot-high ceilings, original poplar floors warmed by Oriental rugs, Italian marble mantels, and a color scheme of Colonial blue emphasize the area's New England heritage. Four guest rooms with private baths feature four-poster beds, antique chests, and desks. Room 3 was inviting with floral applique coverlets on twin beds, chairs pulled up to the fireplace, flower prints, and an antique chest and writing table. Down the hall, Room 4 was furnished with a white iron bed, white wicker chairs, an antique chest, and a quilt in shades of blue. The cheery color scheme was repeated in the bath with blue and white checked wallpaper. Ginny's whimsical collection of china hens is displayed on an antique chest in the hallway at the top of the stairs, where guests will also find a collection of videos and tapes.

THINGS TO DO: Nearby Poland Village Woods offers hiking trails and cross-country skiing. Visit in May and you'll find the woodland carpeted with bluebells. If time allows, the Meloys suggest a visit to the Butler Institute of American Art, with 12,000 works of American art in the permanent collection. Take time to stop at Mill Creek Metropark's Fellows Riverside Gardens in the spring, when 40,000 bulbs are in bloom.

Dining options range from local favorites to national chains in the area west of Poland Village. We chose the Springfield Grille, a few miles away in Boardman, featuring a wide menu selection including Cajun jambalaya and fire-grilled entrees. The dining room was relaxing, with an art collection highlighted on dark, gleaming mahogany walls. For a lighter meal of soups, salads, and sandwiches, try the Mocha House, featuring specialty coffees, teas, and an in-house bakery. Returning from this busy commercialized area, I was grateful that idyllic Poland Village seems to remain intact. The Inn at the Green welcomed with candle-size lights shining from the windows and a glass of sherry on the sideboard.

DIRECTIONS: I -80 to exit 224B for SR 680; south on SR 680 to Main St.; right on Main St.; on left

NEARBY ATTRACTIONS: Butler Institute of American Art, Mill Creek Park, Pennsylvania's Amish country,

Inn of Chagrin Falls

A small-town retreat with all the comforts of a fancy private club

Cynthia Phelps, Innkeeper
87 West St.
Chagrin Falls, OH
(440) 247-1200

RATES & RESERVATIONS:
Hours: 24 hours;
Season: Year round;
Rates: $$$$;
Reservations recommended;
Visa, MC, Disc, Amex,
Diner's Club accepted

ACCOMMODATIONS: 15 rooms
w/bath; 3 suites w/bath

AMENITIES: Cable TV,
phone in room, air cond.

MEALS: Continental breakfast;
May not accommodate
all special diets;

SPECIAL CONSIDERATIONS:
Not fully handicapped accessible;
Parking available: Lot

The rambling yellow cottages that make up the Inn of Chagrin Falls were once Crane's Canary Cottage, a popular restaurant opened in 1927 by Clarence Arthur Crane, the inventor of LifeSavers candy. Notables who stopped by for lunch or dinner at Crane's Canary Cottage include Charles Lindbergh, John D. Rockefeller, and Duncan Hines. Crane's son, the poet Hart Crane, spent some time at the cottage, which was also his parents' home. Today this charming Western Reserve hostelry offers 15 rooms, including suites and a spacious common room. A gift shop, Hearthside, featuring gifts, clothing, and antiques, occupies a second cottage, and a restaurant, Gamekeeper's Tavern, is attached to the inn.

From the time I entered this New England-style inn, I felt it had the intimacy of a bed and breakfast. Innkeeper Cynthia Phelps, a resident of the village and veteran of 16 years in the travel industry, greeted me at the door by name, as she did with all the guests. The Gathering Room off the lobby is an elegant space done in rich burgundy and green with comfortable seating groupings. A marble fireplace, flanked by bookshelves and several desks, including a tiger maple secretary, makes it a perfect room for business clients to unwind at the end of a hectic day. The inn hosts executive retreats as well as receptions in the Gathering Room.

Guest rooms and suites occupy two floors of the inn. On the main floor, the President Garfield Suite exudes graciousness with a color palette of royal blue and beige, a four-poster king-size bed, and a corner gas log fireplace with a marble surround. There's plenty of space for relaxing in a sitting area furnished with a queen pull-out sofa in blue and beige checks, gleaming mahogany tables, and two pull-up chairs. A large framed photo of Garfield's home, Lawnfield, hangs on the wall. In the Crane Suite, a massive fireplace original to the house centers one wall. Fittingly named for the Cranes, it was the living room for the family. The placement of the Jacuzzi allows for a view of the fireplace. A king brass poster bed covered with a white matelasse spread is accented by colorful flowered pillows. The standard rooms at this inn are also quite spacious. I liked the Trout Run Room, with its queen oak Victorian bed, paisley wall covering, and matched chairs with a flamestitched covering. The Garden Room, a favorite of some returning guests, is a bright, cheerful room with a patina-green wicker queen bed with a green-and-white checked duvet that matches the curtains, a flowered border, and a fireplace.

One of the joys of staying in a full-service country inn is being able to wander down to the dining room for meals. At the Inn of Chagrin Falls, house guests find a continental breakfast in the glassed-in sun porch that overlooks the inn's gardens. The Gamekeeper's Tavern is *the* place for lunch or dinner, with a menu featuring wild game as well as traditional entrees. We enjoyed grilled portabello mushroom salad and chargrilled Cajun spiced chicken breast at lunchtime. The patio with white tables and green market umbrellas has perennially been voted "Best Outdoor Dining Restaurant" in Cleveland.

THINGS TO DO: Chagrin Falls has been called "America's Hometown," and the village has preserved and restored many homes in the residential west side historic district. It's a treat to browse through the shops lining Main Street. A couple of my favorites are the Fireside Book Shop, with three stories of books, Taggart's Toys and Hobbies, and the Chagrin Hardware and Supply Company, which has been serving the village since 1857. Stop in the store for nostalgia's sake: some of the inventory goes back to earlier times; wooden drawers and files line the walls holding cotterpins, brass hose fittings, pumps, and washers. (They also carry current hardware supplies and antiques.) Do as the locals do and stop at the Popcorn

Shop for an ice cream cone and enjoy the tumbling falls and rushing river that gave the village its name.

DIRECTIONS: EAST: I-271 to exit 29 for SR 87 (Chagrin Blvd.); east on Chagrin to Chagrin Falls; right (south) on West St.; on right SOUTH: I-422 to SR 91; north on SR 91 to Chagrin Blvd.; right on Chagrin to Chagrin Falls; right (south) on West St.; on right

NEARBY ATTRACTIONS: Waterfall, shopping, galleries, restaurants, Sea World, Six Flags, Amish country

Red Maple Inn

Seventeen guest rooms look out on either farmland, woodland, or the historic village of Burton.

Sallie and John Cwik, Innkeepers
14707 S. Cheshire St.
Burton Village, OH
(888) 646-2753
www.redmaple.com

RATES & RESERVATIONS:
Hours: 7 a.m.–7 p.m.;
Season: Year round;
Rates: $$$;
Specials: Children, AAA;
Reservations recommended;
Check, Visa, MC, Disc, Amex accepted

ACCOMMODATIONS: 17 rooms w/bath

AMENITIES: Hot tub, cable TV, phone in room, Internet, air cond., balconies off of 12 rooms, fireplaces in 5 rooms, golf green

MEALS: Full breakfast

SPECIAL CONSIDERATIONS:
Handicapped accessible;
Parking available: Lot

Gordon Safran always liked country inns for family vacations, and as the former owner of E. B. Brown Optical he found that business meetings and retreats were more productive in these settings. When he decided to build an inn, he came back to the area where his family had enjoyed Sunday drives—the picturesque Western Reserve village of Burton. Gordon and Evie Safran opened the Red Maple Inn in March 1999 and have seen a steady flow of guests who have discovered their inn as a destination for romantic weekends, business meetings, and family vacations.

Built in Western Reserve style, the inn's white exterior with dark shutters fits its setting next to Century Village in Burton. Amish workers were used in the construction, from the roughing stage to the finished structure, and all of the furniture and cabinetry throughout was made by Amish craftsmen. Gordon has a genuine interest in the sect, and on Friday evenings offers guests an informal talk on Amish culture and suggestions for shopping in this fourth-largest Amish settlement in America.

Guests have access to a number of common areas in the inn. On the first floor, a snug library paneled in red cherry offers a selection of books and a place to sit and read by the fire. Breakfast is served in the dining room, which looks out to a breathtaking view of rolling, wooded hills and farmland. Beautiful in every season, the Red Maple boasted a snow-covered landscape during a winter stay and a haying scene when I visited in July. Coffee and snacks are available on the buffet during the day, and between 5:30 and 7:00 p.m. light hors d'oeuvres are set out. Guests can access a fitness room, pool table, and ping-pong table on the lower level of the inn.

Seventeen guest rooms decorated in a casual country style look out on farmland, woodland, or the historic village. TVs are tucked away in armoires and guests have a choice of king, queen, or twin beds, plus a pull-out sofa. Some rooms open to a balcony, and five have gas fireplaces. The Safrans incorporated all the extras they found in their own bed and breakfast stays into the Red Maple. A Jacuzzi tub, robes, and fine toiletries are part of the pampering. Those who bring work along to the inn find desks, comfortable upholstered chairs, and good reading lights. The expansive suite features a kitchenette, bedroom with king-size bed, and a sitting area that opens to a large deck.

Innkeepers Sallie and John Cwik bring years of professional experience to their roles at the Red Maple and keep the inn running smoothly. They help plan business meetings and retreats, using the Burton room, which can accommodate 100 guests. Meals are catered in-house, and audio-visual equipment, fax, and telephone-messaging services are available.

THINGS TO DO: Burton is typical of early Western Reserve communities with a center village green. You can walk to the century homes, shops, and restaurants clustered around the green. March brings the Geauga County Maple Festival to Burton and signals the start of festivities built around maple syrup production. The Sugarhouse on the green opens its doors, and pancake breakfasts bring many visitors to the village.

The inn provides a handy guide to trips within the area by auto, bike, and foot. A few steps away you can take a leisurely walk through history at the Century Village Museum, a restored village with five houses and 20 other buildings from the nineteenth century. Shopping opportunities abound in this Amish area. Follow the inn's guide with a listing of trips to shops with hand-crafted furniture, cheese, and quilts. Or leave the driving to a guide who will take you on a private coach tour through the countryside. Golfers can choose from seven golf courses; antiquers find shops throughout the area.

For fine dining, Fowler's Mill Restaurant and Tavern and Bass Lake Tavern are within a 15-minute drive of the inn. For casual fare, take your choice of Belle's Colonial Restaurant, Cogan's, and Joel's Italian Grille right around the corner on the green. Stop for coffee and pastries at Coffee Corners, where you can also browse the antique selections.

DIRECTIONS: I-480 to US 422; east on US 422; north on SR 700; on left

NEARBY ATTRACTIONS: Century Village, Amish country

Spread Eagle Tavern and Inn

A canal-era hostelry with a welcoming, open hearth

Peter and Jean Johnson, Innkeepers
10150 Historic Plymouth St.
Hanoverton, OH
(330) 223-1583

RATES & RESERVATIONS:
Hours: 9 a.m.–10 p.m.;
Season: Year round;
Rates: $$$$; Reservations required;
Check, Visa, MC, Disc, Amex accepted

ACCOMMODATIONS: 5 rooms w/bath;
1 guest house w/bath

AMENITIES: Cable TV,
phone in room, air cond.

MEALS: Full breakfast, lunch, dinner;
Beer, wine, and liquor served

SPECIAL CONSIDERATIONS:
Not fully handicapped accessible;
Parking available: Lot

The first time I visited the Spread Eagle Tavern the setting took my breath away. This canal-era hostelry stands on Hanoverton's tree-lined Historic Plymouth Street along with 21 other houses that appear to be frozen in time. The Johnsons' son, David, shared the history of the inn with me on a recent visit.

Built in 1837, the Spread Eagle Tavern is recognized today as one of the area's finest examples of Federal-period architecture. Plans for the inn were taken from the pattern books of the preeminent Boston architect Asher Benjamin. Evidence of his designs can be seen in the finish work—raised-wood window and door frames, fluted column casings, and intricately carved mantels. The stairway, with continuing handrail, extends 72 feet to the fourth floor.

During the canal era, Hanover (it became Hanoverton in 1828) was situated midway between the mouth and tail of the 73½-mile-long Sandy and Beaver Canal. This early village became the depot for the canal system, with three large warehouses, and it also served as a busy commercial center with travelers coming to Hanover to purchase goods staying at the Spread Eagle. When the canal era wound down and the railroad bypassed Hanover, the town went to sleep for 150 years.

David's parents, Peter and Jean Johnson, purchased the inn in 1988. A painstaking two-year restoration project included gutting the building down to the stud walls and incorporating beams from old barns and hand-chiseled stone in an addition. The renovation was done so expertly that it is hard to tell where the old building ends and the addition begins.

Today, guests find a full-service country inn enhanced by the Johnson family's love of history and appreciation of fine antiques. Seven restaurants offer dining options. We had a leisurely lunch on a winter day in the rustic Barn Room, warmed by the crackling fire in the massive fireplace nearby. While longtime favorites like chicken potpie and clam chowder remain on the luncheon menu, newer dinner entrees include grilled bison skewers and slow-roasted half-chicken with andouille sausage and pine-nut dressing. Pan-roasted half-pheasant and smoked rack of New Zealand lamb are featured on Friday and Saturday evenings.

Pewter lines the mantel, and a 1770 Cowpens, South Carolina, Revolutionary War battle flag hangs on the wall of the Patriots Tavern Room. Check out the hand-painted tiles behind the bar depicting the history of the canal era, and take time to see Gaver's Rathskeller patterned after an eighteenth-century wine cellar. Hanover served as a safe haven for runaway slaves, and the Johnsons reinstalled a slave tunnel that wraps around the wine cellar.

After dinner, head upstairs to the second and third floors to one of the guest rooms named for United States presidents. The Washington room is a study in blue and white, with a king-size four-poster bed, and

a sitting area with blue-and-white-checked wing chair and sofa set against wallpaper and fabrics using the same colors. The Lincoln Room is elegantly appointed with an early nineteenth-century four poster encased in a flowered fabric from Costan & Tout. As in many of the rooms, hand-painted tiles from the family-owned Summitville Tiles frame the fireplace. The spacious bath is fitted with a tub and sink with gold fixtures, a bidet, and yet another fireplace repeating the bird motif of the bedroom tiles. House guests are treated to a full breakfast in the Barn Room.

A new accommodation located behind the inn, the Hanover House, offers an upscale guest house. With a great room, several smaller parlors, a kitchen on the main floor, and two guests rooms and bath on the second, it provides an ideal space for gatherings like weddings, cocktail parties, and receptions. The Johnsons furnished the Hanover House with beautiful period pieces, including a mirror in the parlor from the John Quincy Adams collection and a nineteenth-century mahogany Plantation canopy bed in the bedroom.

THINGS TO DO: The receptionist at the desk handed me a list of places to visit in the area—such as Columbiana (to shop for antiques), the Pro Football Hall of Fame in Canton, or Beaver Creek State Park. But if I had the gift of a weekend stay at the Spread Eagle, I wouldn't leave the peace and quiet of this historic inn. I would head to the charming parlor, the Asher Benjamin Room, and snuggle down in a deep wing chair by the fire to read for the afternoon. In the evening, I would sample the chef's best in the Patriots Tavern Room and wander up to spend the night in a presidential guest room. The next morning I would stroll down historic Plymouth Street on the brick footpath, past buildings from the nineteenth century, and take home a weekend to remember.

DIRECTIONS: I-77 to exit 176 for SR 30; east on SR 30; left (north) on Plymouth St.; on right

NEARBY ATTRACTIONS: Pro Football Hall of Fame, Beaver Creek State Park, antiques

Walker–Johnson Inn

*Serious fans of Victoriana
will truly adore this inn.*

Judy and David McDowell, Innkeepers
15038 S. State Ave..
Middlefield, OH
(440) 632-5662
www.walkerjohnsoninn.com

RATES & RESERVATIONS:
Hours: 8 a.m.–11 p.m.;
Season: Year round;
Rates: $$–$$$;
Specials: Corporate rates Sun–Thu;
Reservations recommended;
Check, Visa, MC, Disc accepted

ACCOMMODATIONS:
4 rooms, 2 w/bath

AMENITIES: Cable TV, air cond.

MEALS: Full breakfast, snacks

SPECIAL CONSIDERATIONS:
Dog living at inn;
Not fully handicapped accessible;
Parking available: Lot

Judy and David McDowell are the fifth owners of this house built in 1887 by lumber-mill owner Abraham Walker. Located in the heart of Middlefield, on South State Avenue, this "Painted Lady's" exterior is a pleasing combination of green, cream, and burgundy with a touch of gold.

Previous owners made alterations to the structure, but the ambiance remains Victorian throughout the Inn. Potted ferns on stands, oak woodwork, a Kimball pump organ, Victorian settees, and side chairs fill the parlor. Judy, a serious collector of antiques, has placed her treasures around the house. A tall, glass-fronted walnut bookcase with raised fruit and nut drawer pulls is a focal point in the parlor.

Antique bedsteads, chests, and marble-topped tables along with some reproductions grace the guest rooms. It's a few steps down to the room at the end of the hall that overlooks the garden. Family groups as well as business travelers request this room with queen-size bed, queen pull-out sofa, sitting area, and large adjoining bath. Judy's love of things from centuries past includes collectibles that she has grouped as accents here and there in the rooms. I found ladies' beaded and mesh bags arranged on

the wall, two little girls' dresses on a coat rack, a red and white quilt embroidered by Dave's aunt in 1904, and antique dolls in the upstairs rooms.

It's easy to find a quiet place of your own at the Walker-Johnson Inn. There's a TV room off the parlor with comfy chairs, snacks, and a refrigerator stocked with juices and soft drinks. Judy has furnished the enclosed porch with wicker, plumply padded for comfort, reading lamps, magazines, and books. And then there's the back garden. When we parked the car at the end of the driveway, I couldn't wait to peek at what looked to be a refuge behind the fence. Through the gate I found a gazebo, fountain, perennials, and outdoor wicker. The house is sheltered by big old maples, and Judy's green thumb is evident in the flower beds bordering the front walk.

Although located 35 miles southeast of Cleveland in a farming community, the Walker-Johnson Inn is busy with business travelers. I often hear from innkeepers that frequent guests become friends, and this is the case with the McDowells. It helps explain the trend for those who are in the business milieu during the day to seek out a home-like environment for their stay. I would bet that Judy's breakfasts are one of the reasons folks return. She offers a quick continental—fresh-squeezed orange juice and homemade caramel rolls—for guests who take off early on weekdays. For those who can indulge in a more leisurely repast, she serves hearty main dishes like twice-baked breakfast potatoes and a breakfast pizza.

THINGS TO DO: Middlefield is home to the fourth-largest Amish population in America, and the Amish influence helps suggest what to do while visiting Geauga County. Head out to the Middlefield Nauvoo Road Shops to find baskets, antiques, quilts, and country furniture, plus a year-round flea market. We noticed folks on tour buses loading up on Amish-made pies and breads at A & K Bakery on Nauvoo Road. Settler's Farm is another grouping of shops including crafts, needlework, and wood accent pieces on Old State Road.

Stop at Middlefield Cheese, where you can pick up some of their award-winning Swiss cheese and spend some time in the Visitors Center. A small museum and film are free to visitors. When I come to this area, I always try to stop at End of the Commons General Store in Mesopotamia. It's not far from Middlefield, and you'll find it with a 26-star American flag (emblematic of the year the store was built) flying from the porch. Shop side by side with the Amish who come to stock up on staples like 100-pound sacks of flour and sugar. Pick up some lunch items or a hand-dipped ice cream cone and sit on the porch, where you can gaze at the nineteenth-century homes that cluster around the Commons.

For an Amish meal, stop at Mary Yoder's Amish Restaurant in Middlefield; for gourmet cuisine, the Bass Lake Tavern is within a short drive.

DIRECTIONS: I-271 to exit 34 for US 322 (Mayfield Rd.); east on US 322 (Mayfield Rd.); right (south) on SR 608; on right

NEARBY ATTRACTIONS: Middlefield Cheese House, Settlers Farm, Century Village, Pioneer Waterland and Dry Fun Park, Six Flags, Sea World, Amish shops

Chapter 2

A Short Drive—Amish Country

*The gentle peacefulness of the countryside; windmills on the horizon;
the purple and green of women's dresses contrasting with the dark pants
and vibrant blue of men's shirts flapping in the wind; sweet
Amish children, miniatures of their parents in bonnets and straw hats.*

These are some of the things we like about visiting Ohio's Amish country, the largest Amish settlement in the world we are told, right here in the four-county area of Holmes, Wayne, Tuscarawas, and Stark. Plan to stay in your pick of a turn-of-the-century house, a full-service inn, a cabin in the woods, or several bed and breakfasts in countryside settings.

The Amish houses are sprawling affairs, often with a grandfather or "dawdy haus" attached to the main house. You'll see martin houses in the yard (martins take care of the mosquitoes), colorful flower gardens, and an occasional telephone booth along the road. Simple, hand made signs announce quilts or hickory rockers for sale. Follow the lane to the house or barn and you'll have the opportunity of talking one-on-one with an Amish person as well as getting a good buy on a hand crafted item. There are no sales on Sundays in these private homes.

To gain some understanding of Amish and Mennonite history, take time to tour Behalt, a 265-foot cyclorama mural at the Mennonite Information Center.

Explore Amish country in all seasons. Winter presents a very different picture from the clogged highways that autumn visitors find. You see the snow-covered landscape with a wider lens. Barns and trees are silhouetted against the rolling hills, and life is at a slower pace. Horses covered with blankets wait patiently for their owners outside restaurants, and shops are not crowded; the clerk in the quilt shop has time to talk, and there are no lines in the bulk food stores. Spend some time at an auction, where the activity in the sale barn provides an opportunity to observe the Amish going about their business.

Amish country gives you a chance to get off the fast track, sit on the porch, and hear the crickets and the clip-clop of a passing horse and buggy.

A Valley View Inn

Savor the quiet country view from a porch stretching across the back of the inn.

Dan and Nancy Lembke, Innkeepers
32327 S.R. 643
New Bedford, OH
(800) 331-8439
www.ez-page.com/valleyview/

RATES & RESERVATIONS:
Hours: 9 a.m.–9 p.m.;
Season: Year round;
Rates: $$;
Reservations recommended;
Check, Visa, MC accepted

ACCOMMODATIONS: 10 rooms w/bath

MEALS: Full breakfast, snacks

SPECIAL CONSIDERATIONS:
Dog living at inn;
Handicapped accessible;
Parking available: Lot

I am always looking for new accommodations off the beaten track, and when I arrived at A Valley View Inn near New Bedford I knew I had found a rare spot deep in the country. No highways, no shopping centers, no noise. The reason folks come to this inn is the destination. Set off the road, Valley View is a neat, light gray structure with white shutters and porches. Belgians graze in the pasture as you drive to the front door. And those draft horses are the reason owners/innkeepers Nancy and Dan Lembke first came down this way from their previous home in Toledo. The Lembkes raise Belgians, and when they came to Holmes County to sell their horses, they got to know the Amish community, fell in love with the rolling hills, and built an inn on a steep hillside overlooking a spectacular valley. A porch across the entire back of the inn offers a place to sit and savor the view. One guest writes of watching the mist lift off the valley; another remembers viewing a sunrise while sipping coffee on the deck. And while sitting quietly at dusk in a swing on the porch, guests can usually spot their share of deer. Perhaps the most loyal guests are a couple who have come to Valley View 54 times—possibly a record for a bed and breakfast, and certainly the best kind of recommendation for this country inn.

The inn's style has been described as "elegant country." Nancy says they built the inn to be homelike, and they try to keep clutter to a minimum. Each of the 10 guest rooms uses a different quilt pattern as the focal point, complemented by simple window treatments and locally made furniture. The rooms—Alabama Star, Country Lily, and Country Song Bird, to mention a few—are named for these hand-pieced and quilted works of art made by Amish friends. Two rooms, Star Spin and Broken Star, look out on that magnificent view of the valley. There are no televisions or phones in the rooms to disturb the quiet of the place.

There's a common sitting room on each floor. The upstairs sitting room is a welcoming space with a sofa and matching velvet-covered wing chairs in front of the fireplace. Family photos cover the wall, and a selection of books and magazines is available. The family room downstairs is the place to sit by the fire and chat, play chess or ping-pong, or take out some rolls for the old player piano. The inn also has a large map with colorful pins marking the home towns and states of the guests.

Lizzie, the Amish cook, has been with the Lembkes since the inn opened in 1993. Her homemade bread brings many compliments from guests. The full country breakfasts feature dishes like ham and potato casserole, eggs and sausage, and fruit slush. On Sundays, a large continental breakfast is available.

THINGS TO DO: I never would have discovered the little town of Baltic if Nancy hadn't suggested stopping for dinner at Miller's Dutch Kitch'n. Open for breakfast, lunch, and dinner, Miller's serves up roast beef with real mashed potatoes, dressing, Swiss steak, and homemade pies with ice cream for dessert. While in Baltic, stop at Baltic Mills for flour, bulk foods, and Amish crafts, and take home some smoked meats from Baltic Meats. Nancy says guests like to visit Roscoe Village and the Longaberger factory on day trips from the inn.

DIRECTIONS: I-77 to exit 83 for SR 39; right (west) on SR 39; left (south) on SR 93; right on SR 643; on right.

NEARBY ATTRACTIONS: Amish country, Longaberger Basket Factory, Roscoe Village, Berlin, Walnut Creek, Sugarcreek

Barn Inn

*Spend a night in an old barn
transformed into a Victorian inn.*

While in Holmes County in late 1997, I noticed a new bed and breakfast, a red barn structure, just before the entrance to the Inn at Honey Run. I was curious because although the barn looked new, I could tell the foundation had age. Innkeeper Loretta Coblentz welcomed me to the Barn Inn on that cold, dreary, late-November day with a cup of tea and some homemade cookies. We settled down in front of the slate fireplace and she described her search for a bed and breakfast property.

After living in Florida for 27 years, Hartville natives Loretta and Paul Coblentz decided to return to Ohio. They found this turn-of-the-century farmhouse and barn on County Road 203, between Berlin and Millersburg. As they were beginning to decide the decor of the guest rooms in the house, Loretta's mother came to visit, and when she saw the barn she suggested it would make a perfect bed and breakfast. The farm was once the Honey Run Dairy, site of a cheese-making company. Loretta and Paul had the vision to take this old barn and transform it into a Victorian inn.

From the time they started construction in January 1997 until they opened for business in September 1997, the Coblentzes, their family, and

Paul and Loretta Coblentz, Innkeepers
6838 C.R. 203
Millersburg, OH
(877) 674-7600
www.bbonline.com/ohio/thebarn/

RATES & RESERVATIONS:
Hours: 24 hours;
Season: Year round;
Rates: $$$–$$$$;
Two-night minimum stay required weekends Sept and Oct;
Reservations required;
Check, Visa, MC, Disc, Amex accepted

ACCOMMODATIONS:
5 rooms w/bath; 2 suites w/bath

AMENITIES: Hot tub, fireplaces

MEALS: Full breakfast

SPECIAL CONSIDERATIONS:
Handicapped accessible
Parking available: Lot

friends expended lots of elbow grease getting the place clean. They spent three weeks just scrubbing the original barn beams now visible in the interior of the barn. Loretta says folks asked how they did it. Her reply: oil soap, paring knives, razor blades, and toothbrushes. Once the barn was clean they encountered a problem typical of those faced when saving old farm buildings: sparrows had nested in the newly installed insulation. Since the windows were already in place, they had to figure out a way to get the sparrows to leave through the only openings—the doors.

As Loretta and I sat chatting in comfy chairs by the fire in the sitting room, where the ceiling height soars to 33 feet, I found it hard to imagine this space as a barn. But it was actually the third barn built on this site; the foundation is original to the first barn built prior to 1867. Now, the open area extends to a large dining table set for breakfast. Loretta serves a full country breakfast with farm-fresh eggs, smoked sausage, quiche, and apple dumplings one morning and perhaps Belgian waffles with real whipped cream the next. She makes her own bread and cookies, kept on the sideboard. The Coblentzes find that conversation flows readily when guests are gathered around the breakfast table.

When I first walked through the door of the Barn Inn, a bright quilt hanging over the railing of the open second floor caught my eye. I learned that Loretta not only made all the quilts in the guest rooms, but also taught quilting when she lived in Florida. Each room opens to a balcony that offers a pastoral scene of the upper Honey Run Valley. Chairs and sap buckets overflowing with flowers make the balcony an inviting place to sit and read a favorite book or do absolutely nothing.

A couple of my favorite rooms include a large room, the French Country, and a pleasant standard room, the Honey Run Hideaway. The French Country is a spacious yet warm room done in apricot and beige with an antique Louis XVI bed as the focal point. A loveseat facing a gas log fireplace, a whirlpool tub, and classic touches like the cherub frieze running along the bathroom wall make it a romantic retreat. On the lower level of the inn, there's a handicapped-accessible room, the Honey Run Hideaway, with a four-poster queen bed covered with one of Loretta's quilts in the Attic Window design.

Guests' comments after a stay at the Barn Inn include: "It was simply serene"; "the breakfast was awesome"; "I didn't want to go home."

THINGS TO DO: It's refreshing to find a good working relationship between inns, and Loretta values her neighboring accommodation, the Inn at Honey Run (a short walk up the hill), where she often makes dinner reservations for her guests.

Loretta and Paul have Holmes County roots and can suggest day trips to Amish quilt and furniture shops on the back roads. Berlin, with its variety of shops and restaurants, is only $5^{1}/_{4}$ miles from the inn. The Coblentzes keep a running schedule of the farm auctions that take place in Mt. Hope.

DIRECTIONS: I-77 to exit 83 for SR 39; west on SR 39; right on CR 201; left on CR 203; on right

NEARBY ATTRACTIONS: Berlin shops, Guggisberg cheese, Miller's Bakery, Rasketter's Woolen Mill, Amish furniture shops, carriage shops, quilt shops, leather shops

Charm Countryview Inn

The philosophy of this inn: a place to "refresh your spirit"

Naomi and Paul Miller, Innkeepers
3334 S.R. 557
Charm, OH
(330) 893-3003
www.charmcountryviewinn.com

RATES & RESERVATIONS:
Hours: 7 a.m.–8 p.m.;
Season: Year round; Rates: $$$;
Reservations recommended;
Check, Visa, MC accepted

ACCOMMODATIONS: 15 rooms w/bath

AMENITIES: Air cond.

MEALS: Full breakfast, snacks

SPECIAL CONSIDERATIONS:
Not fully handicapped accessible;
Parking available: Lot

It was one of those perfect Indian-summer evenings. We sat in gliders on the wide porch of the Charm Countryview Inn, taking in the pungent smells of autumn lingering in the air and enjoying the quiet of the country setting. The inn was totally booked, and guests spilled out to the porch to chat awhile after stopping in the dining room for the homemade snacks and popcorn. Talk centered on the best routes for "leaf peeping," the activity that brought most of us to Holmes County this time of year. There was a general consensus from this randomly assembled group that we wanted to find the back roads and leave anything that smacked of tourists behind. One gentleman, extolling his particular route that day through hillsides covered with rich rusts and golds, said, "It doesn't get any better than this, does it?" Nods of agreement were his answer.

Perhaps it is the philosophy of the Amish-Mennonite hosts, Paul and Naomi Miller—that their inn be a place to "refresh your spirit"—that brought about the easy conversation and lingering on the porch reminiscent of earlier times. In the absence of television, guests seem more inclined to spend evenings playing board games or chatting with strangers.

Breakfast the next morning was a major happening—an hour-and-15-minute event in the sun-filled dining room. Once we were gathered for the meal at tables for six or eight covered with lace tablecloths, innkeeper Paul Miller offered thanks. And then the parade began—platters of thick ham, a bubbling sausage-and-cheese casserole, baskets of muffins and rolls, and hash brown potatoes accompanied by cheese sauce were all brought to the tables, with seconds served all around. A refreshing fruit slush finished the meal, and once again Paul asked for our attention. When the chatter and laughter ebbed, he asked each table to introduce themselves. We learned there were anniversary celebrants, a small family reunion, and a table of women who had been friends for years, who come back to the inn each October. Guests find a continental breakfast on Sundays, a day of rest for the Miller family.

The inn, a silver-gray Colonial with classic navy shutters, is set off the road on beautifully landscaped grounds. The view from the porch is one of rolling hills interspersed with fields and woodlands. It's a picture-postcard scene of passing Amish buggies and horses grazing in the white-fenced pasture.

The Charm Countryview Inn, owned by the Mast family, was one of the first Amish-area inns; it opened for business in June 1990. It is a family affair, with the 15 guest rooms named for family members. Dorothy's Domain is done up in pink and green with hearts as the dominant motif, while Leon's Lookout, an upstairs room with windows looking out on the Amish countryside, has a more masculine feel. Quilts provide colorful accents in the guest rooms with patterns like Double Wedding Ring, Log Cabin Star, and Boston Commons; the furniture is solid oak. Guests are free to wander the inn's 40 acres, and might choose to go stargazing on a clear night.

After 10 years of innkeeping, Paul Miller finds guests returning every year to the Charm Countryview Inn to experience once again the peace and quiet of the country setting. Paul says, "They just want to soak it all in and, perhaps, take a little of the tranquility they find home with them."

THINGS TO DO: Travel in either direction from Charm Countryview Inn to find Amish-made products. Miller's Dry Goods in Charm carries a large selection of fabrics, quilts, and notions. Stop in Ole Mill Furniture, another Mast family enterprise, for a fine selection of solid oak furniture. In the rolling Doughty Valley, you can watch cheese being made at Guggisberg Cheese and sample the original baby Swiss. Need a break from shopping? The Chalet in the Valley, across Route 557 from the cheese factory, serves Swiss and Austrian dishes. In Charm, the Homestead Restaurant often has a line of folks snaking out the door, but it's worth the wait to taste the pot roast or meatloaf and finish up with pie topped with homemade ice cream. If you're lucky, you may happen upon a local event like an auction while visiting Charm. On our October stay, we had the delightful experience of watching the children of Charm School compete in a Woolly Worm Derby. East of Charm, stop at Hershberger Antique Mall and browse through rooms filled with carnival glass, cast iron banks, and furniture.

DIRECTIONS: I-77 to exit 99 for US 62; west on US 62; left on SR 557

NEARBY ATTRACTIONS: Charm, the Amish Farm, antique mall

Cricket Hill Cabins

*Whisk away to the rustic
simplicity of a cabin
in the woods.*

Paul Weaver Family, Innkeepers
6109 T.R. 310
Millersburg, OH
(330) 674-1892

RATES & RESERVATIONS:
Hours: 7 a.m.–6 p.m.;
Season: Year round; Rates: $$$;
Specials: Children;
Reservations recommended;
Check, Visa, MC accepted

ACCOMMODATIONS: 3 cabins w/bath

AMENITIES: Jacuzzi,
fireplace, kitchenette

MEALS: Continental breakfast;
May not accommodate
all special diets

SPECIAL CONSIDERATIONS:
Not fully handicapped accessible;
Parking available: Lot

When innkeepers Paul and Orpha Weaver decided to build a cabin behind their home near Berlin, it became a family project. Their daughter, Julia, and sons Jeremy, Andre, and Jon Anthony helped with the construction. The original cabin was so successful, the Weavers built two more on a wooded tract of land two miles from their house on Township Road 310. Julia acts as hostess for the cabins, making sure everything is clean and tidy before guests arrive.

As I followed Orpha on the path to this snug little cabin (#1) tucked into the woods, I could see why it has become a popular getaway spot for romantic weekends as well as family vacations. The exposed log walls of the interior are softened by small-paned windows with a touch of lace and a sofa and chair grouping around the fireplace. A kitchenette with microwave and refrigerator, and a grill on the front porch, make preparing meals easy. I found cupboards stocked with cereal, coffee, tea, snacks, and enough dishes and utensils for a family meal. Stairs lead up to a loft with a queen bed. Glancing down from this level on the neatly organized room below—table set with a centerpiece, towels hung by the Jacuzzi, sofa bed made up for the night—I felt like Goldilocks coming into the Three Bears' cottage for the first time.

There's no TV or radio in this log cabin. Guests sit on the porch in rocking chairs and watch the Amish buggies pass by—a peaceful pastime in contrast to their usual busy schedules. And in the evening, it can be the most romantic of settings, with the cabin bathed in candlelight and the glow of the gas log fire. I woke to the sound of rain bouncing off the roof and came downstairs to find a misty fog concealing the road and nearby farm. It was the excuse I needed to leisurely fix my breakfast and linger by the fire with a book until the fog cleared. Some who come to stay in Cabin 1 have always dreamed of living in a log cabin, and others hope to build one of their own someday.

Orpha likes to book families into Cabins 2 and 3, where children have the freedom to explore the woods and generally run around on acreage located off a gravel road. Baseball bats and balls are on the front porch for a quick pick-up game. The interiors of these cabins are similar to Cabin 1 with a little different color scheme. Cabins 2 and 3 are set high on a hill, and parking space is available at the base; the path and steps to all the cabins are well lit. Coming back after dinner and climbing the steps to your very own cabin, you understand why the Weavers describe their getaway as "a quiet spot in the country."

The Weavers, an Amish/Mennonite family, request no alcohol and do not check in guests on Sunday (although you can stay until 12:00 noon). The guest book in my cabin showed a consistent occupancy, and many returning guests feel they have found the perfect hideaway in the

Cricket Hill Cabins. Guests say, "We came for our anniversary and plan to make it an annual affair," and, "It was a great place to reorganize our lives without the interruptions of phone and TV."

THINGS TO DO: There are so many crafts available in the Berlin area that you might want to select specific shops to visit. About midpoint between Millersburg and Berlin there's a historic landmark, Rasketter Woolen Mill, which has been in operation since 1840. Stop in for a tour and look over the variety of colorful rag, braided, and hooked rugs. You can watch the quilt-making process almost every day at the Helping Hands Quilt Shop in Berlin, in business since 1974. You'll find a wide selection of quilts for sale there as well. The Boyd & Wurthmann Restaurant on Main Street in Berlin advertises itself as the place "where the locals eat," and we found this to be a bustling eatery with a choice of light meals or a full dinner.

DIRECTIONS: I-77 to exit 83 for SR 39; west on SR 39; west on US 62; right on TR 310; on right

NEARBY ATTRACTIONS: Amish country

Fields of Home Guest House

*Awaken to a dawn chorus
from the spring-fed pond.*

Mervin and Ruth Yoder, Innkeepers
7278 C.R. 201
Millersburg, OH
(330) 674-7152
www.bbonline.com/oh/fieldsofhome

Ruth and Mervin Yoder, conservative Mennonites, built a log guest house behind their home on County Road 201. This is not a small log cabin, but a large six-unit structure with solid log walls. It's one of a few bed and breakfasts I've visited that allow children, and I could see how it would work, as the suites and rooms are large and nicely spaced. A porch with overflowing flower boxes encircles this log building, which has one of the prettiest views in Amish country—a spring-fed pond and cows grazing in a nearby field. Set against gently rolling hills, it offers a serene refuge from the busy outside world. Entries in guest books at this inn rhapsodize about the simple activity of sitting in rocking chairs on the porch and the solitude it allows.

RATES & RESERVATIONS:
Hours: 7 a.m.–10 p.m.;
Season: Year round; Rates: $$;
Specials: Seasonal specials;
Seasonal minimum stay
requirements, please inquire;
Reservations recommended;
Check, Visa, MC, Disc accepted

ACCOMMODATIONS:
6 rooms w/bath; 2 suites w/bath

AMENITIES: Phone in room, air cond.,
hot tub, CD players and radios

MEALS: Expanded continental
breakfast; May not accommodate
all special diets

SPECIAL CONSIDERATIONS:
Dog and cat living at inn;
Handicapped accessible;
Parking available: Lot

Fields of Home offers three guest rooms and three suites. Cheers for the Yoders in making two of the rooms handicapped accessible with wide doorways, grab bars, and oversize showers. The Maple Suite, a two-level unit, offers generous space that allows for couples traveling together or for small families. A queen bedroom with adjoining bath in the loft, a second queen bed on the ground level, and a sleeper sofa altogether sleep six comfortably, while the kitchenette with microwave, refrigerator, and sink make meal or snack preparation easy. The sitting area is particularly inviting, with a warm blue plaid sofa and chair grouping facing the corner gas fireplace. I loved the Wicker Room; a glorious Palladian window centers the room under the sloping log ceiling of the second story. The room is light-filled and offers a second look at that view of the pond and countryside. Two white wicker queen beds are covered in pristine white comforters, with the only accent a few rose-colored pillows on the bed and in the wicker rockers. A crystal light fixture sparkles at the apex of this log room, and the seemingly strange bedfellows of simple log ceiling and crystal mix just fine. The bathroom, papered in mauve and white against a black background, makes a nice contrast with the white wicker. A recently added suite, the Hickory Room, is furnished in Shaker style with a queen high poster bed. A fireplace, two-person Jacuzzi, and kitchenette complete the unit. The remaining rooms are uniquely decorated and all are stocked with reading materials, CD players, and radios. A selection of games, books, soft drinks, and ice are available on the lower level. Around the corner, a family room where guests can watch videos offers comfortable seating around a fireplace. An expanded continental breakfast is set out each morning from 7:30 until 9:00. Fresh fruit, bagels, and cereals including granola are always available. One of Ruth's specialties is chocolate chip coffee bars.

This Mennonite family invites you to "return to simpler times, to an unhurried world of gentle people depending upon and sharing with each other"—and they have provided the setting at their Fields of Home Guest House. Hint: the porch is not only for daytime sitting; the evening

provides a concert from the pond and, once darkness descends, a chance to reach for your favorite star.

THINGS TO DO: There is so much to see and do when you're in Holmes County that sometimes a little guidance is appreciated. The Yoders suggested some destinations that I did not know well; upon exploration, I found new favorite places to return to. If you've never been to an Amish livestock auction, head over to Mt. Hope on Wednesdays to watch the action and the participants, then move on to the produce and flea markets that are part of the scene. Bulk food stores are also worth a stop, and Ruth suggests you'll find some of those groaning-board–type Amish restaurants on the way such as Mrs. Yoder's in Mt. Hope. To help visitors better understand the Amish and the Mennonites, the Mennonite Information Center near Berlin provides a guided, 30-minute tour of "Behalt," a mural by artist Heinz Gaugel that tells their story in a vivid cyclorama.

DIRECTIONS: I-77 to exit 83 for SR 39; west on SR 39; north on CR 201; on right

NEARBY ATTRACTIONS: Restaurants, craft shops, furniture shops, cheese factories, antique stores, Amish country, flea markets, auctions, bulk food stores

Hasseman House Bed and Breakfast

A sedate Victorian at the gateway to Amish country

Ellen and Harvey Kaufman, Innkeepers
925 U.S. 62
Wilmot, OH
(330) 359-7904
www.amishdoor.com

RATES & RESERVATIONS:
Hours: 8 a.m.–10 p.m.;
Season: Year round;
Rates: $$$;
Specials: Winter packages;
Reservations recommended;
Check, Visa, MC, Disc, Amex accepted

ACCOMMODATIONS: 3 rooms
w/bath; 1 suite w/bath

AMENITIES: Cable TV, air cond.,
use of indoor pool and hot tub at
nearby Inn at the Amish Door

MEALS: Full breakfast, snacks

SPECIAL CONSIDERATIONS:
Not fully handicapped accessible;
Parking available: Lot

Near Wilmot at the northern gateway to Amish country stands a turn-of-the-century house alongside U.S. Route 62—the Hasseman House Bed and Breakfast. The dwelling has known three owners: the Serquet brothers, who came from France and built the house in 1900; the Hassemans, who purchased the house in 1919 and stayed on the land for 75 years; and Milo and Kathryn Miller, who purchased the house at auction in 1994.

Approaching the Hasseman House for the first time, I was reminded of the stately houses that lined the main street of the small Indiana town where I grew up. This farmhome-turned-bed and breakfast is a pale yellow Victorian with dark green trim surrounded by manicured lawns. A brick path bordered by well-tended gardens leads to the wrap-around porch. Its groupings of white wicker chairs and tables provide a perfect spot for afternoon tea or a leisurely breakfast. The Hasseman House is located on 75 acres of farmland just outside Wilmot. Guests can take a nature trail through the woods or relax on the porch and watch the world pass by on U.S. 62.

The original stained glass and warm oak woodwork and floors remain, and guests are taken back to the early 1900s as they step inside the entrance hall. A working fireplace with a cozy seat to the side invites you to sit and get acquainted with this house. To the left of the entrance, a spacious parlor welcomes with floral wallpaper, an antique settee and side chairs, a walnut secretary with curly maple accents, and an early Victrola. Pocket doors with the original beveled glass open to the dining room. At the end of the hall, an oak staircase leads to a landing with a stained glass window. A fine collection of antiques appropriate to the era and a number of original re-brassed light fixtures can be found throughout the house.

A tour of the upstairs reveals three guest rooms, with two carrying the names of the Hasseman children. Rhea's Room, named after the only Hasseman daughter, is a true girl's room with lace curtains, a white iron-and-brass bed, pink wallpaper, and a tan-and-floral rug on the hardwood floor. A sweet childhood picture of Rhea hangs on the wall; an oak chest and chairs with needlepoint seats complete the room. The private bath is a few steps down the hall. Across the hall, the Boy's Room, once the domain of Thereon and Doyle Hasseman, is furnished with a curly maple armoire, a marble-top washstand, and a Victorian high-backed walnut bed. An extra-large bathroom, thought to be the original playroom, adjoins the room. The third guest room at the front of the house is a real charmer, with rose patterned wallpaper, a floral rug on the painted floor, a set of rocking chairs, and a claw-foot tub and pedestal sink in the bath. The afternoon I visited, sunlight filled the room and made me wish I had time for a nap. Steps up to the attic lead to the Honeymoon Suite, a generous space with tongue-and-groove wainscoting in the bedroom portion and a cozy sitting area behind a wicker screen. Honeymooners and family groups alike enjoy the smallest room in this attic suite, furnished

simply with a mattress placed on the floor to offer a view of the stars through the low half-window.

Resident innkeepers Ellen and Harvey Kaufman make sure that guests find snacks when they arrive. Cakes, cookies, and popcorn are waiting in the kitchen. Weekdays, guests are given breakfast vouchers for the Amish Door Restaurant down the road. On Sundays, Ellen serves breakfast in the dining room; thick French toast and waffles come to the table accompanied by Ohio maple syrup and Winesburg sausage. At dinnertime, feast at the Amish Door Restaurant.

THINGS TO DO: Antiquers will be delighted to find antique shopping next door to the inn at the 1881 Antique Barn, filled with a quality collection of furniture, glass, pottery, kitchen collectibles, early toys, and primitives. Browse the nearby Amish Door Shoppes, where you'll find wooden toys, vintage collectibles, bulk foods, and Amish furniture.

DIRECTIONS: I-77 to exit 87 for SR 250; west on SR 250; west on US 62; on left

NEARBY ATTRACTIONS: Amish country, shops, restaurants, bakery, nature center

Inn at Honey Run

*A contemporary inn
with a focus on nature*

Marge Stock, Innkeeper
6920 C.R. 203
Millersburg, OH
(800) 468-6639
www.innathoneyrun.com

RATES & RESERVATIONS:
Hours: 8 a.m.–11 p.m.;
Season: Year round;
Rates: $$–$$$$;
Two-night minimum stay required
on weekends and Thanksgiving;
Reservations recommended;
Check, Visa, MC, Disc, Amex accepted

ACCOMMODATIONS:
37 rooms w/bath; 3 cottages w/bath

AMENITIES: Phone in room, air cond.

MEALS: Expanded continental
breakfast, lunch, dinner, snacks

SPECIAL CONSIDERATIONS:
Dog and cat living at inn;
Handicapped accessible;
Parking available: Lot

Our first visit to the Inn at Honey Run was on a brilliant, crisp October afternoon that showcased this woodland getaway in its autumnal glory. During my next stay, for a February symposium, a huge winter storm gave me a view of the inn cozily encased in snow. Guests gathered around the fireplaces and watched the drifting snow and birds at the feeders. Both these experiences explain the reason for the inn's location off the beaten track in Holmes County—it fits naturally into the landscape and offers serenity and comfort to arriving guests. This was owner Marge Stock's dream when she opened this country inn in 1982.

The approach to the Inn at Honey Run takes you up a winding road to a contemporary structure of wood, stone, and glass nestled in 60 acres of woodland and pastures. A welcoming common room, with hickory Bentwood rockers by the fireplace and a wall of windows connecting you to nature, sets the scene for your stay.

This inn's focus is nature. We stayed on the second level, where the tall corner windows gave us the feeling of living in the treetops. Bird feeders are close to the windows, and bird guides are placed in each room. Binoculars and trail maps are available at the front desk. The decor ranges from Shaker and Early American styles to contemporary, with simple handcrafted furniture and locally made quilts. Returning guests seem to take ownership of their particular rooms and request them for the next visit.

The dining room, hung with colorful quilts that are changed seasonally, is where guests have breakfast and lunch. Reservations are requested for lunch and dinner. The inn relies on locally grown ingredients and homemade breads and desserts. Farm-raised trout, prize-winning Holmes County cheeses, and fresh vegetables are standard fare, along with the inn's own chicken noodle soup, chicken potpie, country-baked pork chops, and chocolate silk pie. From early June through early September, the Milkhaus Cafe deck is open to all for lunch, with soup, salad, sandwiches, and a dessert bar.

A short walk from the main inn building are the Honeycombs—12 earth-sheltered rooms built into the side of a hill with a view overlooking pastures of grazing sheep, goats, and profuse wildflowers. Each unit has a fireplace (gas log on the first level, wood-burning on the second), whirlpool jets in the bath/shower combination, and a stone patio. An expanded continental breakfast of fresh fruit, juices, cereals, and coffeecake is delivered to the door.

Situated high on a hill overlooking a valley, two guest houses, Cardinal and Trillium, afford spectacular views and complete privacy. The Cardinal has a natural stone fireplace in the living room, with a peaked wood ceiling rising up to the skylight. A rainy night brings the staccato sound of rain, and a winter stay provides a snug spot by the fire from which to watch the whirling snow outside. Popular with honeymoon and anniversary couples, the guest cottages have a deck with gas grill, separate living room and bedroom, equipped kitchen, and laundry area. The Trillium offers a hot tub/whirlpool for two. A recently opened accommodation, the Woods House, provides a private stay with two bedrooms, gas fireplace, kitchen, and screened-in porch, making it suitable for four.

With its beautiful setting and attention to detail, the Inn at Honey Run attracts guests year round. Some come for Thanksgiving, others for the fall foliage or the breathtaking beauty of spring. Traditions abound at this inn. The annual decorating of the Christmas tree is literally for the birds—a massive Douglas fir is secured on the large deck outside the dining room, and staff and guests string popcorn and cranberries on the tree and fill grapefruit halves with suet and peanut butter.

The Inn at Honey Run has been a member of the Independent Innkeepers' Association since 1984.

THINGS TO DO: Stop down the road from the inn at the gift shop, "Birds, Books, Blooms," where you can pick up plants and birding supplies, or settle down to peruse the book selection. For information about shops in the Amish area, ask at the desk.

DIRECTIONS: I-77 to exit 83 for SR 39; west on SR 39; right (north) to CR 353; left (west) on CR 203; on right

NEARBY ATTRACTIONS: Amish community, canoeing, golfing

Miller Haus

*A peaceful setting atop
one of the highest points
in Holmes County*

A poem on the Miller Haus brochure describes this bed and breakfast's setting just perfectly:

> *Oh, I live in a house
> at the top of a hill where
> the clouds go drifting by.
> And each lovely flower
> in the garden there, lifts its
> smiling face to the sky.*

While it's only a mile from busy State Route 39, the Miller Haus is approached by a narrow lane off County Road 135, which takes you up a winding hill to the bed and breakfast. Open the gate and step inside the picket fence for a magnificent view from this property, on a ridge overlooking Charm to the

Lee Ann and Daryl Miller, Innkeepers
3135 C.R. 135
Walnut Creek, OH
(330) 893-3602
www.millerhaus.com

RATES & RESERVATIONS:
Season: Closed January;
Rates: $$$;
Specials: Children;
Reservations recommended;
Check, Visa, MC, Disc,
traveler's checks accepted

ACCOMMODATIONS:
9 rooms w/bath

AMENITIES: Air cond., whirlpool tub

MEALS: Full breakfast, snacks

SPECIAL CONSIDERATIONS:
Dog living at inn;
Not fully handicapped accessible;
Parking available: Lot

west and Walnut Creek to the northeast. Miller Haus claims one of the highest points in Holmes County. It's a peaceful scene with llamas, emus, Jacobean sheep, and horses in the pasture on the hillside and Amish farms dotted here and there in the valley below. A roomy porch with twig furniture and padded swings is a perfect spot to take in the panoramic view. And are there flower gardens! The Miller family loves to garden, and the walkways are bordered by sweet-smelling alyssum, petunias, and snow daisies, while the porches overflow with pots and hanging baskets of green and flowering plants. The Miller Haus gardens were featured in *Country Women* magazine.

Daryl and Lee Ann Miller share the innkeeping duties with Lee Ann's mother, Ann DeHass, who lives nearby. Daryl, raised in an Amish family, married Lee Ann, an English girl who came back to the area after graduating from college in Florida. Theirs is a love story that took them to Switzerland for their wedding and back to Holmes County to establish the bed and breakfast. Daryl, a mason/carpenter, and his uncle built the Miller Haus. When I arrived, I met the Miller's young son, Teddy, playing in the yard. The newest addition to the family is baby Joey. The Millers represent a new breed of bed and breakfast hosts—young and ambitious—finding success in the business.

The inn has nine individually decorated guest rooms, and it's hard to pick a favorite. Furnished with oak, cherry, and mahogany reproduction and antique pieces, quilts hand-stitched by relatives, and homey decorative touches, the rooms have their own personalities. Grandpa's Nap Room, with its king-size bed, is popular. Grandma's Spring Room is pretty with pink quilts and curtains, a four-poster bed, and an antique rocker. I wasn't surprised to find quilt squares on the wall, a spool holder, and early advertising signs in the Quilting Corner Room. I stayed in the Log Cabin Room, which was reminiscent of grandma's day with a glass-fronted bookcase filled with quart jars of homemade applesauce, grape jelly, and tomatoes. On the lower lawn level, two luxurious suites open onto private porches. The suites, Tea Time and Garden Party, share a common area with comfortable seating, a gas log fireplace, and a pump organ.

The evening I stayed at the Miller Haus, a group of guests gathered near the fireplace in the large sitting area. As a solo midweek traveler, I found the group friendly and soon learned we hailed from three states. For those who are hesitant to stay at a bed and breakfast on their own, be assured that this evening of quiet conversation beside the crackling fire, and breakfast the next morning with the same folks, were positive experiences. Grandchildren's pictures were shown around and addresses exchanged before we parted.

The dining area in this inn, with its soaring cathedral ceiling and windows to the spectacular view, has tables for four or six. Lee Ann prepares a full country breakfast including fresh fruit, a hot entree made with eggs from the Miller hens, whole hog sausage from the local butcher, homemade bread, and fresh jams. Flower garnishes from Lee Ann's garden, lace tablecloths, and linen napkins make for a gracious table-setting. Whenever guests feel like a snack at the Miller Haus, they find tea and coffee makings and homemade sweets waiting on an old wood cookstove.

One couple who discovered this quiet getaway said, "I could have stayed a week," while another said, "I've had the best sleep I've had in months."

THINGS TO DO: Although the Miller Haus address is Charm, the inn is also very close to Walnut Creek and its bevy of shops and restaurants. Lee Ann knows the area well and is happy to give suggestions and directions to specific shops. Ann DeHass owns the Homestead Restaurant in Charm, which is a short drive from the inn and a popular spot with tourists and locals.

DIRECTIONS: I-77 to exit 83 for SR 39; west on SR 39; right on CR 114; right on CR 135

NEARBY ATTRACTIONS: Walnut Creek shops, Homestead Restaurant, Yoder Amish Home

Oak Ridge Inn

A masterful display of a different type of wood in each room

Joe Miller traveled frequently and used his "on the road" research to plan the country inn he built in Walnut Creek. His goals for the new accommodation included a serene setting, spacious, beautifully decorated rooms and suites, and an unusual idea: using a different wood for each room. His idea was a great success. The Oak Ridge Inn is set in a stand of oak trees on a slight rise overlooking a valley. When the excavation for the inn was started, the builders were careful to save the old oaks, including one that is well over 250 years old. I was a guest in late fall, and the rustling of the dried, brown oak leaves in those tall trees was one of the first things I noticed. The suites are as spacious and inclusive as any I have seen, and the use of wood is exquisite. Joe has created a getaway that appeals to business travelers as

Kenny Hamsher and Karen Burden, Innkeepers
T.R. 403
Walnut Creek, OH
(800) 723-6300
www.valkyrie.net/~cat

RATES & RESERVATIONS:
Hours: 7 a.m.–10 p.m.;
Season: Year round;
Rates: $$–$$$$;
Reservations recommended;
Check, Visa, MC, Disc accepted

ACCOMMODATIONS:
8 suites w/bath

AMENITIES: Hot tub, cable TV, phone in room, air cond.

MEALS: Continental breakfast; May not accommodate all special diets;

SPECIAL CONSIDERATIONS:
Handicapped accessible;
Parking available: Lot

well as those marking a special occasion. Since opening in 1997, the inn has hosted business meetings, family reunions, religious conferences, and anniversary and wedding celebrations. Children are welcome. As you approach Walnut Creek, watch closely for a small sign for Township Road 403, turn left, and the inn is just 500 feet from State Route 39. The inn may be close to a highway, but the rooms are well insulated—another of Joe's concerns based on his many business stays.

The use of a variety of rich woods is the hallmark of the Oak Ridge Inn. Schrocks of Walnut Creek, a well-respected local company, made all the cabinetry and woodwork for these showcase wood rooms. Joe used other local companies, including Weavers of Sugarcreek for the upholstered furniture and Amish craftsman Paul Miller's family-run business, Rainbow Bedding, for the mattresses and bed springs. Returning guests often request the Walnut Room, a corner room with a view in two directions over the valley. Features of this room with a cathedral ceiling are a king-size bed, two plaid recliners, a gas-log fireplace, a Jacuzzi, and a kitchenette. French doors open to a brick patio. The largest room, the Miller Farm Suite, looks out over the Miller family barn, which has been in the Miller family for four generations. A separate living room with a sofa and wing chair grouping in front of the fireplace, a Jacuzzi tub in the bedroom, and a formal dining table that doubles as a conference table

make it a popular room for business guests. Step through the French doors to enjoy the view on a patio, featuring a glider swing and a small waterfall. The Sam P. Schrock Suite honors Mr. Schrock's grandparents. The wood is 1-foot, 4-inch sawed oak, and the reproduction furnishings harken back to 1918. Decorative details like oil lamps and an oak clock continue the theme. All rooms have kitchenettes and decks or patios, and five have two-person Jacuzzis and fireplaces. An expanded continental breakfast is available in the lobby. Innkeepers Karen Burden and Kenny Hamsher keep the place running smoothly.

As I was leaving the Oak Ridge Inn, I asked owner Joe Miller what people like best about their stay. His answer didn't surprise me: "The quiet." Another guest who travels all over the world for business says this inn rates with the best.

THINGS TO DO: Finding a nearby place to eat and shop is easy. The Oak Ridge Inn is across the highway from the little village of Walnut Creek, where you can have an Amish feast or a lighter meal of sandwiches and salad at Der Dutchman. Carlisle House Gifts carries a large selection of teapots and teas, collectible villages, garden items, and a Thomas Kinkade Show-

case Gallery. On the shop's lower level, Global Crafts (SELFHELP Crafts of the World), stocks items from around the world. The elegant Carlisle House specializes in Victorian gifts, and next door the Farmer's Wife shop carries candles, 100 percent cotton home textiles, wreaths, and swags. To satisfy your sweet tooth, stop at Coblentz Chocolates where you can smell the chocolates being made while you pick your favorites from the wide selection of chocolate and old-fashioned candies. If you have children along, consider visiting Yoder's Amish Home, not far from Walnut Creek. This 116-acre working Amish farm offers guided tours of the home, an animal-petting area, and hay and buggy rides. Golfers can hit the links at Willendale Golf Course in nearby Sugarcreek.

DIRECTIONS: I-77 to exit 83 for SR 39; west on SR 39 to Walnut Creek; left on TR 403; on right

NEARBY ATTRACTIONS: Amish country

Olde World Bed and Breakfast

*Enjoy delicious downhome fare
in this Victorian house
in the country.*

Jonna Cronebaugh, Innkeeper
2982 S.R. 516 NW
Dover, OH
(800) 447-1273
www.oldeworldbb.com

RATES & RESERVATIONS:
Hours: 8 a.m.–9 p.m.;
Season: Year round;
Rates: $$$;
Specials: Seniors, AAA (weekdays);
Reservations recommended;
Check, Visa, MC, Disc accepted

ACCOMMODATIONS:
4 rooms w/bath; 1 suite w/bath

AMENITIES: Hot tub, cable TV, air cond.

MEALS: Full breakfast,
lunch, afternoon tea, dinner

SPECIAL CONSIDERATIONS:
Cat living at inn;
Not fully handicapped accessible;
Parking available: Lot

My first impression of the Olde World Bed and Breakfast was of a stately, well-cared-for Victorian standing on a rise in the countryside. And then I talked to innkeeper Jonna Sigrist, another of the new group of young, enthusiastic innkeepers I've met lately. I've heard many a story from those who have purchased houses in need of a tremendous amount of work. As Jonna chronicled the history of this house, I mentally added the Sigrist family to the honor roll I keep of those who rescue old houses.

Built by George Stauffer in 1881 of sun-baked brick with a sandstone foundation, the house remained in the Stauffer family until the 1960s, when it became a rental. Condemned in the early 1970s, the house stood vacant until Jonna's parents, John and Linda Sigrist, purchased the property in 1992. They cleared years of undergrowth from the exterior and tackled the interior after getting rid of the animals who had taken up residence. No windows remained, and new walls had to be built over the existing ones. They were able to save the solid walnut stairs, four-panel pine doors, and pocket doors from the original home. The Olde World Bed and Breakfast opened to their first guests on June 1, 1993.

Jonna grew up on a nearby dairy farm and dreamed that she would someday fix up this old farmhouse and live here. Once the renovation was completed, Jonna and her mom had the fun of selecting furnishings. Those who love period bric-a-brac will enjoy the lace, dresser scarves, and pretty china, along with claw-foot tubs, family antiques, and reproductions filling the four rooms and a suite. The Victorian Room on the first floor is lovely, with bay windows, the original wood floor, a slate fireplace mantel, and a marble-top dresser. A smaller but still very popular room is the cheerful Alpine Room, reflecting the Sigrist family's Swiss heritage. It's done up in country style, with a four-poster topped with a quilt that was hand-stitched by Jonna's grandmother, wooden shutters, and geraniums spilling out of a window box. The Mediterranean Suite on the second floor can accommodate four adults with its sitting room with a day bed, a king-size bed, and a bath. The decor, in shades of green, peach, and ivory echoes the Mediterranean-influenced faux wall finish and pillars. Guests have use of the two parlors downstairs as well as a ve-

randa and the front porch—all good spots to enjoy the fields and forests surrounding the bed and breakfast. Head to the cabin at the side of the house to soak in the hot tub.

Jonna loves to cook and proudly showed me her Elmira's Cooke Delight stove. Everything is prepared from scratch. Specialties served at breakfast include eggs Benedict casserole and peach and butter-pecan muffins. This ambitious innkeeper doesn't stop with breakfast. Make reservations for a "Queen's Tea" served Tuesdays and Wednesdays at noon and 2:00 p.m. Think lunch rather than tea, as her menu offers a variety of sandwiches and salads, along with scones, tea biscuits, and desserts. She has collected her recipes in a book, *Dawn to Dusk*, which also includes photos and history of the house. Romantics reserve the Winter Wonderland package, which includes a carriage or sleigh ride, a candlelight tea for two, a bottle of local wine, and breakfast in bed. December visitors find the house beautifully decorated for the holidays.

THINGS TO DO: Summer guests can make the short drive to see Paul Green's *Trumpet in the Land* at the Schoenbrunn Amphitheater in New Philadelphia. In Dover, take time to tour the J. E. Reeves Home, built in the classically inspired Italianate style—you can have a peek at the lifestyle of a turn-of-the-century industrialist and his family. This grand house is furnished with Reeves family furnishings as well as donated furniture and decorative objects from the Dover Historical Society. As I toured the house, I was pleased to find I could walk into all the rooms—there are no roped-off areas—allowing a closer look at the library, with walnut woodwork and oak parquet flooring, or the third-floor ballroom. Another must-stop while in Tuscarawas County is Warther Carvings in Dover. It's a delightful place on a terraced hillside with stone paths and raised beds of flowers. Ernest "Mooney" Warther carved the *History of Steam* and perhaps is best known for the *Lincoln Funeral Train*, carved of ebony and ivory with mother of pearl accents.

DIRECTIONS: I-77 to exit 83 for SR 39; right (west) on SR 39; right (west) on SR 516; on left

NEARBY ATTRACTIONS: Ohio's Amish country, antiquing, Warther Carvings, Trumpet in the Land outdoor drama, Zoar Village, Atwood and Tappan Lakes, J.E. Reeves mansion

Chapter 3

CENTRAL OHIO—THE HEARTLAND

*South of Cleveland to Columbus, Ohio's rich Heartland
stretches out spanning the mid-section of the state and dipping
in and out of Amish country at its borders.*

The varied topography invites meandering the back roads. Gentle hills give way to pastures and cultivated fields, red barns dot the landscape, and small towns showcase well-kept historic houses. In contrast to the farmland, Mohican State Park offers extraordinary scenic drives through the forest and the Atwood Lake area is often referred to as "the Edge of Paradise."

Take a walking tour of historic Zoar village or plan to come for one of the many festivals. Spend a day at The Longaberger Homestead sampling the entertainment on the main street, a variety of shops, and the restaurants in this new entertainment destination. Loudenville is recognized as the canoe capitol of the Midwest, and you'll find a choice of canoeing, kayaking, rafting or tubing the river. Stop at Malabar Farm and venture into Mansfield to walk the trails and visit the greenhouses of Kingwood Center. This is Johnny Appleseed country, and the fruits of the farms are available at the roadside. Folks like to stop at the National Heisey Glass Museum in Newark and the Granville Historical Museum.

Take your pick of accommodations in the Heartland reviewed in this chapter: a getaway at several proud Victorian homes, a farm setting offering fields and woodland for exploring on foot or horseback, an early railroad pioneer's home, and an inn overlooking Atwood Lake. Along the way, discover small towns where folks still come to shop on Main Street, take in a movie, and stop for a hamburger or an ice cream.

Blackfork Inn

A wonderful old Victorian
filled with antiques and books
in a small-town setting

Sue and Al Gorisek, Innkeepers
303 N. Water St.
Loudonville, OH
(419) 994-3252

RATES & RESERVATIONS:
Hours: 24 hours;
Season: Year round;
Rates: $$;
Reservations recommended;
Check, Visa, MC, Disc accepted

ACCOMMODATIONS:
6 rooms w/bath; 2 suites w/bath

AMENITIES: Air cond.

MEALS:
Expanded continental and
full breakfast

SPECIAL CONSIDERATIONS:
Not fully handicapped accessible;
Parking available: On street

When I first became interested in visiting Ohio's bed and breakfast inns, friends recommended the Blackfork Inn, describing it as a wonderful old Victorian filled with antiques and books in a small-town setting. I finally made my way to Loudonville and found the house and town as described—only now there's Blackfork I, the original 1865 three-story structure listed on the National Register of Historic Places, and Blackfork II, a recently renovated 1847 building across the street. Sue and Al Gorisek bought the inn and property at auction and have been welcoming guests for 18 years.

There's a quiet elegance to the place. It is furnished with English and American antiques, including many family pieces. Sue took time to take me on a tour and related the story of various antiques as well as the history of the house. Al collects Garfield Drape glassware, which is displayed in a back-lighted, velvet-lined case in the first of two parlors. In the formal parlor, a Mason & Hamlin organ is set in the deep bay windows under a Byzantine arch. Sue invited me to touch the silk and linen reproduction wallpaper in this room, which seems quite true to its period with Sue's artistic flower arrangements and a stereopticon with a box of slides—the amusement offered to children of that era. In the evening, as I worked at the dining room table, the lamplit parlor looked like a stage set for a Victorian play. And my friends were right: there are books throughout the house—in the dining room, in a quarter-sawed oak bookcase Sue found on Millionaires' Row in Cleveland; in shelves that line the hallway; in a secretary in the parlor; and in the guest rooms. I found several Ohio books on my night stand and a selection of early *Ohio* magazines in the bathroom.

Six rooms and two suites make up the Blackfork Inn, and it's hard to pick a favorite. The Josephine is memorable, with Sue's great-grandmother's bedroom suite. So is the Margaret, on the third floor, a departure from the Victorian decor with a tropical canopy and a folk-art wardrobe.

Across the street at Blackfork II, it's a completely different look—early Victorian country. I sat awhile in the garden next to the house, enjoying the heavenly fragrance of Sue's herb and flower garden. Two suites and a small antique shop make up the Blackfork II. The Landmark Suite, on the second floor, includes a bedroom with gas fireplace, a sitting room with coffee-making corner, and a huge bathroom with a clawfoot tub. Guests are charmed by the rocking chair and stack of books in this bathroom.

An easygoing innkeeper, Sue is not concerned about exact check-in and -out times. She has placed a clever information piece in the rooms in which she refers to the house as "a grand old lady" and explains the setting of the house so close to the railroad tracks. It seems the man who built the house, Phillip Black, liked to be as close as possible to the tracks to catch the train for his business trips. Guests find earplugs within reach on the bedside table.

Breakfast at the Blackfork is likely to include Amish sausage, cheese, blueberry pancakes with locally made maple syrup, and homegrown raspberries—they might even serve pie.

THINGS TO DO: Downtown Loudonville is three blocks from the inn, and lined up on Main Street are the kinds of stores some of us remember from our small-town childhoods. Visit Raby Hardware, in business since 1885, or sit at a marble counter at the Village Pantry and enjoy a hot fudge sundae. Just around the corner at Loudonville's Ohio Theatre, you can purchase a ticket for $2 to see a movie

in the midst of the ornate decorative touches in this 1910 opera house. The Sojourner Cafe at the end of Main Street offers a surprising selection, from potato-pancake appetizers and pasta combinations, to steak, to a chicken breast and apples Normandy entree, to rich chocolate desserts like chocolate mousse bombe.

Sue is tuned in to what is going on in the area and is happy to help plan a tour for her guests. Bikers and hikers find two of the best trails in the state, and the inn offers golf packages. Mohican State Park and Malabar Farm are nearby. Four times a year, Malabar Farm hosts barn dances, and if you go earlier in the day you can tour Louis Bromfield's home, the Big House, where Humphrey Bogart and Lauren Bacall were married.

DIRECTIONS: I-71 to exit 186 for US 250; left (west) on US 250; right on US 42; left on SR 511; straight on SR 60; right on SR 3; straight on SR 39; right (north) on Water St.; on left

NEARBY ATTRACTIONS: Malabar Farm State Park, Mohican State Park, Amish country

Cowger House #9

Stay in an 1817 log cabin, an 1833 house, or an Amish cottage in historic Zoar village.

Mary and Ed Cowger, Innkeepers
197 4th St.
Zoar, OH
(800) 874-3542
www.zoarvillage.com

RATES & RESERVATIONS:
Hours: By appointment;
Season: Year round;
Rates: $$$;
Reservations recommended;
Visa, MC, Disc, Amex accepted

ACCOMMODATIONS:
10 rooms, 7 w/bath

AMENITIES: Hot tub, cable TV

MEALS: Full breakfast, dinner

SPECIAL CONSIDERATIONS:
Handicapped accessible;
Parking available: Lot

Mary and Ed Cowger have been in the bed and breakfast business for 16 years in the historic village of Zoar. They offer visitors a choice of accommodations: an 1817 log cabin, an 1833 house, or an Amish cottage. The Cowgers find that many of their guests come to celebrate a special occasion; they have also noticed a trend of multiple couples traveling together and requesting use of an entire accommodation—particularly the log cabin and oak cottage.

The Cowger's first bed and breakfast was the 1817 log cabin, which served the early Zoar community as the brewmaster's house. The dining room of the log cabin is the setting for breakfast for guests from all three accommodations. The exposed interior log walls, early tavern tables, and a fireplace give a sense of earlier times. Mary serves a full country breakfast featuring homemade biscuits, muffins, and an egg dish, or German apple pancakes, fried potatoes, and sausage or ham. A candlelight dinner, with a choice of entrees, is served by reservation in the same room.

Three guest rooms in the log cabin are rustic and cozy. Mary's stenciling decorates the rooms furnished with antiques and quilts. The

Cowger Manor, a post-and-beam structure built in 1838, was the first schoolhouse in Zoar. On my July visit, a Christmas tree in the corner of the hallway was festooned with red, white, and blue decorations; Ed explained the tree stays up all year and Mary changes the decorations for various holidays. At the top of the house, the Honeymoon Loft has welcomed many a bridal couple as well as those marking an anniversary. The bathroom may at first surprise and then bring a chuckle from guests. The Cowgers had some fun and installed an oak "two-seater" and an old pitcher pump in a dry sink. Although a spacious room with a queen bed and Jacuzzi, it has the cozy feel of staying in a loft. On the second floor, the Honeymoon Suite—a spacious, light-filled room—is done up in soft floral fabrics.

The final accommodation, the newer Amish Oak Cottage, has a central living room with a wood-burning stove, a sofa, and a table for games and snacks. Four guest rooms are furnished with either oak or white iron-and-brass bedsteads. Two-person Jacuzzis or extra wide showers, pillow-top king beds, and wood-burning fireplaces make the Amish Oak Cottage a luxurious stay.

THINGS TO DO: Festivals and special tours bring visitors to Zoar throughout the year. The Zoar Harvest Festival happens in August with a German beer tent, German music, an established antiques show, and an American folk art show. On September and October weekends, you can learn about Zoar's resident spirits while taking the Lantern Tour of the Ghosts of Zoar. Applefest features apple-butter stirring, open-fire cooking, crafts, and food. Experience an old-style German Christmas during Christmas in Zoar, the first weekend of December.

You don't have to go far to dine while in the village. You'll find lunch or dinner at the Zoar Tavern and Inn, originally House Number 23, where they feature vegetarian entrees along with steaks and seafood. An 1830 canal inn, the Inn on the River, is close by on Towpath Road.

DIRECTIONS: I-77 to exit 97 for SR 212; east on SR 212 to 4th St.; check in at 197 4th St.

NEARBY ATTRACTIONS: Zoar Village, Amish country, Pro Football Hall of Fame, Atwood Lake, Canoe Livery, Roscoe Village, Trumpet in the Land, Ft. Laurens, Reeves Mansion, Warther Museum

Frederick Fitting House

Once a railroad pioneer's home, this comfortable inn boasts lovely gardens.

Barb and Jim Lomax, Innkeepers
72 Fitting Ave..
Bellville, OH
(419) 886-2863

RATES & RESERVATIONS:
Season: Year round;
Rates: $$;
Reservations required;
Check, traveler's checks accepted

ACCOMMODATIONS: 3 rooms w/bath

AMENITIES: Cable TV, air cond.

MEALS: Full breakfast, snacks

SPECIAL CONSIDERATIONS:
Not fully handicapped accessible;
Parking available: On grounds

Hostas and ferns border the front porch of the Frederick Fitting House, a stately 1863 Italianate structure at the corner of Fitting Avenue and Ogle Street in Bellville. The house, built by Frederick Fitting, a prominent Bellville businessman and promoter of the area's first railroad, was established as a bed and breakfast in 1982. When Barbara Lomax purchased the property in 1997, landscaping was one of her first projects. Twenty-one bushes and five trees were removed, allowing more light to fill the high-ceilinged rooms of this Victorian home. Evidence of Barbara's love of gardening can be found in the herb and flower gardens scattered across the large yard.

When the Lomaxes started the interior decoration, they removed seven layers of wallpaper in the foyer and had the floors throughout the downstairs refinished, resulting in warm pine floors. The parlor is a restful room with a chess table set up in the bay window area, where light streams through the stained glass panels. On winter days, the parlor is welcoming with a wood-burning fireplace.

Guests often settle down for the evening in the library off the parlor and sample the inn's collection of classical and big band music on 78-rpm records. There's a library ladder to reach the books on the top shelf

and a comfy plaid loveseat available for reading, watching television, or taking a nap.

At the Frederick Fitting House, mornings start in the sunny dining room, where breakfast is served at the long oak dining table. Barbara likes to prepare Aunt Ruth's Cheese Bake with a side of ham or sausage and homemade muffins. Other favorites of returning guests are buttermilk pancakes and warm cherry or apple crisps. A collection of postcards with scenes of Mansfield from the 1880s is arranged on the wall of the dining room, and Barbara is assembling a similar collection of historic Bellville postcards. The art of Ken Shogren, a Mansfield native, is showcased in the dining room and parlor. Shogren painted scenes familiar to many Ohioans—Malabar Farm, Kingwood Gardens, and Oak Cottage.

In the foyer, a stunning circular staircase of walnut, butternut, and oak leads to three guest rooms. At the top of the stairs, guests find an old General Electric console radio, which belonged to Barbara's grandparents, and glass panels in the windows, which came from a 100-year-old church. A queen four-poster rice bed and matching green velvet chairs are set against burgundy walls with a flower and fruit border in the Colonial Room. Barbara's collection of antique doorknobs is cleverly displayed in the Victorian Room, a charming smaller room with an antique armoire and a queen sleigh bed. I liked the simplicity of the Shaker Room, with early utensils hanging from pegs on the wall, rag rugs, and reproduction Shaker beds covered with rose and green quilts. The bath for the Shaker Room features an Italian marble floor, claw-foot tub, and stenciled walls.

Fans of the Mid-Ohio Sport Car Course have discovered the Frederick Fitting House. Barbara also has returning guests who come to shop for trees and plants at Wade and Gatkins or to access the bike trail.

THINGS TO DO: When visiting small Ohio towns, I like to stop at restaurants frequented by the locals. In Bellville, I was directed to the V & M Restaurant, which advertises "Home-style Cooking—Just Like Mom's." It's an eatery where bean soup and open-face roast beef sandwiches headline the menu and dessert means man-size portions of lemon or fruit pie. A few steps from the V & M, I found one of four antique shops in downtown Bellville.

DIRECTIONS: I-71 south to exit 169 SR 13; south on SR 13; left (west) on Ogle St.; left (south) on Fitting Ave..; on right

NEARBY ATTRACTIONS: Malabar Farms, Mohican State Park, Mid-Ohio Sport Car Course, antiques, bike trail, Kingwood Center

Heartland Country Resort

Ride the trails on resident horses at this country retreat.

Dorene Henschen, Innkeeper
2994 Chesterville-Sparta Rd.
Fredericktown, OH
(419) 768-9300
www.heartlandcountryresort.com

RATES & RESERVATIONS:
Hours: 24 hours;
Season: Year round;
Rates: $$$$; Specials: AAA,
multi-night discounts and packages;
Reservations required;
Check, Visa, MC, Disc, Amex accepted

ACCOMMODATIONS:
7 rooms w/bath; 5 suites w/bath

AMENITIES: Pool, phone in room,
air cond., Jacuzzis, fireplaces, movies,
horseback riding, pool table

MEALS: Full breakfast,
lunch, dinner, snacks

SPECIAL CONSIDERATIONS:
Dog, horses, cats, cattle,
chickens living at inn;
Guest pets allowed;
Handicapped accessible;
Parking available: Lot

Nestled in the rolling hills and beautiful woodlands of central Ohio is the Heartland Country Resort, an upscale guest ranch offering luxurious accommodations in a remodeled 1878 farmhouse, a carriage house suite, and three log units built into the hillside. For true equestrians or occasional riders, this is the place for a getaway where you can ride the resident horses in an insulated indoor arena, a large outdoor arena, or through the meadows and woodland trails.

Dorene Henschen, who designed this private country retreat that covers more than a hundred wooded acres, says, "I welcome the opportunity to share my love of nature with others." Also an elementary schoolteacher, she is aware of the joy and learning that children gain from spending time with animals. Kids love being able to wander out to the barnyard to pet a kitten or visit the horses in the barn.

Couples will enjoy the Kelly Room in the main house, with traditional cherry furniture, love seats, and a window seat overlooking the farm. Relax by the fire in your private Jacuzzi. House guests enjoy breakfast in the dining room, with its wide-plank floors, where a romantic dinner by the fireplace can also be reserved.

The Heartland is truly an intergenerational place. I visited on a warm June day and observed a family group of children, parents, and grandparents unloading two vans for a long-weekend stay. It wasn't long before the kids jumped into the pool and the grandparents settled under an umbrella table on the large deck. In the farmhouse, guests find a recreation room with pool table, television, and games. Picnic lunches, hayrides, bonfires, and riding lessons are available for an additional charge.

If you like to have your own space, check out the log suites on the hillside nearby. Each unit was designed and decorated to fit in the natural setting. The view from the Wildflower Unit is of meadows of wildflowers; the Woodland Unit perches above a meandering stream and looks out to the woods. The Native American Suite has yucca plants outside, while inside dreamcatchers dance from the cathedral ceiling. Art, deco-

rative pieces, and books selected especially for each log home reflect each suite's theme. Guests find a complete kitchen (with refrigerator stocked with breakfast items and snacks), a Jacuzzi for two, a glass-front stove, and a TV/VCR. Guests love the porches with charcoal grills, swings, and the friendly farm dogs and cats that come by for a visit.

Every time I return to visit the Heartland, Dorene has added something new; on my third visit since she opened in 1994, I noticed the Carriage House Suite. Ideal for a family stay or a business retreat, it has a living room with a solid oak table that can double for a meeting space. A separate bedroom with queen bed, queen sleeper sofa, gas fireplace, and complete kitchen make up the unit, which is handicapped-accessible. A gift shop in the same building, Heartland Country Gifts, carries a line of horse-related gifts, afghans, antique toys, and books.

Dorene's goal is to make a stay here unforgettable. She backs up her philosophy with an attentive staff ready to give personal attention. Guests say, "We experienced the most beautiful ride through the woodland heavy with beech trees providing a light dappled trail. Thank you for the friendly smiles and terrific food. We'll be back." And come back they do for special occasions, family reunions, and retreats.

THINGS TO DO: Nearby attractions include Malabar Farm, Mid-Ohio sport car course, and Mohican State Park. Antique buffs can look forward to browsing the many shops in the area.

DIRECTIONS: I-71 south to exit 151 for SR 95; east on SR 95; south on SR 314; south on CR 179; on right

NEARBY ATTRACTIONS: Amish country, Kingwood Garden Center, Mohican and Malabar Farm state parks, golfing, fishing, canoeing

Inn at Dresden

*This 10,000-square-foot
Tudor is ringed with decks
for enjoying the view.*

Patricia Lyall, Innkeeper
209 Ames Dr.
Dresden, OH
(740) 754-1122
www.theinnatdresden.com

RATES & RESERVATIONS:
Hours: 9 a.m.–10 p.m.;
Season: Year round;
Rates: $$$–$$$$;
Specials: Children, seniors,
singles, AAA;
Reservations recommended;
Check, Visa, MC, Disc, Amex accepted

ACCOMMODATIONS: 10 rooms w/bath

AMENITIES: Hot tub, cable TV, phone in
room, air cond., fireplace, deck

MEALS: Full breakfast, snacks

SPECIAL CONSIDERATIONS:
Handicapped accessible;
Parking available: Lot

The Inn at Dresden, a Tudor home perched high on a hill overlooking a village below, was built in 1980 by Longaberger basket company founder Dave Longaberger. It is a favorite accommodation for Longaberger basket collectors who come to Dresden. Longaberger didn't cut any corners in building this 10,000-square-foot home ringed with decks—five private decks and an 8,000-square-foot multi-level deck across the back of the house.

Although the Inn at Dresden is massive, the staff extends a warm welcome. Upon arrival, guests are given a tour of the place and then invited to help themselves from the cookie jar on the kitchen counter. Every evening there is a wine-and-cheese social hour from 6:30 to 7:30 p.m. in the small den off the veranda.

The decor for the 10 guest rooms reflect the history of the area and local attractions. Innkeeper Pat Lyall says the most requested room is City Lights, at the top of the inn, with a panoramic view of Dresden and the surrounding countryside. With upbeat, contemporary decor, the room features a king-size bed, leather swivel rockers, and a heart-shaped, two-person Jacuzzi. Devotees of Victoriana request the Dresden

Suite, an elegant space with a king-size four-poster and a gas-log fireplace viewed from the double Jacuzzi. Both of these rooms open to a private wraparound deck. The Zane Grey has a library ambiance with dark paneling, a massive stone fireplace, a sleigh bed, and collector editions of the author's works. Golf enthusiasts can settle in the Clubhouse, and safari-goers might choose the Wilds Room. The Lodge, the former sauna, gives a nod to Western decor; the Gallery takes you to Key West.

Pat says that along with midweek business travelers and those who come for special occasions she also books groups who take over the entire inn for church retreats, and organizations like the group of quilters who recently met there. Guests have access to the Dresden fitness center and pool.

Breakfast is a casual affair at this inn. After making your selections from the breakfast buffet (with a choice of three hot entrees), you can choose to eat on the enclosed veranda or dine in style in the formal dining room, with its hand-painted American Heritage mural (the same mural/wallpaper can be found in the White House). We savored the freshly made cinnamon rolls that have a place on the buffet daily.

The Inn at Dresden is a member of the Independent Innkeepers' Association, joining in 2000.

THINGS TO DO: For a special dinner, the innkeepers can arrange a meal at the Highlands, a large A-frame building next door. Though the Highlands mainly caters special events, if space is available they will work in guests from the inn. We were treated to a bountiful buffet and that same panoramic view that we loved at the inn. For lighter fare in Dresden, stop at Popeye's, a flashback to the "Fabulous Fifties" featuring chrome chairs with padded leatherette seats, neon signs, and a hostess in a poodle skirt.

We spent a day visiting nearby destinations, but found there was not enough time to do it all. At the Longaberger Manufacturing Campus, you can take a self-guided tour and watch the basket makers at work. A day can easily be spent at the Longaberger Homestead with its retail shops, variety of restaurants, and the Crawford Barn. Nearby Roscoe Village and Zanesville Pottery Outlets also beckon.

Don't overlook little Dresden. It's a great walking town with baskets of flowers and benches along the main street. The shops offer crafts and items for those collectible Longaberger baskets—you are in "Basketville," after all.

DIRECTIONS: I-77 to exit 65 for US 36; west on US 36; right on SR 16; left on SR 60; right (east) on Dutch Hill Rd.; left (south) on Jody Dr.; right (south) on Ames Dr.; on left

NEARBY ATTRACTIONS: Longaberger basket factory, Zanesville Pottery Outlets, Amish country, Roscoe Village

Mainstay

*A Civil War veteran's home
with gunsights on the parlor's
bay windows*

In 1886, Civil War veteran Joseph Folk built the house on East Main Street in Louisville that is now the Mainstay Bed and Breakfast. Folk left a few reminders that he once lived here, such as gunsights on the bay windows in the parlor, which were shown to me by owners/innkeepers Joe and Mary Shurilla, who enjoy sharing the history of their house with visitors. This Queen Anne was likely built from a design found in *Shopwell's Modern Houses* pattern book. Architectural details that were preserved include the original tin ceiling in the dining room, pocket doors, colored glass in the front door, and rich dark oak woodwork—the first thing I noticed. It appeared to be carved, but Joe explained that the designs in the wood came from a process known as wet press. The Shurillas say that almost everyone notices and comments on the beautiful detail of the woodwork.

Joe and Mary Shurilla, Innkeepers
1320 E. Main St.
Louisville, OH
(330) 875-1021
www.bbonline.com/oh/mainstay

RATES & RESERVATIONS:
Hours: 8 a.m.–9 p.m.;
Season: Year round;
Rates: $$;
Reservations recommended;
Checks accepted

ACCOMMODATIONS:
2 rooms w/bath; 1 suite w/bath

AMENITIES: Oversized whirlpools in 2 rooms

MEALS: Full breakfast, snacks

SPECIAL CONSIDERATIONS:
Dog living at inn;
Not fully handicapped accessible;
Parking available: Lot

The parlor offers a slice of Victoriana with curio cabinets filled with Mary's collections of bells and china. A Lincoln chair and claw-foot rocker are pulled up near the bay windows. A collection of antique hat pins, family pictures, and history books fill table tops. Another common room is the cozy library with matching wing chairs, an antique settee, and a gas fireplace.

A full country breakfast is served in a dining room with a wonderful cream-colored tin ceiling and a floral patterned carpet that belonged to Mary's grandmother. The table is set with antique dishes in an Old Rose pattern, and Mary adds little touches like individual flower vases. For health conscious guests, she offers yogurt and cereal, but she also serves her special quiche along with fresh fruit and sweet rolls. Upon arrival, guests receive a complimentary fruit, cheese, and sparkling-beverage basket.

The South Suite features a bedroom with a queen four-poster bed and an antique chest. Guests can relax in the oversize whirlpool tub with a Franklin stove nearby. There's also a traditional bath with a claw-foot tub.

A spacious second suite down the hall has a four-poster queen rice bed and a wide window seat in the upstairs bay window. The East Room, furnished with a waterfall bedroom suite some of us remember from the 1940s, has a luxurious bath with a black marble whirlpool tub. At the end of the hall, a sitting room offers television with cable and VCR, a refrigerator with fruit drinks and bottled water, and the kind of chairs you can kick back and relax in. Joe is especially proud of his mother's antique barrister's bookcase that has a place in this room.

THINGS TO DO: Canton is 10 miles from Louisville, so the Shurillas host guests who are in town to visit the Pro Football Hall of Fame, the National First Ladies' Library, and the Canton Classic Car Museum (filled with cars from 1904 to 1981). The town of Louisville, settled by French and Germans in the early 1800s, has several interesting buildings listed on the National Register of Historic Places, such as St. Louis, a Gothic-style church. Charles Julliard made his fortune in the Gold Rush and returned to build a fine Victorian home in Louisville. Julliard brought the first piano to Louisville, and after his death the Julliard School of Music was established in New York City. The Julliard mansion now serves as a community center for seniors, and tours can be arranged. Golf enthusiasts can choose from 40 public and private golf courses within 50 miles of Canton.

Guests can enjoy an evening meal at the Brickyard Steak and Ale in

Louisville or take the short drive to Mulligan's Pub in Belden Village. If the Mainstay is booked, the Shurillas have a second accommodation in Canal Fulton—a 1865 Georgian-style post and beam home called the Canal House Bed and Breakfast.

DIRECTIONS: I-77 to exit 107B for SR 62; east on SR 62; south on SR 44; left on SR 153 (Main St.); on right

NEARBY ATTRACTIONS: Pro Football Hall of Fame, The National First Ladies' Library, Classic Car Museum

Pitzer-Cooper House

*A beautifully restored
Greek revival house on
gently rolling farmland*

Joe and Teresa Cooper, Innkeepers
6019 White Chapel Rd. SE
Newark, OH
(740) 323-2680
www.pitzercooper.com

RATES & RESERVATIONS:
Hours: negotiable;
Season: Year round; Rates: $$;
No Fri-night-only stays;
Reservations required;
Check, Visa, MC, Disc, Amex accepted

ACCOMMODATIONS:
2 rooms w/bath; 1 suite w/bath

AMENITIES: Cable TV,
phone in room, Internet, air cond.

MEALS: Full breakfast

SPECIAL CONSIDERATIONS:
Cat (outdoors only) living at inn;
Not fully handicapped accessible;
Parking available: Lot

The first time I came to the Pitzer-Cooper, I thought of it as the quintessential early house in a rural setting. A second visit five years later reinforced the impression. The innkeepers, Joe and Teresa Cooper, kept the historical integrity of the dwelling when they renovated it. Built in 1858 by Anthony Pitzer, Jr., the house is of Greek Revival design but has some Italianate features. Only two families have lived in this house, which is listed on the National Register of Historic Places: the Pitzer family, for nearly 130 years, and the Coopers, since 1985. Joe and Teresa honored the Pitzer family by naming rooms after them.

I immediately noticed the quiet of this country setting with its manicured lawn and fragrant herb garden. There's a feeling of space inside; tall windows in the dining room remain uncurtained, providing an unobstructed view of the gently rolling farmland. The colors and prints in the fabrics are just right for this nineteenth-century house with wide moldings, six-panel doors, and oak and pine floors.

The front doors of the Pitzer-Cooper House retain the original colored glass. Once inside, you'll find a music room with a baby grand piano, floor-to-ceiling bookcases, a window seat, and wing chairs. An informal TV room and a dining room are also found on the first floor.

A winding cherry staircase leads to the Melissa Pitzer Suite, made up of a large sitting room, a bedroom with a queen-size bed, and a bathroom. A second guest room is the Major Anthony Room, with views to the countryside in two directions. This room has some lovely antiques, including a Pennsylvania Dutch Sheraton chest, an antique cherry desk, and a four-poster bed made up with a floral quilt and checked bedskirt. Hearts and flowers cover the walls in an adjoining bath with an angle shower and an oak wardrobe. I asked about the Shaker light fixtures and learned that the Coopers designed the beautifully simple lights.

You can tell by the sparkle in his eye when he talks about those who come to stay at the Pitzer-Cooper House that Joe enjoys the guests, and the Coopers have many who return again and again. One business traveler who stayed with them for several months became so comfortable he felt he was part of the family and offered to mow the lawn.

Teresa's full breakfasts include healthful entrees like baked egg souffle and freshly made breads. She uses herbs from her garden in recipes and fresh flowers for garnishes.

THINGS TO DO: Heisey glass was produced in Newark from 1896 to 1957, and the National Heisey Glass Museum, with hundreds of patterns on display, brings many visitors to the area. Nearby in Utica, Ye Olde Mill is a good place to stop for lunch on the picnic grounds or to sample Velvet Ice Cream in the old-fashioned ice cream parlor. The mill was built in 1817 and is home to a museum that tells the story of ice cream from Roman times to the present. The bed and breakfast is also close to the Dawes Arboretum, with 1,150 acres of virgin forest, meadows, and formal gardens. Landscape architect Makoto Nakamura designed the beautiful Japanese Garden.

DIRECTIONS: I-77 to exit 44B for I-70; west on I-70 to exit 132 for SR 13; right (north) on SR 13; left on White Chapel; on right

NEARBY ATTRACTIONS: Dawes Arboretum, Longaberger basket factory, Moundbuilders State Memorial, Ye Olde Mill, National Trails Raceway, Blackhand Gorge, Flint Ridge, Institute of Industrial Technology, National Heisey Glass Museum, outstanding golf courses

Searle House

*Check out famous Ohioans
honored in this resplendent
"Painted Lady."*

Ken and Victoria DiBiagio, Innkeepers
49 Railroad St.
Plymouth, OH
(419) 687-2222
www.searlehouse.com

RATES & RESERVATIONS:
Season: Year round;
Rates: $$; Specials: Seniors;
Reservations required;
Check, Visa, MC accepted

ACCOMMODATIONS:
9 rooms w/bath; 1 suite w/bath

AMENITIES: Cable TV,
phone in room, Internet, air cond.,
fishpond, flower garden

MEALS: Expanded continental and
full breakfast, lunch, dinner, snacks;
Beer, wine, and liquor served

SPECIAL CONSIDERATIONS:
Handicapped accessible;
Parking available: Lot, on street

Some people who have fond memories of growing up in a small town leave a monument in the park or endow a scholarship. Eleanor Searle Whitney McCollum restored a house in her hometown of Plymouth, Ohio, providing a fine bed and breakfast for visitors to the heart of Johnny Appleseed country.

The Searle House, named for Eleanor's family, who have been part of the community for more than 150 years, is a Second Empire structure and the only house of this style remaining in Plymouth. It's set close to the railroad, because it once served as a guest house for VIPs and passengers on the Baltimore and Ohio Railroad. It took two years to paint the house gray with gingerbread trim in hot pink, lavender, purple, and green. For those who love Victorian splendor, the exterior trim is worth a look. The spring day of our visit, an amateur photographer and history buff was taking pictures from all angles of the Searle House. Built between 1876 and 1870, the house has been placed on the National Register of Historic Places.

Ken and Victoria DiBiagio are not what you might consider typical innkeepers. Ken comes from the hotel industry, having served as a certified hotel administrator for 28 years, a position that required frequent moves. When the couple learned about the opening for innkeepers in this small Ohio town, they decided to make a lifestyle change. Ken says it's all the same whether you're dealing with large hotels or a bed and breakfast: "It's how you treat the guests." Gourmet cooks, the DiBiagios serve a full breakfast and offer dinner by reservation. Victoria says that while they prepare a variety of entrees, their specialty is homemade pasta. Guests can be seated on the spacious lawn for refreshments or dinner. A large umbrella shelters a fishpond and flower gardens. Dinner is also served in the dining room, which features Victorian decorative touches. The DiBiagios will also help plan weddings, family reunions, and other special occasion events. The inn has a full liquor license.

Nine high-ceilinged guest rooms are furnished with quality antiques, quilts, and simple window treatments. I found recessed windows, deep window seats, original oak woodwork, and stacks of books. There's an unusual theme to this bed and breakfast: Each room is named for an important Ohioan, with rooms dedicated to authors, entertainers, Native Americans, and historical and sports figures. Outside each room, newspaper clippings, lists of honors, and books are available about that particular honoree. There is a handicapped-accessible room on the first floor and a family suite on the second. Common rooms include a parlor with deep rose walls, antique velvet settee, and marble-top tables. Guests also have use of the dining room and large enclosed porch.

THINGS TO DO: The small town of Plymouth has an antique clothing shop worth checking out: "Stitches in Time" specializes in vintage clothes and alterations and brings folks from far and wide. The town hosts a small festival, the Silver King Festival, that celebrates the manufacture of Silver King tractors in Plymouth. During a recent festival, a croquet tournament was staged on the Searle House grounds, with the players in period dress.

DIRECTIONS: I-71 to exit 176 for SR 30; west on SR 30; west on SR 39; north on SR 314; north on SR 61; west (left) on Broadway; left (south) on Railroad St.; on left

NEARBY ATTRACTIONS: Mid-Ohio sport car course, Cedar Point, antiques, canoeing, museums, theater, free outdoor concerts (in Shelby), many area festivals

Whispering Pines Bed and Breakfast

A "two million dollar view" overlooking Atwood Lake

Bill and Linda Horn, Innkeepers
1268 Magnolia
Atwood Lake, OH
(330) 735-2824
www.atwoodlake.com

RATES & RESERVATIONS:
Season: Year round;
Rates: $$$$;
Reservations recommended;
Check, Visa, MC, Disc, Amex,
money order, cash accepted

ACCOMMODATIONS:
4 rooms w/bath; 1 suite w/bath

AMENITIES: Jacuzzi, air cond.

MEALS: Full breakfast

SPECIAL CONSIDERATIONS:
Not fully handicapped accessible;
Parking available: Lot

L inda and Bill Horn refer to the vista from their bed and breakfast as "a million dollar view." The Horns came down from their home in Michigan in 1987 to pick up some antiques and discovered the Atwood Lake area. They bought this Italianate house with a magnificent overlook of Atwood Lake without ever stepping inside. Linda says, "We bought the view and the house came with it." After two years of extensive renovations and 10 years in business, Linda suggests it may have become a "two million dollar view."

Whispering Pines is set on a rise above Atwood Lake sheltered by rows of pines. The house, built in 1880 by John and Christina Hunter, is a fanciful "Painted Lady" in deep blue with maroon and pink trim. The lake beyond presents a peaceful scene with sailboats floating by. A brick path bordered by lush flower beds leads up to the screened-in porch. Bill has laid thousands of old bricks he found on the property, the pleasing result being a circular courtyard and brick paths.

The Horns have furnished their house with quality antiques from the mid- to late-Victorian era. A gift from Bill's grandmother of 500 glass top

hats started them on the road to collecting antiques, and their first serious find was the glass-fronted cabinet that now displays these collectibles
in the parlor. Other special collections include Linda's beaded and mesh
handbags—displayed on the wall of the downstairs guest room, the
Dryer Room, and Wallace Nutting prints in the Linder Suite. All the light
fixtures and lamps are authentic, and a pleasing color scheme of blue,
pink, and rose mixed with greens flows through the house. I loved the
Huffmann Suite at the top of the winding staircase; this unusual six-
sided room is furnished with an antique walnut bedroom set including
an ornate armoire, and affords spectacular views of Atwood Lake. The
Hunter Room echoes the Victorian age with a high-backed walnut bed,
wood-burning fireplace, and claw-foot bathtub, while the Honeymoon
Suite is a lavish space with oversize Jacuzzi, wood-burning fireplace, a
king-size bed, and a balcony.

Linda loves to cook and claims she has such a variety of menus that
a person could stay for 45 days and be served 45 different breakfasts. She
has collected her recipes into a book, *Taste Sensations from Whispering
Pines Bed and Breakfast* (Bill and good friends were the lucky taste-
testers). Breakfast is served on the screened-in porch in pleasant
weather; on cooler mornings folks gather in the dining room. Favorites
include frittatas and blintzes.

Some guests return bearing plants, which get re-planted and are
identified by small signs with the donor's name in the flower gardens
along the brick path—a typical personal touch by these experienced
innkeepers.

THINGS TO DO: When you're ready to play during a stay at Whispering Pines,
the Atwood Lake region waits to be explored—28 miles of lake shoreline, fishing, swimming, boating (ask about renting the Horn's pontoon
boat), and hiking/biking trails in this protected natural environment. A
big summer spectacular is *Trumpet in the Land* outdoor drama. Watch
the July Fourth fireworks over the lake from your box seat on the porch
of Whispering Pines or the Christmastime light show on the water.
(Then you get to see the six Christmas trees Linda decorates the house
with during the holidays.)

Don't miss a chance while you are in the area to dine at the charming
Bluebird Farm Restaurant near Carrollton. After turning onto a lane off
Alamo Road, follow the little bluebird signs marking your way to the
century-old red brick farmhouse. The menu features homemade soups
and daily specials like quiche, chicken casserole, and barbecued beef.
Save room for homemade cream puffs or a piece of cherry macaroon
pie. Check out the gift shop loaded with items for the garden, including

bluebird houses, and stop at the new museum on the grounds, Susie's Museum of Childhood.

DIRECTIONS: I-77 south to exit 103 for SR 800; south on SR 800; left on SR 183; right on SR 542; on left

NEARBY ATTRACTIONS: Atwood Lake, Trumpet in the Land, Amish country, Dennison Railroad Festival, Riverfront Antique Mall

94

White Oak Inn

Mystery Weekends in the "middle of nowhere"

Ian and Yvonne Martin, Innkeepers
29683 Walhonding Rd.
Danville, OH
(740) 599-6107
www.whiteoakinn.com

RATES & RESERVATIONS:
Hours: 24 hours;
Season: Year round;
Rates: $$$;
Specials: Midweek, 2-night packages;
Two-night minimum stay required on weekends;
Reservations required;
Check, Visa, MC, Disc, Amex accepted

ACCOMMODATIONS: 10 rooms w/bath

AMENITIES: Phone in room, air cond.

MEALS: Full breakfast, dinner, snacks

SPECIAL CONSIDERATIONS:
Dog living at inn;
Not fully handicapped accessible;
Parking available: Lot

The White Oak Inn, a lovely turn-of-the-century farmhouse sided with white oak and fronted with a wide porch, stands surrounded by fine old trees in the beautiful Walhonding Valley near Mount Vernon. When Ian and Yvonne Martin decided to leave their career positions in Canada to become innkeepers, they looked at many properties before purchasing this ideal getaway in the middle of 14 wooded acres.

Upon entering the inn, we were greeted by classical music. Fresh flowers and antiques throughout the house lent a gracious feel to the place. Timbers from the inn property were used for the red oak floors and white oak woodwork. Guests like to gather in the common room, where a restored Chickering grand piano is the focal point. Rocking chairs are pulled up to the fireplace, an abundance of reading material is at hand, and jigsaw puzzles wait to be completed.

A padded window seat on the stair landing provides a quiet place to curl up with a book or watch the birds at the feeders in the backyard. Seven guest rooms in the house are named for the type of wood featured in them. At the top of the stairs, the Cherry Room is a sun-filled room furnished with an antique cherry bed. Simple white tie-back curtains and chenille bedspread are brightened by floral accents in the rug and comforter. Down the hall, the Walnut Room welcomes guests with a rose color scheme, a marble-top chest, and a Victorian settee in the bay window. The Martins converted a former chicken house into three spacious suites, the largest of which is the Dogwood Room, with a high queen bed and a comfortable chair by the fireplace. With luxurious interiors and a porch running the length of the structure, you would never know it once was home to chickens.

At the White Oak Inn, dining is an experience to be savored. Yvonne has appeared on PBS's *Country Inn Cooking with Gail Grecco* and seems to produce fantastic meals effortlessly. Starters for our breakfast were a delicious juice combination and hot-from-the-oven muffins all served in a pleasant dining room set with pink linen centered with small bouquets. Yvonne favors farm-fresh eggs and local meats and cheeses. Breakfast entrees might be broccoli cheese strata or Belgian waffles with pecans and bananas. Plan to reserve a gourmet dinner when Yvonne serves main courses like chicken with apricot glaze or mushroom-stuffed ravioli followed by almond cake with raspberry coulis. Her recipes are collected in a cookbook, *Cinnamon Mornings and Chocolate Nights*.

The White Oak Inn brochure invites you to escape to "the Middle of Nowhere." Many guests find such a satisfying stay in this country setting that they don't want to leave. The Martins offer a full schedule of special weekends. Choose from their popular murder mystery, spring wildlife, or big band weekends. Packages for these events include an overnight stay, dinner, and breakfast. You have to book early for the Yuletide program, a Dickens Christmas, which begins with an afternoon tea, moves on to a performance of Charles Dickens' classic story presented by one actor(!), and finishes with a light supper.

The Martins have done such a fine job of making the comfort and feeding of their guests top priority that they have garnered quite a list of accolades, including being named one of the top 50 inns by *American Historic Inns* and *The Road Best Traveled* newsletter, and being featured in *Midwest Living* magazine. The inn has also been a member of the Independent Innkeepers' Association since 1989. They welcome small business meetings and retreats.

THINGS TO DO: Should you want to take a day trip, Roscoe Village, Amish country, and Longaberger Homestead are not far from the inn. Hikers, bikers, and roller bladers will enjoy Kokosing Gap Trail, only 10 minutes away. (Rocky, the White Oak Inn's friendly resident black Lab, might come along for a hike.)

DIRECTIONS: I-71 south to exit 169 for SR 13; south on SR 13 to SR 36; east on SR 36 to SR 715; left on SR 715; on left

NEARBY ATTRACTIONS: Roscoe Village, Amish country, Longaberger Basket Factory, The Wilds, Kokosing Gap Trail, antiques

Winfield Bed and Breakfast

Every comfort and luxury are extended in this stunning country house.

Bill and Sally Davidson, Innkeepers
1568 S.R. 60
Ashland, OH
(800) 269-7166
www.bbonline.com/oh/winfield

RATES & RESERVATIONS:
Hours: 8 a.m.–10 p.m.;
Season: Year round;
Rates: $$–$$$;
Reservations required;
Check, Visa, MC, Disc, Amex accepted

ACCOMMODATIONS:
2 rooms w/bath; 1 suite w/bath

AMENITIES: Cable TV, phone in room, air cond., fireplace (in some rooms)

MEALS: Full breakfast

SPECIAL CONSIDERATIONS:
Not fully handicapped accessible;
Parking available: Lot

When innkeepers Sally and Bill Davidson were looking for a bed and breakfast property, they had three criteria: it had to be a century house, in the country, and not too far from family. The search ended when the former Lakewood residents found an 1876 Italianate home near Ashland. Approaching the Winfield Bed and Breakfast for the first time, I was impressed with this formal house, painted the palest of pinks with green shutters and surrounded by sweeping lawns and gardens. A pergola in the green center of the circular drive welcomes with clematis, peonies, and roses.

Once they took possession of the house, the Davidsons—he an artist, she a skilled seamstress—started to remake this nineteenth-century structure room by room. After an initial stay, I was so charmed with their style that I stop back whenever I have time to see what they're doing next. During a two-year stay in England, when Bill was with the Air Force, they gained an appreciation for antiques and sought out quality pieces for the bed and breakfast. We stayed in the Garden Suite, which looked out through French doors to a terrace and beyond to a bucolic scene of grazing sheep. The light-filled sitting room and bedroom in English country decor showcase some of the Davidsons' fine English and American antiques. The canopied Shaker bed is one of those you access by a small stool (or the run and leap method). Snuggle into the cushy sofa by the fire and watch a classic video from the innkeepers' collection.

Upstairs in the East Room, you begin to appreciate some of the architectural interest provided by fine crown moldings and rich faux marble bordering the thick carpet. Wingback tapestry chairs in the bow window and an eighteenth-century French armoire add to the elegant formal feel. In the Crow's Nest at the top of the house, the cocoa walls contrast with white molding, pine armoire, a mahogany four-poster, and white louvered shutters at the window. A turndown service and French chocolates at bedside are some of the extras guests appreciate.

The Davidsons are naturals at innkeeping. You end up sitting on a Louis XV chair at the kitchen table talking to Sally while she cooks, or walking through the house with Bill to look at his next project. Upon arrival, guests are offered a beautifully arranged fruit and cheese tray, which many take out to the patio in warm weather. The patio is another of the Davidsons' improvements. Typical of their quest for the "old," they searched until they found brick that looked weathered for the patio, added Lutyens benches and market umbrellas, and created an alfresco dining spot.

Sally serves breakfast in a classically inspired dining room highlighted with crown molding and a faux marble floor in green and ivory with a black border. After a starter of freshly squeezed orange juice and fresh fruit topped with yogurt, she likes to serve a family-favorite "comfort" food: eggs goldenrod, with a white sauce over toasted French bread and a rasher of bacon on the side. Or she might prepare a sweet red pep-

per strata or gingerbread pancakes with lemon sauce.

Sally and Bill genuinely extend every comfort and luxury in this stunning country house. Others who have discovered it and return include conservators who come to Ashland University as well as many midweek business guests. Those who have to be on the road should access the Winfield's "Business Traveler's Express Page" on the Web to get a sense of the Davidsons' style and humor!

THINGS TO DO: For an evening meal, the Davidsons recommend Casa Fiesta, serving a regional Mexican menu, just three miles from their house. For antique lovers, Sally suggests specific shops: Delegrange Antiques in Jeromesville, and Antiques on Main and the Gleaner in Ashland. If time allows, head over to Kingwood Center in Mansfield to enjoy the gardens, greenhouses, and nature trails.

DIRECTIONS: I-71 to exit 186 for US 250; left (west) on US 250; right on US 42; left on SR 60; on left

NEARBY ATTRACTIONS: Amish country, Mohican State Park, Kingwood Center, Malabar Farm State Park, antique shops

Chapter 4

EAST AND WEST
ALONG THE NORTH COAST—
LAKE ERIE STAYS

Ohioans can choose from many destinations for getaways, and Lake Erie is one of the best. In fact, visitors from other states often express surprise at finding quaint coastal towns reminiscent of New England along Lake Erie's shore, where impressive homes built by lake captains and shipping magnates look out over the Great Lake. These landmark dwellings showcase exquisite woods and interior decor that mirror the style of the era.

The Lake Erie Islands beckon with an offer of an active day or a leisurely stay at one of the island hostelries. Opt for a quick trip on the Jet Express or take your time on the ferry, which gives you the feeling of separation from the mainland. You'll find scenic trails and historic sights on Put-in-Bay and Kelleys Island. And then there are the views of the lake from the porches of the inns or, a short distance away, beach. An island visit can be a busy time or a chance for a quiet retreat.

Lighthouses provide the perfect photo opportunity on a drive along the lake. Stop at the Marblehead Lighthouse, one of the most photographed scenes in Ohio, and climb to the top for another view of the lake. There's an octagonal lighthouse in Vermilion, and the Ashtabula Lighthouse can be viewed from the waterfront park. Festivals bring visitors to the area year round. Of note are Vermilion's Wooly Bear Festival in October and Port Clinton's Walleye Festival in May. Wineries dot the shoreline from Port Clinton to the eastern-most location at Conneaut.

Come explore Lake Erie and enjoy her many moods in the daytime and the sound of the pounding surf at night. Plan a stay at an early ship captain's home, a winery, a historic home on the bay, or an inland town with fine old houses lining the main street. Walk out the door at one inn and dip your toes in the lake or pull up a beach chair at another and watch the sun set over Lake Erie.

Michael Cahill Bed and Breakfast

A "stick style" Victorian within view of Ashtabula's historic harbor

Paul and Pat Goode, Innkeepers
1106 Walnut Blvd.
Ashtabula, OH
(440) 964-8449

RATES & RESERVATIONS:
Season: Year round;
Rates: $$;
Reservations required;
Check, traveler's checks,
money order accepted

ACCOMMODATIONS: 4 rooms w/bath

AMENITIES: Cable TV,
phone in room, air cond.

MEALS: Full breakfast

SPECIAL CONSIDERATIONS:
Not fully handicapped accessible;
Parking available: Lot

The brochure for the Michael Cahill Bed and Breakfast, in Ashtabula's historic harbor district, features a quote from Augustine of Hippo: "Adjuvat discere peregrinatio." I asked Paul Goode, the former Latin teacher who runs the inn with his wife, Pat, to translate the quote, which says: "Travel helps one to understand." The Goodes have traveled extensively in Europe and the United States and particularly enjoy sampling all kinds of accommodations, including bed and breakfasts, convents, and country inns. In their 14 years of innkeeping, they have hosted many international guests.

The Michael Cahill Bed and Breakfast, a "stick style" Victorian built in 1887, stands at the corner of Hulbert Street and Walnut Boulevard. This tree-lined street in a quiet residential neighborhood figures prominently in Ashtabula's history. The community was settled by Irish, Swedish, and Finnish immigrants. Cahill, an Irish saloonkeeper, joined other Ashtabula Harbor businessmen and ship captains in choosing to build his house on the street that came to be known as "Captains' Row."

After purchasing the house in 1983, the Goodes spent three years restoring the place. For starters, the original "stick style" exterior was covered up with a material called Insulbrick, which had to be stripped away. In striving to remain true to the original architectural details, Paul had to recreate portions of the wood exterior that were beyond repair, upgrade the electricity and plumbing, and add two bathrooms. In 1988, the Michael Cahill House was placed on the National Register of Historic Places.

Two adjoining sitting rooms feature beautiful cherry woodwork and the original gas light fixtures, which have been converted to electricity. A fireplace in the front room and a bay window in the second room are typical of the era. Guests gather in the dining room for a full breakfast. Eggs Benedict, fresh fruit in season or the Goode's home-canned peaches in winter months, and Finnish nisua bread are favorites. At the top of the stairs, a common room provides a comfortable place to relax with a television and games. You can spend the evening reading or watching a video in the Morris chair, and make some popcorn in the kitchenette provided for guests' use. To learn a little of the history of the house, check out the collection of photographs from its second owner.

There are three guest rooms on this level. A favorite is the front bedroom, which offers a cherry four-poster with lace canopy, an antique rocker, and a small desk. At the opposite end of the hall, there's a cheerful room with three-quarter spool beds covered in bright quilts. There's an additional guest room on the first floor.

THINGS TO DO: It's an easy walk to several museums in this historic district. The Great Lakes Marine and U.S. Coast Guard Memorial Museum is a block away. Built in 1898 and originally the residence of the lighthouse keeper and the Coast Guard chief, the museum showcases paintings, ship models, photos of early Ashtabula Harbor, and a working-scale model of a Hulett ore-unloading machine. Across the street, there's a wonderful view of the harbor from the observation point at Point Park. The Hubbard House Museum is a short walk in the opposite direction on Walnut Boulevard. This 1840s brick house was used as the northern terminus of the Underground Railroad. Walk along the public beach at Walnut Beach where folks gather for the fireworks on the Fourth of July.

Special events in this waterfront community include the Blessing of the Fleet, the first weekend in June, and Christmastime in the Harbor, when Santa arrives by boat the first weekend in December. There's an interesting mix of shops on nearby Bridge Street. Four Flags of Scandia carries beautiful Finnish and Swedish crystal, Danish stainless, and Scandinavian jewelry. The Riverfront Trader has a good selection of nautical gifts including clothing, lighthouse items, and the work of local artist Bernie Baker. Stop for lunch or a snack at Doxsie's Deli Eatery, where you can enjoy a view of the historic Lift Bridge. At the top of the hill, HilMaks is the locals' favorite for seafood. If you enjoyed the bread at the Michael Cahill Bed and Breakfast, stop at the Squire Shoppe Bakery before leaving town for a loaf of Finnish nisua, Swedish llmpa, or skorpes, a treat that this small bakery in Ashtabula sends all over the United States.

DIRECTIONS: I-90 to exit 228 for SR 11; north on SR 11; left on SR 531; right on Hulbert St.; left on Walnut Blvd.; on left

NEARBY ATTRACTIONS: Lake Erie beaches and parks, harbor historical museums and shopping, Ashtabula County covered bridges and wineries

Warner-Concord Farms

*An impressively restored,
155-year-old barn along
Lake Erie's wine trail*

Kay Herdman, Innkeeper
6585 S. Ridge Rd. W
Unionville, OH
(440) 428-4485

RATES & RESERVATIONS:
Hours: By arrangement;
Season: Year round;
Rates: $$$;
Reservations required;
Check, Visa, MC, Disc accepted

ACCOMMODATIONS: 3 rooms w/bath

AMENITIES: Cable TV,
phone in room, air cond.

MEALS: Full breakfast

SPECIAL CONSIDERATIONS:
Dog and cat living at inn;
Not fully handicapped accessible;
Parking available: Lot

The air was heavy with the fragrance of ripening grapes on the September afternoon we arrived at Warner-Concord Farms, a bed and breakfast overlooking a 50-acre vineyard near Unionville. Innkeeper/owner Kay Herdman welcomed us to the converted, 155-year-old barn, built in post and beam construction. As I entered the great room from the foyer, the first thing I spotted was a massive brick fireplace straight ahead, reaching 30 feet to the ceiling. Various-size furniture groupings soften the room, and a wall of bookcases house collectibles, books, and a collection of early radios. A grand piano, antiques, and whimsical items like rocking horses and the suit of armor Kay refers to as her "Tin Man" add interest to the room. There's even a hay cradle in the foyer—a reminder of the building's first use.

The king suite on the lower level opens through French doors to the deck. It's an elegant space with oak floors, a deep window seat, a fireplace, Tudor molding, and a luxurious camel leather sofa. Upstairs, one room has a grape motif carried through in the comforter design and the stained glass window. There's a mix of antique tables and bed, an art deco piece on a chest, and—another reminder of the barn—a piece of barn siding running the width of the bed. Special features of the second room on this level are a private balcony overlooking the vineyard and a fireplace. When we arrived, we were welcomed with a bottle of locally produced wine in our room—a nice touch. The vineyard is only part of the acreage at Warner-Concord Farms. If you like to hike, you'll find 130 more acres of woodland and pastures waiting to be explored.

Kay invites guests into her kitchen/family room for breakfast. She served our group crème brûlée French toast, melon, and freshly squeezed orange juice, along with excellent coffee.

THINGS TO DO: Although the mailing address of Warner-Concord Farms is Geneva, the inn is in Unionville. Lunch or dinner can be found nearby at the Olde Tavern at Unionville, an antique-filled tavern built in 1798. Dine in a room that looks out to the garden, and enjoy the round corn fritters in a pool of maple syrup traditionally served with meals. Another dining option is Season's Grill in Geneva, serving a contemporary menu in a casual atmosphere. Salmon with fruit salsa and grilled Asian chicken salad are popular entrees. Bread is baked daily by the pastry chef who also turns out fantastic desserts. Antique stores nearby include a pair of shops, the Red Button and the Green Door.

This is Lake Erie wine country, and you can easily spend a day stopping at vineyards of all sizes. And they all have their charm. Stop for lunch at Ferrante Winery & Ristorante, where you can dine by the fireplace on a winter day and move out to the patio with a view of the vineyards in warm weather. At Harpersfield Winery, an estate winery with a European feel, settle down in the tasting room while owner/winemaker Wes Gerlosky bakes bread in a stone oven. Yet another kind of winery visit is available at Chalet Debonne Vineyards, where you're likely to find a hot-air balloon festival one weekend and an outdoor concert the next.

Take a left out of the Warner-Concord drive, and about a mile down State Route 84 you'll find Shandy Hall, a frontier Federal-style house built in 1815. Three generations of the Harper family lived in the 17-room home, and the original antique furnishings remain. Our last stop on State Route 84 was the Spring Hill Farm Market to pick up some fresh cider and homegrown vegetables.

DIRECTIONS: I-90 to exit 212 for SR 528; left on River St.; right on Main; becomes SR 84; on left

NEARBY ATTRACTIONS: Lake Erie, wineries, antiques, museum

Captain Gilchrist Guesthouse

Sit a spell on the Captain's veranda just 200 feet from the city docks and public beach.

Dan and Laura Roth, Innkeepers
5662 Huron St.
Vermilion, OH
(440) 967-1237

Vermilion was home to many ship captains in the late 1800s; on Huron Street, the Captain Gilchrist Guesthouse, a grand house from this era, remains. With the requisite archhead and bay windows, and decorative trim such as carved tulips near the roofline, it's a fine example of the Italianate style that swept the country at that time. Nine colors enliven the exterior. The inn was included in the 1992 book, *America's Painted Ladies,* and is listed on the National Register of Historic Places. Built by lumber and shipping magnate J. C. Gilchrist in 1885, it has served as a private home for Gilchrist's family, as a hotel in the early part of the 1900s, and as a

RATES & RESERVATIONS:
Hours: 7 a.m.–Midnight;
Season: Year round;
Rates: $$;
Reservations recommended;
Check, Visa, MC, Disc, Amex accepted

ACCOMMODATIONS:
2 rooms w/bath; 2 suites w/bath

AMENITIES: Hot tub, cable TV, phone in room, Internet, air cond., 200 feet from public beach and boat docks

MEALS: Expanded continental breakfast

SPECIAL CONSIDERATIONS:
Dog and cat living at inn;
Guest pets allowed;
Not fully handicapped accessible;
Parking available: Lot, on street

four-unit apartment house when Dan and Laura Roth purchased the property. It's an ideal location for vacationers, as it stands just 200 feet from the city docks and public beach; the Inland Seas Maritime Museum and historic lighthouse are adjacent to the grounds.

Guests were sitting in rockers and swings on the wraparound porch when we arrived at Captain Gilchrist's Guesthouse. Innkeeper Laura Roth says she thinks the wide front porch is everyone's favorite part of the house.

The newest suite features a cathedral ceiling and is furnished with a mix of antiques and reproductions. With a bedroom and a separate sitting room with a sleeper couch, it will easily accommodate a family of four or two couples. Three other rooms, which the Roths refer to as staterooms, are on this floor. I stayed in a high-ceilinged room with antique furnishings and a good selection of Lake Erie lore to read for an evening. A large "ballroom" is divided into a dining room, where an extended continental breakfast is set out each morning, and a living room with television, games, and books. A small cottage at the back of the house sleeps four.

THINGS TO DO: We found a variety of gift and craft items in Old Jib's Corner, where you can also stop for lunch; the Herb Garden Tearoom in this 1860 home serves gourmet luncheons and desserts. Warm afternoons and evenings find locals and visitors alike stopping by Ednamae's Ice Cream Parlor for a cone or sundae. Two fine dining options are Chez Francois and Old Prague Restaurant. Also, plan to spend some time at the Inland Seas Maritime Museum next to Captain Gilchrist's.

Vermilion hosts a number of yearly festivals, starting with the Festival of the Fish on Father's Day weekend. The Historic Summer Fare features a tour of historic homes, antiques, and crafts in the park along with a gathering of antique boats. The Woolly Bear Festival in October honors woolly bear caterpillars with a major parade. The final event of the year is the Christmas Walk in the Historic District. Vermilion is proud of historically correct street lamps purchased to line the downtown streets.

DIRECTIONS: SR 2 to SR 60; north on SR 60; left on Huron St.; on right

NEARBY ATTRACTIONS: Adjacent to Inland Seas Maritime Museum

Georgian Manor Inn

Experience a grand stay in a Georgian Revival mansion.

Judy and Gene Denney, Innkeepers
123 W. Main St.
Norwalk, OH
(800) 668-1644
www.bbhost.com/georgianmanorinn

RATES & RESERVATIONS:
Hours: 8:30 a.m.–10 p.m.;
Season: Year round; Rates: $$$;
Specials: AAA, corporate rates,
"Two-Night Romantic Getaway,"
golf packages;
Reservations recommended;
Check, Visa, MC, Amex,
Diner's Club accepted

ACCOMMODATIONS: 4 rooms w/bath

AMENITIES: Cable TV, phone in room,
Internet, air cond., private balcony, five
public rooms with library,
fireplace, two patios, gardens with
stone paths, stream with waterfall

MEALS: Full breakfast

SPECIAL CONSIDERATIONS:
Not fully handicapped accessible;
Parking available: off street, paved
and lighted

Gracious living. That's how I describe my stay at the Georgian Manor Inn in Norwalk's West Main Street Historic District. While this Georgian Revival-style mansion, built in 1906, gives a first impression of elegance, it is also a warm and welcoming home. Entering the foyer, you'll grasp the sense of space as your glance moves from the crystal chandelier upwards to the dentil moldings highlighted with gold. Straight ahead is a burl-walnut cylinder desk—one of many antiques you'll discover here.

Innkeepers/owners Gene and Judy Denney invited me into the library for a chat and a cup of tea soon after I arrived. A Governor Winthrop secretary, floor-to-ceiling bookcases, a leather sofa, and an overstuffed chair make this a popular room where guests who love history can be found at all hours sampling the Denney's extensive collection of books. The living room/parlor is highlighted by a wall of oak—an oak mantelpiece, oak pillars, and built-in oak glass-fronted bookcases. Comfort is again the key in this room, with its plumply cushioned sofa and chairs grouping. In this house of beautiful rooms, perhaps the most stunning is the dining room, with rich mahogany paneling and beamed ceiling offset by a deep red wall covering sprinkled with white dogwood blossoms. This room opens to the wicker-filled sun porch, which in turn looks out to the rear garden. As we were leaving the dining room, Gene pointed out the pocket doors with oak on the parlor side and mahogany on the dining room side.

The Denney's individual tastes are evident throughout the house and grounds. Gene collects the work of marine artist John Stobart, while Judy favors Alan Maley's work. On their leisure trips and business stays in England, Judy took notes on the interiors of inns and transferred some of those ideas into the decor of Georgian Manor. The result is sumptuous use of fabric, such as in the "crown" of fabric over the antique burled walnut bed in Lady Katherine's room. Throughout the house, coordinating fabrics and wall coverings are used. A slant-top secretary and marble-top tables complete this room. One of the joys of staying in a house from this era is discovering little nooks like the dressing area that connects this bedroom to the luxurious bath with a whirlpool/Jacuzzi. As I toured the house, I marveled at the extra space from large walk-in closets (12 in all!) to the wide hallway on the second floor hung with hunting prints from England.

You soon understand the decision to use "Lady" and "Lord" in naming the suite-size rooms in this inn. The Lord Sheldon provides a restful decor with a light floral wallpaper, overstuffed chairs in front of the white painted fireplace, and a cherry pediment rice four-poster bed. Business travelers will find workspace for a laptop at the cherry secre-

tary and good lighting for reading. Lady Anne's room is the favorite for bridal couples and anniversary celebrants, with a canopied bed, wedding pictures from past decades, and a balcony overlooking the gardens, stone patio, and pond. Gene designed and built a pergola—a white lattice-work structure—in the garden, which has been the setting for some lovely weddings.

Through their extensive travels, the Denneys became acutely aware of the difference personal service can make, and they provide special touches with class—turndown service includes a carafe of ice water by the bedside, wake-up coffee arrives on a silver tray, the bath is stocked with almond-scented toiletries and fluffy robes. For those who get the "hungries" in the middle of the night, apothecary jars filled with snacks can be found on the library table in the upstairs hall.

THINGS TO DO: A loose-leaf binder in each room is organized with descriptions of area attractions. The Firelands Museum and Library is in downtown Norwalk, and Thomas Edison's birthplace, Milan, is a short drive away. Take off for Lake Erie and the islands, or ask Judy to recommend the best antique shopping in the area.

The Denneys suggested a local restaurant, Berrys, within walking distance of the inn, and I found it to be a lovely walk through this neighborhood of historic homes. A Norwalk landmark, Berrys has been in business since 1946. The walls of this eatery are lined with photographs and memorabilia of earlier years in the city. This is the place to enjoy comfort food like chicken and biscuits and macaroni and cheese, as well as steaks, seafood, and sandwiches.

DIRECTIONS: I-80 to exit 7 for US 250; south on US 250; right on SR 61 (Main St.); on left

NEARBY ATTRACTIONS: Lake Erie Islands, Cedar Point Amusement Park, Norwalk Raceway Park, Hayes Presidential Center, wineries, lighthouses, antiques, gift shops, Edison's birthplace, Firelands Museum, Kingwood Center

Captain Montague's Bed and Breakfast

This quiet lake retreat features Irish touches, including delicious Irish scones.

Judy and Mike Tann, Innkeepers
229 Center St.
Huron, OH
(800) 276-4756
www.bbhost.com/captainmontagues

RATES & RESERVATIONS:
Hours: 8 a.m.–11 p.m.;
Season: Year round;
Rates: $$$–$$$$;
Specials: Corporate rates, multiple nights (min. 4);
Two-night minimum stay required on weekends; Reservations required;
Check, Visa, MC, Disc accepted

ACCOMMODATIONS: 5 rooms w/bath

AMENITIES: Cable TV, pool, Internet, air cond.

MEALS: Expanded continental breakfast, snacks

SPECIAL CONSIDERATIONS:
Not fully handicapped accessible;
Parking available: Lot

Captain Montague's is a quiet retreat in Lake Erie's vacationland. The house, with white pillars in Southern Colonial style, is in the Old Plat portion of the original village of Huron. John Wickham, a shipbuilder who also owned a lumber company, built the house in 1880. As might be expected of a lumber magnate, exquisite woods are used in the interior. The front staircase is hand-carved solid black walnut, and the same beautiful wood is used for mantels in the front parlor and the dining room. There's a double set of entry doors, one made of white oak and another of ruby glass, which innkeeper Judy Tann explains is the forerunner of one-way glass. Several chandeliers, pocket doors, and marble sinks original to the house remain despite the fact that in 1958 it was converted into apartments and offices. Judy and her husband, Mike, Huron's city manager, purchased the place in 1994 and give credit for the restoration to former owners Bob and Shirley Reynolds.

And who was Captain Montague? When Wickham fell on hard times in 1892, Captain Charles Montague purchased the property. Montague and his wife, Sarah, were known in the Firelands area for the gala parties they hosted in their reception room, currently the dining room of the inn.

Judy says guests sometimes ask if anyone else is staying at the bed and breakfast, it is so quiet. Two sets of stairs, one at the entry hall and one in the back, allow guests staying in the suite private access. I stayed in Edith's Room, a sunny front room named in honor of the Captain's daughter, with a queen-size brass bed and one of the original gas light fixtures converted to electricity. The Captain's Room has a masculine feel, with a steamer trunk at the end of the rice four-poster bed. This room has two of the original marble sinks, one in the bathroom and another in the guest room, cleverly hidden behind doors. The romantic setting of Jenny's Room, a two-room suite, makes it a favorite of brides or those coming to celebrate an anniversary. Victorian flowered wallpaper, a four-poster queen-size bed swathed in a full curtain treatment, and a bath charmingly decorated with hand-painted petite bouquets set the mood. Judy supplies pampering touches, like a basket of fine toiletries and luxurious robes. Another often-requested room is Sarah's Room, named for the Captain's wife, with a full-canopied white-iron queen bed with painted porcelain balls and the original fireplace and mantel.

There are many Irish touches throughout the house—Irish Santas perch on the antique pump organ, Judy's collection of Beleek china is displayed on shelves, and a Waterford crystal chandelier sparkles over the dining room table. The Victorian parlor sports green walls, and Irish music is piped through the house. Judy serves Irish scones and cinnamon coffee for breakfast at the antique dining table or, when weather permits, in the gazebo by the pool.

This busy innkeeper was working in the garden when we arrived; she seems to always have a new project going. The Tanns recently redid the dining room, and they plan to tackle the second sitting room next. I first visited this accommodation six years ago, and it's fun to come back and see the changes they have made.

THINGS TO DO: Huron invites exploration. Lakefront Park and the beach on Lake Erie are a two-block walk from the inn's front door. Huron Playhouse, Ohio's longest-running summer theater, is also close by and offers productions during the month of July. If you head off to Cedar Point or the islands, you can look forward to returning to the quiet of this bed and breakfast. Starting around Halloween, mystery weekends are a popular event at Captain Montague's; plays are written expressly for the place, and every guest becomes an actor for the two-day event.

During a stay in Huron, take time to browse the Wileswood Country Store, with its wide selection of old-fashioned toys, gourmet foods, and children's books. You'll find the Cottage Collection with antiques and gifts across the parking lot from the Wileswood Country Store.

For a leisurely romantic dinner, Judy suggests the Mariner's Club at the Sawmill Creek Resort. A local favorite is Berardi's Family Restaurant, where everything is made from scratch.

DIRECTIONS: I-80 to exit 7A for Baumhart Rd; left on Baumhart; left on SR 2; right on Berlin Rd.; left on SR 6; right on Center St.; on corner of Center and Cleveland Rd.

NEARBY ATTRACTIONS: Cedar Point, Huron Boat Basin and Amphitheater, Lake Erie Islands, Huron Playhouse, Edison's birthplace, Old Woman Creek, Sheldon Marsh, Merry-Go-Round Museum, Marblehead

Wagner's 1844 Inn

An early Sandusky business leader's exquisitely furnished Italianate-style house

Barbara Wagner, Innkeeper
230 E. Washington St.
Sandusky, OH
(419) 626-1726

RATES & RESERVATIONS:
Hours: 8 a.m.–10 p.m.;
Season: Year round; Rates: $$$;
Specials: Corporate;
Two-night minimum stay
required on weekends Memorial
Day–Labor Day;
Reservations recommended;
Visa, MC, Disc accepted

ACCOMMODATIONS: 3 rooms w/bath

AMENITIES: Cable TV, air cond., billiard table

MEALS: Expanded continental breakfast

SPECIAL CONSIDERATIONS:
Dog living at inn;
Guest pets allowed;
Not fully handicapped accessible;
Parking available: On street

Soon after my arrival at Wagner's 1844 Inn near downtown Sandusky, innkeeper Barb Wagner handed me a history of the house. Those of us who love old houses appreciate getting this kind of information as we begin to look over the place where we will spend the night.

The white frame house with black shutters stands close to the sidewalk, bordered by a black iron fence. Built in 1844 by William A. Simpson, president of the Sandusky Gas Light Company, the Italianate-style home is listed on the National Register of Historic Places. When the Wagners bought the house, it was basically a shell with no heat, a cast-iron kitchen sink, no cupboards, and only two electric circuits. It took them 10 years to restore the place.

Wagner's 1844 Inn appears deceptively small when viewed from the street. But just inside the front door, the house unfolds into a series of common rooms, guest rooms, a screened-in porch, and an enclosed courtyard. It's a classically traditional interior with a mix of antiques and reproductions.

The front parlor gives a sense of the age of the house with the original floor-to-ceiling windows, flocked wallpaper, marble fireplace, and an antique Steinway piano. We talked with the other guests in the adjoining living room, in a comfortable seating area in front of the wood-burning fireplace. In the evening, the dining room is illuminated by a beautiful, antique, electrified gas fixture with wine-colored glass. The subtle wine color is continued in carpeting in the downstairs rooms. The carved mahogany dining chairs with the original light olive upholstery were found in New Orleans.

A guest room on the first floor sports painted gold floorboards, wooden shutters, and an antique reproduction bedstead. The fireplace in this room has an interesting history. Three years after William Simpson's death, Mrs. Simpson built a new home on the corner lot, but in order to have enough space for the dwelling a portion of the east side of the old home had to be removed, thus the shortened fireplace wall that remains today in the Gold Room. Barb has been very creative in decorating the inn. When she couldn't find the wallpaper she wanted for the hallway, she used fabric in a fruit design, which brightened the entry and staircase. The Canopy Room, at the top of the stairs, has original wallpaper from France, a crocheted-canopy four-poster bed, a highboy, and a fireplace with electric logs. Across the hall, the Green Room's decor includes a newer iron bed, desk, and green wallpaper with pink roses.

There's an informal room for guests at the end of the hall with a billiard table, small refrigerator, and bar. Cushioned seats under the window and a good variety of books, including travel books and information about the area, make it a popular room.

Barb served a leisurely candlelight breakfast with a first course of melon and grapes with a cream sauce followed by a selection of cereals and an outstanding raspberry marzipan coffeecake. The table was beautifully set in the dining room; guests also had the option of eating breakfast in the screened-in porch.

THINGS TO DO: It's a short walk from Wagner's 1844 Inn to catch a ferry to the islands, and Cedar Point is just down the road. A self-guided walking tour of Sandusky's downtown and nearby neighborhoods takes you past significant nineteenth- and twentieth-century architecture. Limestone was quarried locally for many buildings, including St. Mary's Catholic Church. Take a look back at Sandusky and Erie County history at the Follett House Museum. Antiquers will find four antique shops in downtown Sandusky.

For Mexican-American cuisine, head out to Margaritaville with an outside bar overlooking a waterfall and pond. In downtown Sandusky, you can settle into the comfort of Coffee Temptations for gourmet coffee or lunch. On a summer evening, take a short drive to Tofts Dairy where folks sit out on the patio with super-size cones of delicious ice cream.

DIRECTIONS: I-80 to exit 7 for US 250; north on US 250; left (west) on US 6; right on E. Washington St.; on right

NEARBY ATTRACTIONS: Cedar Point, Lake Erie Islands, museums, Edison's birthplace

Red Gables Bed and Breakfast

Eclectic collections and cozy corners

Jo Ellen Cuthbertson, Innkeeper
421 Wayne St.
Sandusky, OH
(419) 625-1189
www.bbonline.com/oh/redgables

RATES & RESERVATIONS:
Hours: 9 a.m.–9 p.m.;
Season: Year round;
Rates: $$$;
Two-night minimum stay required
on weekends Jul–Aug;
Reservations required;
Check, Visa, MC accepted

ACCOMMODATIONS:
4 rooms, 3 with bath

AMENITIES: Air cond.

MEALS: Expanded
continental breakfast

SPECIAL CONSIDERATIONS:
Not fully handicapped accessible;
Parking available: Lot

Jo Ellen Cuthbertson has welcomed guests to Red Gables, a Tudor Revival home in the historic Old Plat District of Sandusky, since 1989. She knows the house well—it served as her physician father's office. At one time, student nurses from a nearby nursing school stayed in rooms on the second floor.

Summer visitors find pots of flowers lining the front steps of this half-timbered home, built in 1907. Entry is into a wide hallway; the great room on the left. It's a vast room, anchored by a fireplace at one end and a large bay window at the other. Sage green walls set off the eclectic collection of furnishings, and a white molded plaster ceiling contrasts with the oak of the Tudor interior. Jo Ellen's talent as a theatrical costume-maker is evident throughout the house in her use of fabrics as well as in decorative touches like the framed piece of embroidered Chinese silk hanging in the great room.

On the second floor is a cozy, light-filled sitting room furnished with old wicker and stacks of magazines and books. The first of the four guest rooms is Alice's Room, to honor Jo Ellen's mother. It's a beautifully proportioned room with fireplace and sitting area, and the queen-size bed is covered with one of Jo Ellen's creations, a flowered chintz comforter in shades of green and pink. A spacious bath with double marble sinks and white octagonal floor tile adjoins the room.

Jo Ellen, the oldest of eight children, kindly named the other rooms for her sisters. Janet's Room, done up in navy fabrics, has windows facing the street and is connected to Joann's Room by a large shared bath. As we walked down the hall to the last room, Jo Ellen pointed out the change from oak woodwork to white painted surfaces in this end of the house; with access to a back stairway, this area most likely was originally for staff. It makes a charming little suite today, with Jennifer's Room, a small bath with a claw-foot tub, and the use of the hospitality room with refrigerator and a reading area.

Classical music fills the great room at breakfast time, when fresh fruit, yogurt, cereals, and homemade muffins are served at an antique table in front of the bay windows. Jo Ellen's charm and enthusiasm for the innkeeping business is evident. She says that having visitors from all over the world is a little like traveling herself.

THINGS TO DO: We made the short drive to the little community of Bay View for dinner at the Angry Trout, where tables with umbrellas fill the patio and the dining room overlooks the bay. We also ventured into Sandusky and were surprised to find a wonderful green space downtown. Washington Park invites strolling or a light lunch among flower beds, fountains, a gazebo, and statues, including the famous *Boy with a Boot*. Another attraction within walking distance of the bed and breakfast is the Merry-Go-Round Museum. There is an excellent guided tour with displays of fanciful carousel creatures and a woodcarver at work. And when the music of a Wurlitzer military-style band organ fills the air, pick out a proud stallion and have a ride on the 1930s county fair-style carousel.

DIRECTIONS: I-80 to exit 7 for US 250; west on US 250; left on US 6; left on Wayne; on left

NEARBY ATTRACTIONS: Lake Erie Islands, Cedar Point, nature preserves, antiques, museums

Old Stone House on the Lake

Watch the sunset from the top of this house on beachfront property.

Dan and Brenda Anderson,
Innkeepers
133 Clemons St.
Marblehead, OH
(419) 798-5922
www.oldstonehousebandb.com

RATES & RESERVATIONS:
Season: Mar–Dec;
Rates: $$$–$$$$;
Specials: Seasonal rates;
Reservations recommended;
Check, Visa, MC, Disc,
traveler's checks accepted

ACCOMMODATIONS: 13 rooms,
7 w/bath; 1 suite w/bath

AMENITIES: Air cond.

MEALS: Full breakfast

SPECIAL CONSIDERATIONS:
Cat living at inn;
Not fully handicapped accessible;
Parking available: Lot

Imagine ... a stretch of lakefront property you can pretend is your own for a few days. Spend a weekend at the Old Stone House on Marblehead Peninsula, where you can lazily watch the action on the lake from the stone patio. During an hour in this spot, we observed a variety of pleasure craft and freighters and enjoyed the view of Kelleys Island. Chairs are padded for comfort, and lap robes are available for cooler days. It's a quiet retreat with only the crashing of waves and call of the gulls breaking the solitude.

The Federalist-style Old Stone House was built by Alexander Clemons in 1861 with stone from his quarry. To accommodate his family of 14 children, Clemons designed a mansion that rambles over three floors, with 11 guest rooms on floors two and three. And then there's the tower room on the fourth floor—once the widow's walk and now an enclosed room with what owners/innkeepers Brenda and Dan Anderson call "a panoramic view of the entire western basin of Lake Erie." Guests say there's nothing quite like watching the sunset from the top of the house or waking up to the sunrise flooding the room. At the back of the house, a suite with living room, guest room, and bath has a private entrance.

The Andersons have made many improvements since I first visited five years ago, shortly after they had purchased the property. Dan added bathrooms on the second floor, and Brenda placed antiques and collectibles throughout the house. She also did all the stenciling on the freshly painted walls and had fun naming the rooms. On the second floor, the Homestead Room, with a nostalgia theme, is a lakefront room with four large windows—even the bathroom looks out to the lake. I liked Room 4, with its collection of Blue Willow and Flow Blue china as a focal point in an arrangement over the king-size bed; set against the white walls and with blue and white repeated in the quilt, the china lends a crisp, clean look. Although this room isn't a lakefront room, there is a good view of the lake from the window near the wing chair. The adjoining bath has a whirlpool tub.

There's a casual summer-guesthouse air to the six smaller rooms with shared baths on the third floor. Groups traveling together, including families with children over 10, find rollaways available. When Alexander Clemons ran his stone quarry, he offered rooms on this floor to his quarry supervisors, many of whom came from Yugoslavia. The rooms open to a large public room with comfortable seating, a gas log fireplace, and a good selection of books and magazines. Room 6 is the Doll Room, with an antique double bed and dolls on the dresser and in the old-fashioned doll buggy. Brenda placed two family wedding dresses on forms and an old treadle sewing machine in the room she calls the Cinderella Room. There's a bit of Civil War history associated with Room 7, the Military Room: in 1864, Loyalist troops used this room as a lookout after there was a rumor that rebels on Pelee Island were preparing for a "dash" rescue of Confederate prisoners from Johnson Island.

Breakfast is served in the dining room, on the main floor with windows to the lake. Brenda finds guests like her bananas-Foster pancakes and eggs Benedict, as well as down-home offerings like sausage, biscuits, and gravy. Trays are provided for carrying your breakfast out to the patio. Or you can just linger there with a second cup of coffee by the lake.

THINGS TO DO: You can walk from the Old Stone House to catch a ferry to the islands or to visit the shops and historic Marblehead Lighthouse. The day we visited, we found not only the often-photographed white lighthouse with red trim open to visitors but also the recently opened keeper's house on the grounds available for tours. It's 87 steps to the top of the lighthouse, but it's worth the climb for yet another view of the big lake. The Marblehead Lighthouse, built in 1821, lays claim to being the oldest lighthouse in continuous operation on the Great Lakes. Picnic tables are provided in the green park-like space, but stay away from the rocky shore—there is a steep drop-off. The shops nestled along West Main Street are reminiscent of New England seaside towns. We stopped at Richmond Galleries, which offers a good selection of Ben Richmond's watercolors and nautical gifts. In the same building, Matey's is known for its clam chowder and Lake Erie fish entrees and sandwiches. Across the street, Martha and Molly's carries Amish quilts and quilted jackets. The Garden Restaurant in downtown Port Clinton was recommended for lunch or dinner.

DIRECTIONS: I-80 to exit 7 for US 250; west on US 250; west on SR 2; north on SR 2693; west on SR 163; left on Clemons St.; on left

NEARBY ATTRACTIONS: Put-In-Bay Marblehead Lighthouse, Johnson's Island Civil War Site, Kelleys Island, Lake Erie, art galleries, shopping, swimming and fishing on premises

Water's Edge Retreat

*Escape to this island getaway—
sun decks, massage therapy, and
no cars.*

Elizabeth and Timothy Hermes,
Innkeepers
827 E. Lakeshore Dr.
Kelleys Island, OH
(419) 746-2455
www.watersedgeretreat.com

RATES & RESERVATIONS:
Hours: 8:45 a.m.–7:45 p.m.;
Season: Year round, except January;
Rates: $$$$;
Specials: 2, 3, 4, 5, and
6-night packages;
Two-night minimum stay required on
weekends (some exceptions); Reservations recommended;
Check, Visa, MC, Disc, cash accepted

ACCOMMODATIONS:
4 rooms w/bath; 2 suites w/bath

AMENITIES: Hot tub, spa, air cond.,
massage therapy, beach, beach decks

MEALS: Full breakfast, snacks

SPECIAL CONSIDERATIONS:
Dog and cat living at inn;
Handicapped accessible;
Parking available: Lot

Water's Edge Retreat is an upscale bed and breakfast on Kelleys Island. This three-story Queen Anne Victorian, dressed in aqua and coral with touches of lacy white trim, stands tall and proud on a rocky beach. Though this "Painted Lady" was built recently, she has the requisite architectural characteristics of tower, verandas, and gables.

Some guests who return to Water's Edge Retreat say they love the secluded location. Cars are left on the mainland, and a 30-minute ferry ride begins the feeling of escape from everyday life. Other guests remember the luxuriant coddling of their stay at this accommodation, which has a massage therapist available on site.

Innkeepers/owners Elizabeth and Tim Hermes built sun decks that seem to nestle into the rocky shoreline. A wraparound veranda, with white wicker furniture and a gazebo, beckons guests to sit awhile and enjoy the sound of gently lapping waves. Stepping inside the house, guests first see the inviting parlor,

with polished wood floors, quality antiques, and a wood-burning fireplace. The Hermes found the burled oak mantel in a Cleveland antique store. Unadorned windows and a tripod telescope provide views of Sandusky Bay, Cedar Point, and the Marblehead Lighthouse. The feeling of space and the expert craftsmanship evident throughout the house are part of the charm of the place.

Honeymooners and special-occasion celebrants find luxury suites on the second and third floors, with spectacular views of the lake and the small bay in front of the house. Take the private staircase to the Jacuzzi Suite, with a sitting room, guest room with queen bed, Jacuzzi, and walk-in shower. The expansive Charles Lawrence Executive Suite features a sitting area with overstuffed chairs and ottoman, fireplace, queen bed, dressing room, two-person Jacuzzi, sun porch, and a walk-in ceramic shower. The remaining rooms, the Mary Louise and the Paul Francis, are beautifully decorated and offer lake views.

A gourmet breakfast feast served in the formal dining room or out on the veranda might include eggs Benedict, huevos rancheros, or Belgian waffles with pecans. Wine and cheese is available in the parlor every evening from 5:00 to 6:00 p.m.

This adult-oriented Lake Erie island bed and breakfast has won its share of accolades. *Glove Box Guidebooks of America* (June 1998) voted Water's Edge Retreat "Best of the Best" of all B&Bs on Lake Erie, and *Travel & Leisure* (June 1996) rated it as one of the top 50 U.S. beach resorts.

THINGS TO DO: On this island with no traffic lights, folks get around on bikes, motorized carts, or by foot. The downtown shops are only eight minutes away. Hikers find miles of trails in the 800-acre Ohio state park system on the island. The Hermes are happy to arrange fishing charters and full- or partial-day trips to the other islands in Lake Erie. A pleasant stop on a hot day is Kelleys Island Wine Company, where you can sip wine under spreading sugar maples or have a meal in the full-service restaurant. You'll find a selection of imported beers and microbrews, and a steak fry on the "Grilling Deck" on Friday nights.

DIRECTIONS: SR 2 to SR 269; north on SR 269; right (east) on SR 163; left (north) on Francis St to Neuman Ferry

NEARBY ATTRACTIONS: Cedar Point, South Bass Island

Vineyard Bed and Breakfast

Stay on the quiet side of this popular island on 20 acres with a private beach.

Barbi and Mark Barnhill, Innkeepers
910 Columbus Ave.
Put-in-Bay, OH
(419) 285-6181
www.mytreeway.com/vineyardohio

RATES & RESERVATIONS:
Hours: 8 a.m.–10 p.m.;
Season: Apr–Nov;
Rates: $$$;
Two-night minimum stay required, unless specifically approved;
Reservations required;
Check or cash accepted

ACCOMMODATIONS:
3 rooms, 1 w/bath

AMENITIES: Cable TV, air cond., family antiques, 6-acre vineyard next door, 700-foot private beach, complimentary bicycles

MEALS: Full breakfast

SPECIAL CONSIDERATIONS:
Dog living at inn;
Not fully handicapped accessible;
Parking available: On property

We discovered the quiet side of Put-in-Bay on an early June visit to South Bass Island and the Vineyard Bed and Breakfast. Barbi and Mark Barnhill have been in business for 17 years. Mark picked us up at the ferry and gave us a tour of South Bass on the way to their home on the east point of the island. Far from the frenetic activity of downtown Put-in-Bay, this 135-year-old, tree-shaded, white house with green shutters sits on 20 acres. It's a brief, pleasant walk to the private beach, and the six-acre vineyard remains from the family-run E&K Winery established in 1940.

The house is filled with antiques inherited from Barbi's family and accented with treasures the couple found in their various postings while Mark served as a career Air Force officer. A brass heater from Turkey, a mongal, is the centerpiece in the parlor furnished with family pieces, including a Victrola, Victorian settees, and intricately carved Chinese tables. A portrait of Barbi's great-great uncle, Jacob Engels, has a place of honor on the parlor wall.

The stairway, lined with family photographs, takes you up to the three guest rooms. Barbi did all the wallpapering and decorating in the house, using blue as a predominant color. At the top of the stairs, the Concord Room is furnished in bird's-eye maple set off by a Chinese Oriental rug in navy and cream. An Eastlake bed, an Empire chest with glass knobs, and a Turkish rug highlight the front room. White cotton curtains grace the windows with original glass in all the rooms. The most-requested room is the suite-like Catawba Room, with a wood-burning stove and cozy corner sitting area. At one time this spacious room was two rooms; the Barnhills removed a wall and ceiling so that the room extends upwards to the rafters, where 48 pieces of Turkish copper are displayed in a loft area. It's a welcoming retreat softened by blue and peach fabrics. A leaded glass window saved from another family home sparkles in the sitting area. A final accommodation is the honeymoon cottage, with a living room, bedroom, dressing room, and small kitchen.

Breakfast, served at nine o'clock sharp, is a happening at the Vineyard—in fact, it's a culinary experience that can last for hours. Barbi, certified in restaurant management, loves to cook. After a breakfast of fruit compote, buttermilk corn pancakes, or scrambled eggs accompanied by bacon, sausage, or ham, guests sit and chat around the dining room table. The record for this extended meal and conversation was clocked by Mark at four hours and ten minutes!

Guests return to the Vineyard not only to celebrate special occasions but also to help out when it's time to harvest the grapes in October. Loyal guests who have become friends come to stay for at least two days to help the Barnhills, and Barbi rewards them by serving three meals a day. The opportunity to work close to the earth and the interaction among guests

and hosts must be worth the trip and time away from home, as the rooms are booked every year for the event.

THINGS TO DO: The highly recommended Erie Isle Tavern on the second floor of Parker's Inn features entrees paired with wine from their extensive list (300 wines). Owner/chef Rob Morrow says the rack of lamb and macadamia-encrusted walleye are popular entrees. Decadent desserts, including hot chocolate cake and Italian pound cake with fresh berry sauce, are made in house. Take time to browse the shops along Catawba Avenue, and stop in the Lake Erie Islands Historical Society, located behind the fire station. Displays include a history of the 1928 Ford Trimotor airplanes that brought visitors to the island until the 1980s. You can follow the story of the Battle of Lake Erie at the museum and then stop over at Perry's Victory and International Peace Memorial. An elevator will take you to the top for a spectacular view of the lake and surrounding area from the observation tower. Our hosts also suggested touring Stonehenge, a stone farmhouse and wine press cottage. Those who love things nautical will find a large selection of restored marine antiques at the Cargo Net. Furniture pieces, like coffee tables made from ship grating and beautifully restored ship's desks, are lined up with vintage gasoline pumps and antique vehicles.

DIRECTIONS: SR 2 to SR 163; west on SR 163 for Port Clinton; right (north) on N. Jefferson St.; Jet Express Boat for Put-in-Bay; on right
OR: SR 2 to SR 53; north on SR 53 for Catawba Island; left (west) on Sloan St.; right (north) on Crogh St.; left (west) on Water St.; Miller Boat Line for Put-in-Bay; on right

NEARBY ATTRACTIONS: Perry's monument, winery, caves, historical museum, Victorian village, beautiful harbor, historic island, tours, excellent restaurants, shopping, entertainment

Chapter 5

WORTH THE DRIVE

*Sometimes it's fun to explore a little farther away from home;
you'll find some exceptional accommodations
worth a little extra driving time in this chapter.*

These bed and breakfast destinations will take you to southern Ohio, Pennsylvania, Kentucky, New York, Indiana, and Ontario. None are longer than a six-hour drive from Cleveland. Make it an unhurried day trip, with time to stop for a picnic lunch, browse an antique shop, or get off the highway and follow a country road.

Come along for a drive to Pennsylvania's rolling countryside, the Chautauqua region of New York, a genteel Kentucky town and the rolling farmland of Indiana. Visit southern Ohio's Hocking Hills, with its precipitous gorges and spectacular waterfalls. Travel to "Ohio's Outback," and take a walking tour of a historic southwestern Ohio city. Along the way, find significant architecture in an industrialist's elegant home and inns from the eighteenth century. Or book a stay in a log cabin so far from a neighboring cabin that you can pretend the woods are your own. Sample cuisine ranging from Southern cooking and fine continental dining to meals featuring the best of locally grown products.

Head up to western Ontario, a lush agricultural area where endless fields of golden wheat are broken up by patches of green. Sturdy brick farmhouses with the Canadian flag in the air and the family name on the barn show the industriousness and pride of our neighbors to the north. An autumn visit allows you to drive through the countryside and sample the abundant harvest at farmgate markets. Amble along the Lake Erie shoreline and stop at wineries or Point Pelee, a sanctuary for bird watchers, or follow the Bluewater Highway along miles of Lake Huron's golden coastline that make up Ontario's west coast.

Inn at Cedar Falls

Surround yourself with the abundant nature and pure quiet of Hocking Hills.

Ellen Grinsfelder, Innkeeper
21190 S.R. 374
Logan, OH
(800) 653-2557
www.innatcedarfalls.com

RATES & RESERVATIONS:
Hours: 8 a.m.–9 p.m.;
Season: Year round;
Rates: $$;
Specials: Seniors, singles, AAA, mid-week packages for winter and spring;
Two-night minimum stay required on weekends;
Reservations recommended;
Check, Visa, MC accepted

ACCOMMODATIONS: 9 rooms w/bath; 6 cabins w/bath

AMENITIES: Air cond., whirlpool tubs, gas log stoves, Internet hookup in sun room

MEALS: Full breakfast, lunch, dinner; Beer, wine, and liquor served

SPECIAL CONSIDERATIONS:
Cat living at inn;
Handicapped accessible;
Parking available: Lot

William Wordsworth once wrote: "A genial hearth, a hospitable board, and a refined rusticity" make for the best accommodation. He could have been describing the Inn at Cedar Falls. While this country inn deep in the Hocking Hills, with a collection of log buildings, is rustic, it's also an award-winning inn with a reputation for fine gourmet meals. But it's the quiet that you first notice. Walking back to our room on a brisk fall evening after a relaxing and delicious dinner, we heard only the rustling of some small creature in the underbrush and our own footsteps on the gravel path. We marveled at the sky's canvas glittering with stars in that open space.

Nine guest rooms in the contemporary, barn-like inn building are simply but comfortably furnished with antiques, rag rugs, quilts, and good reading lights. Rocking chairs line the porches for a spectacular view of the Hocking Hills. One room in the inn has been set aside as a common room, with a library corner, writing table, snacks and drinks, and chairs to pull up to the wood-burning stove. There are no telephones or televisions. Over the hill, six renovated log cabins offer private retreats. Treehouse Cabin features a living room with a gas log stove, a complete kitchen, and, on the lower level, a cozy bedroom and large bath. Decks with grills and porch swings complete the units. Due south of the inn is an area known as the Quiet Hilltop, with hammocks, a swing, and a fire circle used by groups on retreat as well as guests looking for a meditation spot. An environment that makes it easy to commune with nature was Anne Castle's vision; she built the inn in 1987 as a getaway for urban dwellers. Her daughter, Ellen Grinsfelder, carries on her mother's dream today as innkeeper.

Guests gather for dinner by candlelight in the 1840s double log house. It has 18-inch-thick log walls and original plank floors. The gourmet kitchen is open to the cabin, allowing friendly banter from the chef and the wonderful aroma from cooking to waft through during the four-course meal. Vegetables and herbs from the inn's gardens are used in the ever-changing menu emphasizing American cuisine. On an October visit, we started with a salad of crisp mesclun greens topped with feta cheese, radishes, and a delicious inn-made maple balsamic dressing. We moved on to salmon, wild rice, and fresh asparagus, and finished with a choux pastry filled with Chantilly cream and dipped in chocolate ganache. It was a leisurely feast, with good company around the table. Folks asked for recipes, which can be found in the inn's new cookbook, *INN the Morning, INN the Evening, INN the Kitchen at Cedar Falls*. Take time for a breakfast of homemade granola, fresh-squeezed juice, or a plate of gingerbread pancakes with lemon sauce before heading out to the Hocking Hills, which surround the Inn at Cedar Falls on three sides.

The inn has a busy schedule of self-development programs and special classes. Hike with a naturalist, go stargazing, or learn to make a basket from Hocking Hills "basket lady" Leota Hutchison. Guest chefs come to cook, and you can be a taster for one of the meals. Retreat and conference planners say the absence of ringing telephones and lack of television contributes to the success of their meetings. Groups of 20 meet in a room in the rustic barn-like building and move to the sun room off the dining room for break-out sessions. The serenity of the setting and the genuine hospitality of the inn staff encourage productive thinking.

Visitors come back to the Inn at Cedar Falls for many reasons—its natural, unpretentious setting, the warmth of the innkeeper and staff, sophisticated food, and as one guest told me, "It's the only place I know with pure quiet." Once you're a guest at the inn, Ellen will keep you informed of new happenings in the newsletter, *Inn Connections*. The Inn at Cedar Falls has been a member of the Independent Innkeepers' Association since 1989.

THINGS TO DO: Spend an afternoon browsing the shops in Logan. We stopped at Great Expectations, a restored 1892 home where you can pick out some books and sit down for lunch in their cafe. In warm weather, folks move out to the grape arbor to sip their coffee. Logan offers a wide choice of antiques in malls and individual stores.

DIRECTIONS: I-71 to exit 107 for I-70; east on I-70 to exit 105A for US 33; east on US 33; right (south) on SR 664; left on SR 374; on left

NEARBY ATTRACTIONS: Hocking Hills State Park, Tecumseh, antique and artisan malls, golfing, fishing

Burl Manor Bed and Breakfast

An 1880s Italianate beauty in Lebanon's historic district

Liz and Jay Jorling, Innkeepers
230 S. Mechanic St.
Lebanon, OH
(800) 450-0401
www.lebanon-ohio.com
/burlmanor.html

RATES & RESERVATIONS:
Season: Year round;
Rates: $$;
Specials: Children, seniors,
singles, AAA;
Reservations recommended;
Check, Visa, MC accepted

ACCOMMODATIONS: 3 rooms w/bath

AMENITIES: Cable TV, pool,
phone in room, Internet, air cond.

MEALS: Full breakfast, snacks

SPECIAL CONSIDERATIONS:
Dog living at inn;
Not fully handicapped accessible;
Parking available: On street,
in driveway

We always enjoyed stopping briefly in Lebanon on our way to Cincinnati or Kentucky, and we decided it was time to make this historic city our destination. We visited on the first weekend in December, when Lebanon pulls out all the stops for the annual Christmas Festival and Horse-Drawn Carriage Parade. And we reserved early for our stay at Burl Manor Bed and Breakfast, an Italianate home built in 1884 by William P. Denney, the editor and publisher of Ohio's oldest weekly newspaper, *The Western Star*.

Liz and Jay Jorling became interested in innkeeping after their children gave them the gift of a stay at a bed and breakfast. Jay retired first from the military and more recently from his own business; Liz continues to work as an occupational therapist. The Jorlings seem to adapt to wearing the many hats of innkeepers easily—Jay takes the main responsibility during the week, and Liz helps on the weekends. They welcome their guests warmly and continue to care for them throughout their stay. We shared breakfast with a group of women who had traveled to Lebanon to shop for antiques. It seems this merry crew comes back every December, and they gave glowing accolades to the Jorlings. Since it was the holiday season, Jay served breakfast in a Santa hat and apron.

A crystal chandelier is the focal point in the parlor, surrounded by a period wall covering in the shade of blue used at Monticello, interior shutters, and high ceilings. The staircase in the wide hallway is a combination of rich woods—cherry, oak, and walnut, and the burled walnut newel post helps give the house its name. Breakfast is served in the formal dining room, which features floral wallpaper, windows with the original wavy glass, and a beautifully set table. The Colorado Room, an informal room paneled in cherry, is the kind of place you can relax, put up your feet, and visit or watch TV. Liz previously lived in Colorado and contributed Indian artifacts like a kiva ladder and wedding jar. Snacks are available in the adjoining hospitality room, where guests find games and a bumper pool table.

Four guest rooms, each with queen-size bed and private bath, have individual personalities. Poster beds, antiques, and family pieces fill the rooms, and sitting areas with good lighting are great spots to read.

A plaque by the front door of Burl Manor Bed and Breakfast best states the philosophy of Liz and Jay Jorling: "Be not forgetful to entertain strangers for thereby some have entertained angels unawares" (Heb. 13:2). These innkeepers love the guests who come to stay with them and cherish their neighbors in this friendly town.

THINGS TO DO: Our early December weekend was an exciting time to be in Lebanon. Quite a sight awaited us on Broadway Street, just two blocks from the inn: twinkling white lights outlined the trees, and the streets were lined with people waiting for the horse-drawn carriage parade to begin. Food and gift vendors were set up along the side streets. Once the parade began, we had a curbside view of 134 carriages of many styles and sizes. As darkness descended, the route was marked by flickering candles held by those who came to see this event. A town crier, who is also a fine storyteller, filtered in and out of the crowd. For a winter event, it felt like a summertime county fair.

If you're coming to Lebanon, be sure to stop for lunch or dinner at Ohio's oldest inn, the Golden Lamb—a four-story Federal brick building with white balconies fronting South Broadway Street. The early stagecoach inn offers outstanding regional cuisine and an interior filled with antiques. Take a self-guided tour of the second and third floors, with rooms named for notable guests, and continue on to the fourth floor to view the inn's Shaker collection. If time allows, explore museums including Glendower, a stunning example of 1846 Greek Revival architecture. Lebanon boasts more than 80 specialty and antique shops. Take a rest from shopping and have lunch or an ice cream treat at the Village Ice Cream Parlor.

DIRECTIONS: I-71 to exit 32 for SR 123; west on SR 123; left (south) on Mechanic St.; on left

NEARBY ATTRACTIONS: Kings Island Amusement Park, Beachwater Park, Miami Valley Dinner Theater, Sauerkraut Festival, Renaissance Festival, Old Fashioned Christmas, Harmon Golf & Tennis Center

Outback Inn Bed and Breakfast

A retreat in "Ohio's Outback," a dream land for fishing, hunting, and camping

Bob and Carol Belfance, Innkeepers
171 E. Union Ave.
McConnelsville, OH
(800) 542-7171

RATES & RESERVATIONS:
Season: Year round;
Rates: $–$$;
Specials: Business traveler rates, long-term stay rates;
Reservations required;
Check, traveler's checks accepted

ACCOMMODATIONS: 3 rooms w/bath

AMENITIES: Phone in room, air cond., cable TV in living room

MEALS: Full breakfast

SPECIAL CONSIDERATIONS:
Not fully handicapped accessible;
Parking available: On street

On my first trip to the Outback Inn Bed and Breakfast in southeastern Ohio, I found the drive on State Route 60 from Zanesville to McConnelsville to be a pleasant, meandering route alongside the Muskingum River. When I arrived in McConnelsville in the early evening, a mist rising from the water gave a mysterious aura to this river town. This is "Ohio's Outback," where thousands of acres have been set aside for fishing, hunting, and camping. Three-hundred-and-fifty lakes dot 30,000 acres of reclaimed Ohio Power Company recreation land. A portion of the land is home to The Wilds, North America's largest endangered species preserve, where animals roam freely in large, open-range habitats.

The Outback Inn, built in the Federalist style, is three blocks from the McConnelsville town square. Owners/innkeepers Bob and Carol Belfance have furnished this 1870s banker's home with a pleasing mixture of antiques and contemporary pieces. The interior is graced by original oak woodwork, pocket doors, and beautiful stained glass windows made by local artist Chuck Bosari. The Belfances had fun naming the guest rooms. There's the Roadside Roost on the first floor with a 1930s-era bed and Bob's collection of parrot art. (He says the number of parrot items in this room keeps changing as returning guests bring gifts.) I liked the Hooray For Hollywood room on the second level with its art deco bedroom suite and early movie posters. The Queen's Chamber is a romantic room with a cherry four-poster queen bed, cherry wardrobe, and marble-top dresser. The Belfances' collection of local artist Howard Chandler Christy's work is displayed throughout the house.

Inn guests are served a full breakfast in a dining room furnished with an oak dining set from 1928. Carol describes her breakfast offerings as "savory," and indeed they are—consider Carol's Three Cheese Puff, a blend of eggs, cottage, cheddar and Monterey jack cheeses, ham, and spices, accompanied by homemade breads and fruit. There was a full house when we stayed at the Outback, and lively conversation as Carol cooked and Bob served breakfast. As we were finishing the meal, one couple surprised us by announcing it was their fiftieth wedding anniversary. Only in an intimate setting like this bed and breakfast would we find ourselves part of a special celebration with strangers.

The Belfances co-host a radio talk show, "Breakfast at the Outback," on Mondays and Fridays from their dining room. Programs have included interviews with politicians, McConnelsville citizens, and an occasional visiting Broadway or television star. Sometimes they tackle a topic like, "What to do with all those tomatoes and zucchinis folks have from their gardens."

The Outback is an Ohio treasure. The Belfances provide a comfortable getaway and their guests embrace it—68 percent of their business is from people coming back for another stay.

THINGS TO DO: There's an excellent restaurant, the Howard House, at the edge of town near a small park. Dari and Steve Hann purchased this antebellum mansion in 1989 and spent nine months restoring it. It has an elegant interior filled with family antiques, and the food and service match the decor. Featuring pastas and steaks, the menu also highlights seafood and veal. Two winning entrees are tenderloin Russo served with a cognac sauce, and grilled salmon. Breads and desserts are made in-house.

The Belfances, transplanted Akronites, have entered enthusiastically into the life of this small village. Carol designed a historic walking tour of McConnelsville, and Bob serves as the chair of the Downtown Revitalization Committee, a group that has put a 1.1 million dollar project in place to bring downtown McConnelsville back to the way it was in 1896. And it is a charming downtown. On weekends you can catch a movie at the Opera House Theater, a facility in continuous use since 1890. Carol says they were looking to settle in a quiet community and they found it in McConnelsville, where there's still a walk-up window at the bank and the clerks in the grocery store call you by name.

DIRECTIONS: I-77 to exit 44B for I-70; west on I-70 to exit 155 for SR 60; south on SR 60; right (south) on 8th St.; right (west) on Union Ave..; on right

NEARBY ATTRACTIONS: The Wilds, Zanesville Pottery

Checkerberry Inn

A Georgian style inn in the Amish farmland of Indiana

John and Susie Graff, Innkeepers
62644 C.R. 37
Goshen, IN
(219) 642-4445
www.checkerberryinn.com

RATES & RESERVATIONS:
Season: Feb–Dec;
Rates: $$$$;
Specials: Sun–Thu discounts;
Reservations required;
Check, Visa, MC, Amex accepted

ACCOMMODATIONS:
11 rooms w/bath; 2 suites w/bath

AMENITIES: Pool, phone in room, air cond., Jacuzzis in suites

MEALS: Expanded continental breakfast, dinner, snacks

SPECIAL CONSIDERATIONS:
Handicapped accessible;
Parking available: Lot

French country cuisine, a professional croquet course, tennis courts, a golf chipping and putting green, a Georgian-style inn ... in the Amish country of northeastern Indiana? First-time visitors marvel at the accommodation John and Susan Graff have created on 100 acres of farmland near Goshen, Indiana. It feels like an elegant European hotel, with its mixture of antiques, fine art, and tranquil views of the Indiana farmland from every window. Personal attention starts with check-in and continues in the dining room with a consistently high level of service. We were not surprised to learn the Checkerberry has been rated by *Inn Review* as one of the 10 best inns nationwide.

The Checkerberry Inn has 11 rooms named for flowers. Our quiet room on the main floor was a sophisticated blend of beige and white brightened by colorful pillows and art. A white wicker chaise lounge is comfortably padded with pillows next to a wheeled tray table set with coffee service. The spacious bath is stocked with high quality towels and toiletries. Tall windows with wide wooden slats are curtained with white sheers. There are three luxurious suites, including the Checkerberry

Suite, which features a private staircase, living/dining room, kitchen, two bedrooms, two baths, and a two-person Jacuzzi.

The dining room is reminiscent of a country inn in Brittany, with French tiles around the fireplace, blue-and-white-checked tablecloths, and windows onto the rolling countryside. The Checkerberry Restaurant, which has been featured in *Gourmet* magazine, surpassed our expectations. We were guests on Thanksgiving Day, and restaurants meals on such holidays are usually rushed affairs; this was not the case at the Checkerberry. The pace was leisurely and the presentation outstanding. It was one of those occasions when you feast first with your eyes. The menu, which changes frequently, reflects the use of the freshest ingredients. Favorite entrees include Middlebury duck and roasted Amish chicken. A pastry chef prepares desserts like orange custard apple tart and chocolate espresso fudge cake. Guests find a select wine list. Special events in the dining room include herb luncheons in July and madrigal dinners at holiday time.

A gathering room is a short walk from the dining room through a light-filled hallway lined with green and flowering plants. A massive stone fireplace anchors one end of the room; a wet bar offers a variety of snacks at the other. Cozy groupings of chairs and game tables complete this spacious room. The trophy room near the entrance is equipped with TV and videos.

The Checkerberry Inn has been a member of The Independent Innkeepers' Association since 1990.

THINGS TO DO: If you can pull yourself away from this haven of tranquility, check out the Old Bag Factory, a complex of 17 shops and a cafe, in nearby Goshen, a town that offers excellent antiquing. July brings the Elkhart Jazz Festival, and September sees the Mennonite Relief Sale.

DIRECTIONS: I-80 to exit 107 for SR 13; south on SR 13; right (west) on SR 4; left (south) on CR 37; on right

NEARBY ATTRACTIONS: Old Bag Factory, antiques, festivals

Beaumont Inn

*Tradition reigns in this
Old South setting.*

Tradition and hospitality do reign supreme at the Beaumont Inn, a Greek Revival-style inn that has been owned and operated by four generations of the Dedman family. From the moment you enter the front hall lined with portraits of Robert E. Lee to guest rooms furnished with family heirlooms, you become immersed in Kentucky history and gracious Southern living. Situated in the heart of Kentucky's Bluegrass Country, this 1845 brick building served both as a finishing school for young ladies and a college (Beaumont College) before becoming an inn in 1918. It's chock full of memorabilia from earlier days displayed in cases that line the downstairs hallways. We found well-documented collections of antique fishing lures, glassware, and old letters that tell the history of the inn. Crystal chandeliers, pier mirrors, elegant fireplaces, and a Steinway parlor grand piano grace the twin parlors. Current innkeeper Chuck Dedman says returning guests often request his grandmother's (#8) and great-grandmother's (#28) antique-filled rooms.

Chuck and Helen Dedman, Innkeepers
638 Beaumont Inn Dr.
Harrodsburg, KY
(800) 352-3992
www.beaumontinn.com

RATES & RESERVATIONS:
Season: Mar–Dec;
Rates: $$$;
Reservations recommended;
Check, Visa, MC, Disc, Amex accepted

ACCOMMODATIONS:
33 rooms w/bath

AMENITIES: Cable TV, pool,
phone in room, air cond.

MEALS: Expanded continental and
full breakfast, lunch, dinner, brunch

SPECIAL CONSIDERATIONS:
Not fully handicapped accessible;
Parking available: Lot, on street

A dinner bell calls guests to feast on two-year-old Kentucky cured country ham and Beaumont's famous yellow-legged fried chicken. Traditional desserts include General Robert E. Lee orange lemon cake and

Beaumont Inn prune cake with Bourbon sauce. A Beaumont Cocktail (a glass of ice water) is offered at bedtime for those who indulged in salt-cured, hickory-smoked ham at dinner. You'll know you're in the South at breakfast. The selections include sausage gravy and biscuits, grits, and Beaumont's famous cornmeal batter-cakes.

The inn offers a total of 33 rooms. Besides the original building, guests can book a stay in nearby Greystone House, a two-story Colonial Revival building with four large bedrooms, built in 1931. The Bell Cottage, with two cottage-style suites, is ideal for a family or two couples. Goddard Hall, built in 1935 with 10 rooms, is named for Annie Bell Goddard, founder of the Beaumont Inn. This is truly a family-run inn and a typical Dedman touch is a poem found in every guest room written by Annie Bell Goddard, a former mathematics teacher and dean of Beaumont College. Annie and Glave Goddard turned the former college into an inn in 1917.

The beautiful grounds planted with 37 different tree species invite strolling. April brings out the dogwood and daffodils, and May the tulip poplar, red bud, iris, and tulips. Spring is a popular time to visit the Beaumont Inn so reserve early. The pillared porch of the inn is the place to slow down and enjoy the view. Gift items from around the world fill the gift shop on the lower level of the inn.

Special packages at the Beaumont Inn include Chef Nick's cooking

school weekend, a Kentucky Derby weekend package, and a December "Christmas Season" weekend package. A yearly update, *The Beaumont Inn News*, listing upcoming special events as well as news of this fourth-generation innkeeping family, is sent to those who have stayed at the inn.

The Beaumont Inn has been a member of the Independent Innkeepers' Association since 1979.

THINGS TO DO: Harrodsburg, Kentucky's first town, was settled in 1774 and is filled with architectural treasures. Pick up a map for a walking tour of the historic districts of Harrodsburg or book an Olde Towne Tour, a 50-minute narrated overview of Harrodsburg and Mercer County. Summertime finds *The Legend of Daniel Boone* returning to James Harrod Amphitheater. A pleasant stop is Harrodsburg Kentucky Pottery and Particulars, a mile east of downtown Harrodsburg, offering Kentucky craft items including rag rugs, honeysuckle baskets, and hand-thrown pottery in a century-old building surrounded by fragrant herb and flower gardens.

DIRECTIONS: I-71 to I-75; south on I-75 to exit 115 for SR 922; south on SR 922; south on SR 4 to exit 2 for US 68; west on US 68; left on Beaumont Dr.

NEARBY ATTRACTIONS: downtown Harrodsburg, James Harrod Amphitheater

Inn at Georgian Place

A prestigious Georgian mansion with exceptional antiques

Jon Knupp, Innkeeper
800 Georgian Place Dr.
Somerset, PA
(814) 443-1043
www.somersetcountry.com/theinn

RATES & RESERVATIONS:
Season: Year round;
Rates: $$$–$$$$;
Specials: Seniors, AAA;
Reservations recommended;
Check, Visa, MC, Disc, Amex,
Diner's Club accepted

ACCOMMODATIONS:
9 rooms w/bath; 2 suites w/bath

AMENITIES: Cable TV,
phone in room, Internet, air cond.

MEALS: Full breakfast,
lunch, dinner, afternoon tea;
Beer, wine, and liquor served

SPECIAL CONSIDERATIONS:
Guest pets allowed;
Not fully handicapped accessible;
Parking available: Lot

Traveling along the Pennsylvania Turnpike from Ohio to Philadelphia, I often noticed an imposing building high on a hill at Exit 10 at Somerset. I finally stopped one day to check it out and found a beautifully restored Georgian mansion—the Inn at Georgian Place, a place once described as "Somerset's most prestigious home."

Built in 1925 by Mr. D. B. Zimmerman, a local coal and cattle baron, the 22-room mansion became a bed and breakfast inn in 1993 and earned a spot on the National Register of Historic Places. Stepping into the foyer, I had my first taste of the grandeur of this accommodation, with its marble floor, grand staircase supported by large columns, and brass light fixtures. I learned from the assistant innkeeper that these were the original light fixtures from the New York Brass Company. The common room at the end of the hall is equally elegant with dentil molding, hardwood paneling, and a grand piano. In the Georgian style, asymmetrical wings balance the central portion of the structure. The original tiled-floor conservatory in the south wing is now the sun room, where later we were served an excellent meal, from a menu that featured continental cuisine. With a wood fire crackling away, classical piano music drifting in from the common room, and quietly efficient servers, it was a romantic setting on a cold January night. A delightful way to begin a stay at the Inn at Georgian Place is to stop for afternoon tea in this many windowed room, where inn guests also enjoy a full breakfast.

Each of the nine guest rooms and two suites have a distinct personality. They are furnished with Chippendale, Hepplewhite, and Sheraton style reproductions, and desks and reading lights are provided in the rooms. The Zimmermans' daughter, Sally, had the large corner room on the second floor, where today's guests find a king-size four-poster rice carved bed and a neoclassical-design mantelpiece with carved bell flowers and rosette detail. A settee in front of the fireplace, wing chairs, and a table set for two invite guests to bring a book back to the room or settle down to watch television. The deep burgundy wallpaper in the bath

provides a nice contrast to the original white tile of the era. Down the hall, the Library Suite feels like a library with bookcases, oak paneled walls, a king-size sleigh bed, and a comfy leather chair. A sitting room with overstuffed sofa and club chairs adjoins the bedroom. I liked the Trumbauer room on the third floor, named for Horace Trumbauer, the architect who designed the mansion; dormer windows, sloping ceiling, and matching plaid club chairs make it a snug getaway.

THINGS TO DO: Immediately below the inn is a complex of 35 stores that make up the Factory Shops at Georgian Place. For those who love to shop, this is the perfect setting. You can stay at an elegant inn and shop at the designer outlets and specialty shops within an easy walk. A second shopping option can be found at Pine Haven, a village of restored historic buildings in Somerset showcasing women's clothing, Amish-made goods, children's clothing, and computer equipment. We enjoyed browsing the Walker Room, a restored log home in this complex featuring handcrafted eighteenth-century and Shaker reproduction furniture, candles, and collectibles. Frank Lloyd Wright's Fallingwater and Kentucky Knob are popular trips for guests of the inn.

DIRECTIONS: I-80 east to exit 42 for I-76; east on I-76 to exit 10 for SR 601; left on SR 601; on right

NEARBY ATTRACTIONS: Fallingwater, Kentucky Knob, Seven Springs, Hidden Valley, Laurel Mountain

Felicity Farms Bed and Breakfast

Enjoy the vista from the veranda in this Southern plantation country home.

Anne Mayerich, Innkeeper
2075 Dutch Ridge Rd.
Beaver, PA
(724) 775-0735
www.forcomm.net/bnb-felicity

RATES & RESERVATIONS:
Season: Year round;
Rates: $$$;
Reservations required;
Checks accepted

ACCOMMODATIONS:
3 rooms w/bath

AMENITIES: Cable TV, air cond.

MEALS: Full breakfast

SPECIAL CONSIDERATIONS:
Dog living at inn;
Not fully handicapped accessible;
Parking available: Lot

Felicity Farms stands on the crest of a hill near Beaver, Pennsylvania. Owner Anne Mayerich had always wanted a barn so she could keep horses. When she purchased the property in Brighton Township in 1997, she got not only a barn but also a historic house and eight-and-a-half acres of farmland. After doing extensive renovation work, Anne is now the proud keeper of a bed and breakfast, a great big red barn, and enough pastureland for her horses, sheep, and chickens. Aptly named, Felicity Farms is a pleasant destination and is well-suited to its site on a hill.

The house is a combination of Federal and Southern Colonial-style architecture. The original four-room dwelling, built in 1786, was moved to its present location in 1908, when two bedrooms and a kitchen were added. Elizabeth and John Young built the last section of the house in 1936 and refurbished the large verandas that give the place its Southern feel. In looking back over the months of renovation, Anne relates that there were days when she would come to check on the progress of the work only to find a new problem and sometimes a disaster. The house had stood empty for three years, possums and raccoons had taken up residence in the basement, and she had to jack up the house and gut the kitchen. She had the pleasure after nine months of work to host the Candlelight Christmas Tour in December 1997. Thirteen-hundred people came through to admire her house decorated for the holidays. Fittingly, the first overnight guests at Felicity Farms were the daughter of the last owner and her family. They had followed the renovation of the house and were pleased to find the property intact in this area of encroaching housing developments.

The exterior of this heritage house is sage with cranberry shutters. First time visitors will know where to pull in when they spot the red barn at the bottom of the hill. When I stepped into the kitchen at Felicity Farms, I was transported to Provence—the walls, lined with shiny copper utensils, are interspersed with baskets and greenery, while pine floors and cherry and blue cabinets contribute to the look. A sweet little sun room adjoins the kitchen with a view of the barn and the sheep (Ada, Hulda, and Edna) and horses (Chili and Megan) grazing in the pasture. Weekdays, an expanded continental breakfast with Anne's homemade breads and spreads awaits guests. This busy career woman's avocation is cooking, and her gourmet breakfasts are the event of the weekend. Some of her specialities include crème brûlée French toast, and sausage and walnuts in puff pastry.

The living room, with its original 1786 wide beams and warm, dark paneling, becomes a welcoming retreat with a wood-burning fireplace, family pictures and book lined shelves. The spacious great room, furnished with overstuffed sofas and chairs, provides private conversational groupings. This is the room in which to watch TV, listen to the col-

lection of CDs, or play the grand piano. When weather permits, guests enjoy breakfast on the six-sided screened-in porch overlooking the gardens.

As Anne and I talked about the work and time involved in renovating the place, she said, "All I really wanted to do was decorate the house in the style I love." I found her style to be warm, charming, and unpretentious. The wide upstairs hallway showcases her stenciling and collection of art. When Anne finds an antique that fits her style she works it in with existing traditional pieces. I stayed in Miriam's Room, with

a burnished brass bed, an antique trunk, and a pair of chairs by the fireplace. A second-story porch adjoins the room, and the next morning sun streamed in along with the chirping of birds. All the guest rooms take advantage of the wonderful views of flower gardens and surrounding countryside. Bessie's Room honors Anne's mother, who made the quilts on the twin four-poster maple beds: the quilt's Iris design in pink and green is picked up by pink flowers in the white tile surrounding the fireplace. Elizabeth's Room is a cheerful corner room with folk art, a verdigris bed, and a door to the porch.

Anne's guest book includes visitors from around the world who find this bed and breakfast a short (20 minutes) drive from Pittsburgh's International Airport.

THINGS TO DO: There's a wide choice of dining options at one location at the Sebastian Family of Restaurants in nearby Bridgewater. It's a beautiful drive along the Beaver River to this complex. Take your pick of family dining at Bert's Wooden Indian Bar-B-Q, light meals at the Casual Cafe which features jazz in the evening, or the upscale Wooden Angel, winner of awards from *Travel/Holiday Magazine* and *Wine Spectator* magazine. Continue on from the restaurant to Bridgewater's street of unusual shops.

DIRECTIONS: I-80 east to exit 42 for I-76; east on I-76 to exit 1a for PA 60; south on PA 60 to exit 14 for Brighton Rd.; left (north) on Brighton; right (east) on Dutch Ridge Rd.; on right

NEARBY ATTRACTIONS: Harmony Village, Brady's Run, Pittsburgh (35 minutes)

William Seward Inn

Haute cuisine in a luxurious historic inn

Jim and Debbie Dahlberg, Innkeepers
6645 S. Portage Rd.
Westfield, NY
(716) 326-4151
www.williamsewardinn.com

RATES & RESERVATIONS:
Hours: 8 a.m.–9 p.m.;
Season: Year round;
Rates: $$$;
Specials: Singles, AAA;
Two-night minimum stay required on weekends during high season;
Reservations recommended;
Check, Visa, MC, Disc, Amex accepted

ACCOMMODATIONS: 12 rooms w/bath

AMENITIES: Spa, phone in room, air cond., double Jacuzzi, 2 rooms w/gas log fireplaces

MEALS: Full breakfast, dinner

SPECIAL CONSIDERATIONS:
Dog and cat living at inn;
Handicapped accessible;
Parking available: Lot

High atop a grassy knoll halfway between Westfield and Mayville, New York, stands the William Seward Inn, a nineteenth-century Greek Revival structure. It's nestled in a stunningly distracting setting, so be on the lookout as you travel along Route 394 or you may miss it. At one time it was the home of William Henry Seward, Abraham Lincoln's secretary of state.

Debbie and Jim Dahlberg always wanted to own a country inn and in 1991 realized their dream with the purchase of this inn. The Dahlbergs have furnished the inn's eight rooms, and four deluxe rooms in the coach house, with quality antiques and reproductions. Relax upon arrival with a cup of tea in the parlor in front of the fire, or settle down in one of the wing chairs in the sunny library. On the second floor we found the William Seward Room welcoming with its pleasing combination of fabrics and colors—cream and peach against pale greens, dark woods against a white tile fireplace. We had driven through snow squalls on our trip from northeast Ohio, and we basked in the warmth of the gas log fireplace. This room at the front of the inn has a view of Lake Erie. The four luxurious coach-house rooms, including one handicapped-accessible room, offer double Jacuzzis, vaulted ceilings, and generous sitting areas.

If fine dining is an important part of the country inn experience for you, make a reservation for the prix fixe four-course dinner served

Wednesday through Sunday, with seatings at 5:00 and 7:00 p.m. The evening we dined in the Rose Room, the table was elegantly set with pink roses, place cards, and fine china. A full gourmet breakfast is served to guests of the inn. Memorable breakfast specialties include scrambled eggs with three cheeses and tarragon, eggs Benedict, and apple cinnamon pancakes. On our snowy early January stay, we enjoyed the activity at the bird feeders outside our window.

The Dahlbergs offer special theme packages, including International Wine and Gourmet Weekends. During Women's Escape Weekend, women can leave family and career responsibilities behind for a pampering stay at the inn. These popular weekends fill quickly, so reserve early.

Innkeepers often make the difference in a first stay at an accommodation and are the reason guests return. While the William Seward Inn is a bustling place, I have never stayed without either Debbie or Jim taking time to chat. Their philosophy is a simple one: "If we see something we like, we try it, and if it's not right or to our liking, we either change it or throw it out," says Jim. The William Seward Inn has been a member of the Independent Innkeepers Association for eight years. The inn was the recipient of *Upstate New York* magazine's Fine Dining Award. The *New York Times* says of this classic country inn, "The charm of the Seward Inn is its intimate but comfortable state."

THINGS TO DO: This is an inn for all seasons—when the snow blankets this scenic area, when the spring blooms cover the grounds, in summertime when the nearby Chautauqua Institution is in full swing, and when fall colors kiss the hills of the Lake Erie plain. The Portage Hill Gallery showcases juried regional artwork in all media, in a Colonial home near the inn. Spend an afternoon checking out the antique stores in Westfield or stop at the Johnson Estate Vineyards and Winery, the oldest estate winery in New York State, two miles west of Westfield.

DIRECTIONS: I-90 to exit 60 for SR 394; left on SR 394; on right

NEARBY ATTRACTIONS: Chautauqua, downhill and cross-country skiing, Lilydale, art galleries, wineries, antiques, crafts, boating

Little Inn of Bayfield

A heritage landmark inn tucked along Lake Huron's shore

Patrick and Gayle Waters, Innkeepers
100 Main St.
Bayfield, ONT
(519) 565-2611
www.littleinn.com

RATES & RESERVATIONS:
Hours: 24 hours; Season: Year round;
Rates: $$$$;
Two-night minimum stay
required on weekends;
Reservations required;
Check, Visa, MC, Amex, Disc,
Enroute, Diner's Club accepted

ACCOMMODATIONS:
15 rooms w/bath; 15 suites w/bath

AMENITIES: Double whirlpool tubs,
cable TV, phone in room, Internet,
air cond.

MEALS: Full breakfast,
lunch, dinner, brunch;
Beer, wine, and liquor served

SPECIAL CONSIDERATIONS:
Guest pets allowed;
Handicapped accessible;
Parking available: On street

Traveling along the Blue Water Highway (Route 21), you can easily miss the little village of Bayfield tucked away along the shores of Lake Huron. Our first visit was a short one, a stop to browse the specialty shops that line Bayfield's wide Main Street. But it was long enough to gain an appreciation of the village's nineteenth-century architecture and magnificent maple and locust trees, and to discover the Little Inn of Bayfield. Originally a stagecoach stop on the London to Goderich route, the inn has welcomed guests since 1832. We sat on the veranda, shaded by a huge old willow tree, and watched the parade of visitors march from the park-like Clan Gregor Square at one end of Main Street past the chic shops and then past of our post at the Little Inn. This historic village center has been designated a Heritage Conservation District. It doesn't take long to get the sense of tradition and pride in this enclave along the Huron.

When innkeepers Gayle and Patrick Waters bought the inn in 1981 it had nine rooms. The Waters restored the carriage house and built a Guest Cottage across the street, making a total of 29 guest accommodations. The 16 suites all have double whirlpools, and many have access to verandas. The old inn is a calming retreat with botanical prints, a small settee, good reading lights, and a high bed made even higher with a puffy duvet. A spacious adjoining bath with Jacuzzi stocked with the thick towels and luxurious toiletries one expects to find in a fine country inn.

We settled in the formal front parlor to read the morning newspaper and chatted with guests from Canada and the U.S. It is a delicious room done in Devon cream-colored wainscoting, with cream and raspberry wallpaper in an old-fashioned, elegant ribbon design. A marble fireplace and antique piano highlight the room. The furniture is original Canadiana in walnut, cherry, and butternut. In the cozy back parlor, an eight-foot-high antique cherry armoire filled with puzzles, games, and books makes this the place to relax and pull up a chair to the brick fireplace.

The dining room is perhaps my favorite spot in the Little Inn (which, by the way, is not little—the inn's name came from one of the owners, the Little Family). With floor-to-ceiling windows on to the heritage main street, the exposed brick wall of the early inn, ladder-back chairs, and white linen service, it's a romantic setting in the evening, with flickering candlelight, and is just as lovely the next morning for a breakfast buffet in this sun-splashed room. The inn is known for regional and seasonal dishes. Chef Jean Jacques Chappius selects the best of fresh, country grown produce from Huron County, "the breadbasket of Ontario." A summer meal could start with cold smoked Huron boar, continue with cracked-peppered duck breast with duck foie gras brioche, and finish with fresh ginger creme caramel.

This traditional country inn, cloaked in an almost-unassuming grace and venerable history, has garnered a list of awards, including the coveted CAA/AAA Four Diamond Restaurant designation for four years in a row and *Wine Spectator*'s Award of Excellence. The inn is a four diamond accommodation member of the Independent Innkeepers' Association (member since 1981).

THINGS TO DO: When you finish a leisurely repast at the Little Inn, what is there to do in Bayfield? We took a short walk to Pioneer Park to watch the spectacular Bayfield sunset on Lake Huron along with other visitors and local residents.

Summertime folks walk the golden sandy beaches or try fly-fishing on the Bayfield or Maitland rivers. Evenings can be spent at the theater; the nearby Blyth Festival has earned an international reputation for performing plays by Canadian playwrights, and the Stratford Festival is a

40-minute trip from the inn. Autumn brings the Huron Harvest Trail, an event that offers a chance to see the great variety of food produced in Huron County, with stops at farms and businesses. The innkeepers plan celebrations for both American and Canadian Thanksgiving, and once the snow flies guests can access cleared and pruned cross-country ski trails.

DIRECTIONS: I-80 to exit 5 for I-280; north on I-280; north on I-75; east on I-94 to Blue Water Bridge; east on SR 402; north on SR 21; left on Main St.; on right

NEARBY ATTRACTIONS: Stratford Festival, Blyth Festival, conservation areas for hiking, biking, and fly-fishing

Kingswood Inn

An octagonal-style house surrounded by beautiful gardens

Bob and Barb Dick;
Jay and Helen Koop, Innkeepers
101 Mill St. W
Kingsville, ONT
(519) 733-3248
www.lsol.com/Kingswood

RATES & RESERVATIONS:
Season: Closed Christmas–Feb;
Rates: $$$$;
Specials: Two-night weekend discount May–Oct;
Reservations required;
Check, Visa, MC accepted

ACCOMMODATIONS: 5 rooms w/bath

AMENITIES: Cable TV, pool, phone in room, Internet, air cond.

MEALS: Expanded continental and full breakfast, snacks

SPECIAL CONSIDERATIONS:
Not fully handicapped accessible;
Parking available: Lot

There's a luxurious bed and breakfast on the opposite shore of Lake Erie—the Kingswood Inn in Kingsville, Ontario. Built in 1858 by Colonel James King, the founder of Kingsville, the octagonal house is situated on three acres planted with a beautiful variety of flowers and trees bordered by a stone wall. Guests interested in history and architecture will be intrigued with the design of this place. The house was originally a perfect octagon, but two wings were added to the structure in 1881, and today a veranda runs around the octagonal part of the house. The interior trim was retained, and the swimming pool—the first in-ground pool to be built in Ontario (1926)—is still used. It was purchased in 1996 by Helen and Jay Koop and their daughter and son-in-law, Barb and Bob Dick. The couples share the innkeeping responsibilities, with mother and daughter trading off welcoming and breakfast duties. The Kingswood Inn extends the same offer to today's guests that Colonel James King extended to weary travelers in the 1860s—a warm welcome to "Kingsholme."

Returning guests say they come back because of the inn's romantic and luxurious ambiance. There is an air of graciousness throughout this heritage house, with bouquets of flowers from the garden and gleaming hardwood floors. You can wander at will, and then settle down in the cozy library or find a swing or bench in the superbly land-scaped yard. While the drawing room is more formal, with an 1868 Steinway that belonged to Colonel King, it offers intimate conversational groupings. Canopied beds, fluffy comforters, antiques, and decor ranging from Victorian to the arts and crafts era fill the rooms. The most-requested room is #5, a Victorian-style room with a four-poster queen bed, fireplace, and two-person whirlpool.

Breakfast is served in the dining room, a cheerful sunny room with a table set with colorful linens and fine china. Some of Barb's breakfast specialties are caramel French toast and Octoberfest sausages.

THINGS TO DO: The guest book at the Kingswood Inn includes visitors from many parts of the world who come for the excellent birding and the monarch butterfly migration. Point Pelee National Park, the southern-most tip of Canada's mainland, offers a peaceful refuge for nature lovers and photographers. You can walk the beautiful Marsh Boardwalk, rent canoes, or take a canoe trip into the marsh with a park naturalist. Four local wineries are also a draw, as is the strength of the American dollar.

Stop in at Pelee Island Winery's Kingsville location and meet winemaker Walter Schmoranz. You can sample wines in the cellar barrel room and take home some of Ontario's Icewine. At Colasanti's Tropical Gardens you'll find a wide selection of cacti and tropical plants.

We found a wonderful local restaurant, the Vintage Goose, located in one of Kingsville's oldest buildings. There's a gift shop on the second floor, the Piggery, offering a variety of gourmet foods and gifts. The Victorian Rose Tea Room serves high tea and also is a full-service restaurant.

DIRECTIONS: I-80 to exit 5 for I-280; north on I-280; north on I-75 to Ambassador Bridge; south on Hwy 3; south on SR 29; right on Mill St.

NEARBY ATTRACTIONS: Pelee Island, Winery Tours, Point Pelee National Park, Colasanti's Tropical Gardens, Jack Miner's Bird Sanctuary, Windsor Casino

Chapter 6

CITY STAYS

*We often think of a bed and breakfast as a house set at the end of a
quiet street in a small town or in the countryside. But these destinations
are popping up in the middle of active cities as well. The appeal of a
stay in a metropolitan area is easy access to cultural riches, varied dining
options, and a chance to explore a city's history and neighborhoods.*

Comeback cities like Cleveland and Pittsburgh now offer a fresh face
to visitors. Thanks to urban pioneers, historic architecture is being renovated, and entire neighborhoods are being revitalized. Brownstones,
tudors, and Victorians escaped the wrecking ball, and private homes are
not the only structures given a second chance—preservationists are
restoring the best of the old by bringing back old theaters and other
buildings.

Each city profiled in this chapter has distinctive neighborhoods offering ethnic foods and festivals, like Little Italy in Cleveland, German
Village in Columbus, and the German-American Festival in Toledo.

Planning a city getaway? Think fine museums, professional sports,
galleries, symphony concerts, a day at the zoo. In Cleveland, check into
a bed and breakfast downtown and find the theater district nearby or at
an inn in the University Circle area with its wealth of museums and Severance Hall, home to the Cleveland Orchestra. In Columbus, stay in a
turn-of-the-century house in Victorian Village within easy access of
downtown. Review a little history at the classic Greek Revival Ohio
Statehouse and catch up with technology at COSI, the Center of Science
and Industry. In Akron, stay in a former industrialist's home and explore
another sizable Tudor, Stan Hywet Hall. In Toledo, stay in a suburb or
nearby town—Grand Rapids, Ohio, and Blissfield, Michigan, offer destinations close to Toledo where visitors find a jewel of an art museum
and an outstanding zoo.

O'Neil House Bed and Breakfast

This stately Tudor mansion boasts six working fireplaces.

Gayle Johnson, Innkeeper
1290 W. Exchange St.
Akron, OH
(330) 867-2650
www.oneilhouse.com

RATES & RESERVATIONS:
Hours: 9 a.m.–9 p.m.;
Season: Year round;
Rates: $$$$;
Specials: Singles;
Reservations required;
Check, Visa, MC, Disc accepted

ACCOMMODATIONS: 4 rooms w/bath

AMENITIES: Air cond.

MEALS: Full breakfast

SPECIAL CONSIDERATIONS:
Dog and cats living at inn;
Not fully handicapped accessible
Parking available: Lot

Everything is on a grand scale at the O'Neil House, a half-timbered, 19-room Tudor mansion built in 1923 for William O'Neil, founder of the General Tire Company. This bed and breakfast in west Akron is a showcase of the exquisite workmanship of the era, with leaded glass windows in diamond, octagon, and rectangular patterns; planked oak floors; and six working fireplaces.

A favorite room of guests is the library lined with bookshelves, one of which hides a secret bar. The living room is reminiscent of 1920s, with twin tufted beige leather sofas flanking a low table in front of the wood-burning fireplace, a grand piano, and groupings of chairs and tables that break up the space into conversational areas.

On the second floor, the enormous master suite is made up of a sitting room, dressing room, bathroom, and bedroom. A sitting room with a fireplace, Oriental rug in wine tones, and comfortable seating is spacious enough to host a party. A dressing room with a wall of built-in cabinets opens to the suite's most remarkable feature, an art deco bathroom with classy jade Vitrolite walls and a circa-1932 chandelier. The bedroom, dominated by a mahogany king-size bed, is decorated in beiges and brightened by a floral sofa nestled cozily under the diamond-shaped leaded-glass windows.

In Grace's Room, named for the O'Neil's daughter, a soft rose and beige color scheme complements the light wood furniture. The adjoining bath has a pedestal sink and an interesting Oriental chest. Innkeeper Gayle Johnson has added small touches, like a flapper-era feathered headpiece and old photographs.

At the top of the stairs, there's a suite with a good-size bedroom featuring a sleigh bed, a corner sitting area, and a large bath. The star of this set of rooms is the sunroom at the back overlooking the gardens, with light gold-and-white-striped walls and a floral chintz sofa—a perfect place to settle down with a book or a cup of tea.

Guests gather for breakfast in the formal dining room, a study in blues from the blue painted woodwork to the blue and peach on floral panels and in the Oriental rug. During my visit, one of the resident cats was lazing in the sun on the long window seat. Just beyond the dining room, a many-windowed breakfast room looks out on to a yard with seven distinct gardens. This innkeeper is known for her "Gatsby Breakfast": filet mignon, asparagus tips, and a poached egg in a light wine sauce served with fresh fruit and homemade pastries.

Gayle has been innkeeping for 11 years and has yet to advertise. Returning guests include those who come to Akron on business and couples celebrating special occasions. The O'Neil descendants have gathered at the house for a reunion and other family groups have had a family Christmas celebration at this stately Tudor on West Exchange Street.

THINGS TO DO: You can continue the Tudor experience with a tour of Stan Hywet Hall, a 65-room mansion surrounded by landscaped grounds and formal gardens. Once home to the Frank A. Seiberling family, it is one of the finest examples of Tudor Revival architecture in the United States. To step back to Victorian times, visit the Hower House, a second-empire Italianate-style mansion near the University of Akron campus. Visitors to the O'Neil House also stop at the Akron Art Museum and Inventure Place—the National Inventors Hall of Fame. Don't miss West Point Market, a gastronomical delight where you can sample new products as you stroll the grocery aisles. You might catch a visiting chef or a celebration in this one-of-a-kind market. There's a wide choice of dining spots in Akron, including Gayle's own Amber Pub Restaurant.

DIRECTIONS: I-77 to exit 132 for White Pond Dr.; north on White Pond; right (east) to Mull Ave..; left on W. Exchange; on left

NEARBY ATTRACTIONS: Akron University, Pro Football Hall of Fame, Inventure Place, Akron Art Museum, Stan Hywet Hall and Gardens

Baricelli Inn

*A European-style inn in
Cleveland's cultural center*

The Baricelli Inn is a city inn in the European tradition. Suburbanites come for getaway weekends, business travelers book midweek stays, and it's the site of many a wedding or other special-occasion celebration. This turn-of-the-century brownstone in University Circle offers accommodations and an internationally acclaimed restaurant. Guests can check into a spacious suite, come downstairs for a leisurely meal in one of the intimate dining parlors, and the next morning have breakfast at the inn.

Built in 1896 for Dutch architect John Grant from his own design, the mansion has an interesting history. This was Grant's residence until he sold it to Dr. and Madame Giovanni Barricelli. Dr. Barricelli, a well-known heart and lung specialist at University Hospital, was also a prominent civic leader. Madame Barricelli was a professor of romance languages at what was then Western Reserve College. The Barricellis had many international guests, and students occupied rooms in the house after Dr. Barricelli's death in 1934.

The Minnillo family, longtime Cleveland restaurateurs, purchased

Ursula Garcia and Laura Sabo,
Innkeepers
2203 Cornell Rd.
Cleveland, OH
(216) 791-6500
www.baricelli.com

RATES & RESERVATIONS:
Season: Year round;
Rates: $$$$;
Reservations recommended;
Visa, MC, Amex accepted

ACCOMMODATIONS: 7 rooms w/bath

AMENITIES: Cable TV,
phone in room, air cond.

MEALS: Continental and
full breakfast, dinner;
Beer, wine, and liquor served

SPECIAL CONSIDERATIONS:
Not fully handicapped accessible;
Parking available: Lot

the mansion in 1981, changing the spelling to "Baricelli." In December of 1985, the inn opened with a restaurant and guest suites, and the tradition of welcoming visitors to this lovely old home was continued.

Chef/Owner Paul Minnillo, who represents the third generation of the Minnillo family in the restaurant business, started his cooking career standing on a milk crate in the kitchen of his father's restaurant. Minnillo trained in New York and London. Although the restaurant is located in Little Italy, where Italian restaurants prevail, the Baricelli emphasizes fine American and European cuisine. A first course might include pistachio-crusted soft-shell crab, with a main course of caramelized diver scallops or stuffed Australian venison rack.

The Baricelli Cheese Co., opened in 1999, offers 40 varieties of cheeses "bloomed" in the affinage cooler in the lobby of the inn. Minnillo hopes to educate people about cheeses; stepping into his cooler is a good start. Our server suggested a plate of cheese following our main course and preceding dessert. Other diners may order the platter of aged-to-perfection cheeses to share at the table for a starter. The extensive wine list reflects Minnillo's knowledge of American and European wine producers, and winetastings and winemakers dinners are some of the special events at the inn. The Baricelli received the *Wine Spectator* Award of Excellence.

Reservations are strongly suggested at this four-star restaurant. This is fine dining at its best, and you might spend three hours at dinner in one of the parlor dining rooms. The Villeroy & Boch place settings pick up the purple, green, and orange colors of the striped chairs. The green plants in the main dining room and abundant use of fresh flowers warm the interior. Fireplaces, a focal point in each parlor, have different mantels: white in one room, oak in another, and, in a third, a blue and white Dutch tile surround. Dining is available in the garden during the summer months with a bistro menu. A European continental breakfast featuring fresh pastries, sheep's yogurt, granola, and fresh fruit is served to inn guests in the glassed-in front porch.

This old brownstone retains its original oak woodwork, and stained glass windows pop up at a turn in the stairway or in the public rooms. Upstairs, seven suites are similarly decorated but have different configurations—a slanted ceiling in one, the sunlit exposure in a corner room, a turret room that juts out from the building. A king suite offers a generous sitting area with matching chairs, a television hidden in an antique armoire, a desk, and a four-poster bed. The floral fabric of the comforter is repeated in the drapes and shower curtain. I liked a corner room with its view over the streets and houses of Little Italy. The Baricelli Inn, a wonderful city getaway, allows visitors a charming and comfortable setting with access to some of Cleveland's best attractions.

THINGS TO DO: The location—Little Italy, in the heart of the cultural center of Cleveland—offers quick access to the Cleveland Museum of Art, the Museum of Natural History, Crawford Auto-Aviation Museum, Cleveland Botanical Garden, and Severance Hall. The inn is adjacent to Case Western Reserve University and University Hospitals of Cleveland.

DIRECTIONS: EAST: I-90 to exit 177 for Martin Luther King Blvd.; south on MLK; left (east) on Euclid; right (east) on Cornell; left on Murray Hill Rd.; on left
WEST: I-90 to exit 173B for Chester Ave..; right (east) on Chester; left (east) on Euclid Ave..; right (east) on Cornell; left on to Murray Hill Rd.; on left

NEARBY ATTRACTIONS: The Cleveland Orchestra, The Cleveland Museum of Art, Cleveland Botanical Garden

Brownstone Inn Downtown

Stay near Playhouse Square in this landmark 1847 four-story townhouse.

Robin Yates, Innkeeper
3649 Prospect Ave..
Cleveland, OH
(216) 426-1753
www.brownstoneinndowntown.com

RATES & RESERVATIONS:
Hours: All day;
Season: Year round;
Rates: $$;
Specials: AAA, seniors
Reservations required;
Check, Visa, MC, Disc, Amex accepted

ACCOMMODATIONS:
4 rooms w/bath; 1 suite w/bath

AMENITIES: Cable TV,
phone in room, Internet, air cond.

MEALS: Full breakfast, snacks

SPECIAL CONSIDERATIONS:
Guest pets allowed;
Not fully handicapped accessible;
Parking available: On street

Business travelers and visitors looking for a city stay have discovered the Brownstone Inn on Prospect Avenue in Cleveland's Midtown Corridor. This 1874 restored red brick townhouse is identifiable from its neighbors by a peacock-blue double door. A plaque on the gigantic elm in front of the inn identifies it is as the last elm of Cleveland's first tree-planting of 1880.

Owner/innkeeper Robin Yates renovated the four-story townhouse in 1976, staying as true to the historic integrity of the structure as possible. Designated as "Cleveland Landmark No. 58," the house is on the National Register of Historic Places. Stepping into the foyer, you'll find a sweeping staircase, 12-foot-high ceilings, and elegant French wallpaper setting the style for this four-story Victorian home. A parlor to the left of the entrance with a player piano and comfortable seating offers a place to read the morning paper or relax with a sherry after the theater. Through the pocket doors, another small parlor opens to the dining room, where Robin serves a full breakfast each morning.

The front room on the second floor is elegant with brown leather walls; a 200-year-old, hand-carved, mahogany, four-poster bed; marble-top table; and matching chairs by the fireplace. Lace curtains and green plants in blue and white cachepots lend a softening touch to the high-ceilinged room. At the other end of the hall, a suite with sitting room and bedroom is popular with business guests who need short-term accommodations. A kitchenette with a well-stocked refrigerator and microwave is shared by the rooms on this floor. Up on the next level, guests have a choice of a midsize room or larger room in front. A skylight brightens the common sitting area in the hallway furnished with wicker rockers and a settee. Business guests have the use of a complete office on the sub-level.

In preparing breakfast, Robin favors fresh ingredients, which he finds at the West Side Market. Fresh fruits, specialty breads, and a choice of egg or meat dishes are prepared in the kitchen on the lower level and served in the dining room or, when weather permits, on the enclosed deck. Coffee and tea are always available on the sideboard; in the evening, complimentary sherry and port are offered. Searching for a place for dinner? Reservations can be made at the nearby University Club. The reception table in the middle parlor has a good selection of menus and guides to the city.

Robin thinks of his inn as an American guesthouse borrowing European traditions. Visitors from Switzerland, England, and Germany have found it to be just that. And guests coming from nearby suburbs for a getaway give it high marks. One couple described their stay at the Brownstone Inn as a visit with dear friends or relatives. Those who stay at the

inn mingle in the common rooms. Robin, a Cleveland native, loves the city and wants visitors to know the treasures it holds. He takes guests on tours of Cleveland and tries to tailor itineraries and restaurants to individual guests. His enthusiasm and caring for his city have not gone without notice. In 1999, he was given the Residential Leadership Award for Commitment and Confidence in Midtown Cleveland.

THINGS TO DO: Both Playhouse Square and the Cleveland Play House are within a mile of the inn. Whether you're returning from dinner or an evening on the town, the Brownstone Inn welcomes you back with a coach lamp designed by the Junior League of Cleveland when the house was the 1976 Decorators Showcase.

DIRECTIONS: EAST: I-90 to exit 173A for Prospect Ave..; left (east) on Prospect; on left
WEST: I-90 to exit 172C for Carnegie Ave..; right (east) on Carnegie; left (north) on E. 30th St.; right (east) on Prospect Ave..; on left

NEARBY ATTRACTIONS: downtown Cleveland, theater district, museums

Harrison House Bed and Breakfast

A historic "Painted Lady" in Columbus' Victorian Village neighborhood

Sandy and Don Davis, Innkeepers
313 W. 5th Ave..
Columbus, OH
(800) 827-4203
www.columbus-bed-breakfast.com

RATES & RESERVATIONS:
Hours: 8 a.m.–9 p.m.;
Season: Year round; Rates: $$$;
Reservations required;
Check, Visa, MC, Disc,
Amex, cash accepted

ACCOMMODATIONS: 4 rooms w/bath

AMENITIES: Cable TV, phone in room, air cond., apartment available

MEALS: Full breakfast

SPECIAL CONSIDERATIONS:
Not fully handicapped accessible;
Parking available: Lot, on street

Harrison House, a cream and turquoise "Painted Lady," hugs the corner of West Fifth and Harrison avenues in Columbus. This is known as Victorian Village, a neighborhood where those who treasure Victorian dwellings find themselves happily in the midst of Italianate and Queen Anne architecture as well as sturdier Foursquare houses. Amos Solomon built the house in 1890, and despite its many reincarnations, architectural details from the Gilded Age—like the hardwood floors and original beveled-glass windows in the dining room and front door—remain in the house. It was placed on the National Register of Historic Places in 1980. Sandy and Don Davis purchased it in 1997. The bed and breakfast is Sandy's domain, but she is quick to mention that Don, who has his own business, is essential to the smooth operation as her handyman.

Your first glimpse of Victorian style is the front porch, furnished with white wicker, potted ferns, and baskets overflowing with flowering plants. There's a feeling of genuine warmth and hospitality when you walk through the door.

The parlor gives a turn-of-the-century feel, with a parlor organ, a conversational grouping of sofa and chairs, and old photos. Sandy loves to share the history of her house. She explained as we toured it that in homes built at that time the main floor featured hardwood floors and ornate woodwork, as this was the part of the house guests would see. On the second level, seen only by the family, the floors become wide pine and the woodwork more plain.

Breakfast is served in the dining room at an antique table that seats 12. On cool days the fireplace sends out warmth, and on bright days sunlight streams through the beveled-glass windows. Sandy insists that her breakfasts are not fancy. She serves the things that people grew up with but don't take the time to fix anymore—scrambled eggs with bacon, homemade muffins, and blueberry pancakes. Returning guests request Sandy's French toast, which she makes with apple cinnamon bread served with pure maple syrup.

The Honeymoon Suite on the third floor is an architecturally interesting set of rooms. The bath is in the tower of this Queen Anne house. Wallpaper with a pattern of dogwood blossoms against a dark green background; a pine, four-poster, queen-size bed; a collection of music boxes; and good reading materials make the suite a snug hide-away at the top of the house. One couple liked it so much that they called after a stay at Harrison House and let Sandy know that they planned to duplicate this room exactly in their own home. On the second floor, Santa is the star in the Christmas Room. A collection of the jolly elf figurines is displayed in an antique oak cabinet, and a deep crimson velvet settee is centered in front of a trio of windows. It's a spacious room with a dressing room connecting to the bath. Sandy says almost no morning goes by without a guest saying, "I slept so well. Where did you get those mattresses?" She purchased new top-of-the-line queen mattresses for all the rooms when she opened the inn and uses only quality bedding.

Sandy Davis received the highest compliment an innkeeper could get from another local innkeeper who said of Harrison House, "If I could manage the time to get away from my own inn, I would go to Harrison House and let Sandy pamper me!"

THINGS TO DO: Along with business and professional guests, those who have discovered this neighborhood treasure include visiting professors who come to the Ohio State University, visitors to the nearby Battelle Institute, participants in the Ohio bicycle tour, and runners in the Columbus marathon. Guests head out to the Wexler Center, the Center of Science and Industry (COSI), and the Short North gallery district. Easton Town Center, a new concept in shopping centers patterned after a village, is a popular destination.

DIRECTIONS: I-71 to exit 110A for 5th Ave.; right on 5th Ave..; on corner of 5th and Harrison

NEARBY ATTRACTIONS: The Ohio State University, Nationwide Arena, Schottenstein Arena, Battelle Institute, Convention Center

Worthington Inn

An elegant and romantic getaway in a historic village near downtown Columbus

Ann Williams, Innkeeper
649 High St.
Worthington, OH
(614) 885-2600
www.worthingtoninn.com

RATES & RESERVATIONS:
Season: Year round; Rates: $$$$;
Specials: AAA, "Weekend Getaway";
Reservations recommended;
Check, Visa, MC, Disc, Amex accepted

ACCOMMODATIONS:
26 rooms w/bath; 4 suites w/bath

AMENITIES: Cable TV,
phone in room, Internet, air cond.

MEALS: Full breakfast,
lunch, dinner, brunch;
Beer, wine, and liquor served

SPECIAL CONSIDERATIONS:
Not fully handicapped accessible;
Parking available: Lot, on street

The Worthington Inn, like so many early inns, served as a major stagecoach stop for weary travelers and also as a meeting place and discussion forum for local residents. Built in 1831, it has served as a private home for various owners, a boarding house, and a hotel. When purchased in 1982 by the current owners, it was one more classic example of a deteriorated structure being saved from demolition. Today this handsome inn, with an exterior of old Ohio glazed brick, mansard roof, and balconies offers guests an elegant and romantic getaway. Located in historic Olde Worthington Village, it's 15 minutes from downtown Columbus and five minutes from Interstate 270.

The inn offers 26 rooms and suites in the original building and in the 1817 Snow House across the street. As I walked through the inn, I kept finding wonderful architectural details that had been left intact: original fireplace mantels, corner cupboards, and doors with handblown glass still in place. Additional pieces of interest include the Griswold window in the lobby, the marble-top bar in the pub, and a white marble stairway from the old Franklin County Courthouse in the entryway. Antique aficionados will appreciate the many pieces found throughout the inn; a few examples are the cherry-paneled registration desk, circa 1850, a rosewood secretary from the 1830s, and the four-chair, bow-front bench with cane seat in the lobby. Check out the Van Loon Ballroom on the third floor with its exquisite Czechoslovakian crystal chandelier. The guest rooms are filled with antiques, as well as reproductions of period wall decorations and draperies. The Grand Suite in the old inn is completely furnished in antiques, including a pedestal sink and claw-foot bathtub. Cocktails upon arrival, turndown service in the evening, and a full breakfast are part of the stay.

The inn is also known for fine dining—its Seven Stars Restaurant specializes in regional American cuisine. At lunchtime, we sampled the butternut squash and apple cider soup, a spinach salad, and an apple tartlet with caramel sauce. Recommendations for dinner include an appetizer of pan-seared crab cakes in a jalapeno and sun-dried tomato remoulade, an entree of New Zealand baby rack of lamb, and a dessert of warm almond and pear tart with creme Anglaise. The work of local artists is displayed on the walls of the dining rooms, along with a permanent collection of James Wallace Baker's paintings reflecting everyday life in America.

THINGS TO DO: Step outside the front doors of the Worthington Inn and you're in Olde Worthington's shopping district. Lined up and down High Street are specialty shops, including clothing boutiques, craft stores, collectibles shops, and antique stores. Stop for coffee at Scottie Macbean Roastery or have a great hamburger or fish and chips at Old Bag of Nails Pub. There's a distinctive New England feel to this village, which retains the original design of the group of Connecticut settlers who came to Ohio in 1802. The village green and many historical sites remain today. Tour the Orange Johnson House, circa 1811, on Sunday afternoons and stop by the Old Rectory, which not only houses a gift shop and library but has one of the most extensive doll collections in the area. Special events include evening concerts on the village green on Sundays in summer, a two-day arts festival the third weekend in June, and Market Day, an all-day downtown celebration in early September.

DIRECTIONS: I-71 to exit 117 for SR 161; right on E. Dublin-Granville Rd.; becomes Granville Rd.; left on High St.; on corner of High and New England Ave..

NEARBY ATTRACTIONS: The Ohio State University, Columbus Zoo, Wyandot Lake, Easton Town Center

Morning Glory Inn

A Civil War-era house on Pittsburgh's South Side

Nancy Eshelman, Innkeeper
2119 Sarah St.
Pittsburgh, PA
(412) 431-1707
www.morningglory
bedandbreakfast.com

RATES & RESERVATIONS:
Hours: 7 a.m.–11 p.m.;
Season: Year round;
Rates: $$$$;
Specials: Corporate and business
travel rates Sun–Thu;
Reservations required;
Check, Visa, MC, Disc, Amex accepted

ACCOMMODATIONS:
3 rooms w/bath; 2 suites w/bath

AMENITIES: Internet, air cond., phone
in room, Swedish pressure-relieving
mattress, "rainsoft" treated bathwater

MEALS: Full breakfast

SPECIAL CONSIDERATIONS:
Guest pets allowed;
Not fully handicapped accessible;
Parking available: Lot

Tourists and business travelers visiting Pittsburgh have found a home away from home at the Morning Glory Inn on the city's South Side. Housed in a red brick, pre-Civil War row house, the Morning Glory Inn stands close to the sidewalk, edged by the original iron fence. Innkeeper Nancy Eshleman named her inn for the Victorian flower, and this motif is repeated in the sign, etched-glass front door, and flowers that now twine up the old fence. Eshleman renovated this Italianate structure so guests could delight in its pocket doors, 12-foot ceilings, music room with an 1890 Chickering grand piano (tuned to concert pitch), and cheerful library with French doors opening to a porch. Five guest rooms are resplendent with antiques, wicker, and floral and pastel wallpapers. At the top of the house, a two-level suite has a sitting room and bath on the first level and a bedroom on the upper level with a view over the rooftops of the city. An unusual feature of the Margaret Jackson Suite is a sizable sitting room/bathroom with a chaise lounge and a working, black slate, faux painted fireplace. This inn's guest book is brimming with comments about the wonderful nights' sleep on the inn's Swedish system of pressure-relieving foam mattresses.

The breakfast room, with the original pine floors and large working fireplace, is set up with tables for two or four, giving guests the choice of chatting with others or concentrating on their morning newspaper. This is an example of the care Eshelman has taken to make both sets of guests comfortable: those who come for a romantic getaway, and business travelers (who also find private telephones with digital answering technology and computer ports, plus the availability of a laser printer and fax machine). Another example of attention to detail at the Morning Glory Inn is soft water, treated to remove chemicals and chlorine. The inn is conveniently situated less than a mile from Pittsburgh's downtown business district and the University/Hospital Complex in Oakland.

Home-economics teacher Eshelman prepares breakfast. Fresh-squeezed juice, homemade biscuits and muffins, German baked eggs, Nancy's Quiche, and cinnamon bread pudding French toast served with bourbon sauce are a few of the favorites.

THINGS TO DO: The Morning Glory Inn is located in Pittsburgh's East Carson Street Historic District, and guests find restaurants, antique shops, art galleries, and theaters a block away.

Have a grand meal at Le Pommier just around the corner from the inn. The dining room, serving country French cuisine, is reminiscent of a European cafe with lace curtains at the window, wainscoting, snowy linens, classical music, and an extensive wine list. The work of local artists lines the walls.

Pittsburgh offers a wonderful variety of artistic and cultural destinations. It's easy to spend half a day at the Frick Art and Historical Center, a complex that includes Clayton, industrialist Henry Clay Frick's mansion; the Frick Art Museum; and the Car and Carriage Museum. Stop for tea or lunch at the cafe located on the grounds, and visit the gift shop, which carries a nice selection of Victorian reproductions, books, and collectibles. Other popular destinations are the

Nationality Rooms in the University of Pittsburgh's Cathedral of Learning and the Phipps Conservatory.

DIRECTIONS: I-80 east to exit 42 for I-76; east on I-76 to exit 1A for PA 60; south on PA 60; east on US 22 to exit 8 for Grant St.; right (east) on Forbes Ave..; right (south) on S. 10th St.; left (east) on E. Carson St.; right (south) on S. 21st St.; left (east) on Sarah St.; on left

NEARBY ATTRACTIONS: downtown Pittsburgh's cultural district, E. Carson St. (a national historic district and Pittsburgh's restaurant and entertainment center), Henry Clay Frick estate, Phipps Conservatory, Carnegie Museum, Cathedral of Learning, Andy Warhol Museum, Carnegie Science Center, National Aviary, Pittsburgh Zoo, Heinz Regional History Center, The "Strip" Marketplace, Kennywood Amusement Park, symphony, ballet, opera, City Theater, the Steelers, the Penguins

Priory— A City Inn

*What was once
a Benedictine priory
is now a fine city inn.*

Ed and Mary Ann Graf, Innkeepers
614 Pressley St.
Pittsburgh, PA
(412) 231-3338
www.thepriory.com

RATES & RESERVATIONS:
Hours: 24 hours;
Season: Year round;
Rates: $$$–$$$$;
Specials: Seniors, AAA;
Reservations recommended;
Check, Visa, MC, Disc, Amex accepted

ACCOMMODATIONS:
21 rooms w/bath; 3 suites w/bath

AMENITIES: Cable TV, phone
in room, air cond., hair dryers,
iron and ironing board

MEALS: Expanded
continental breakfast, snacks;
Beer, wine, and liquor served

SPECIAL CONSIDERATIONS:
Handicapped accessible;
Parking available: Lot

When Ed and Mary Ann Graf first visited what was then St. Mary's German Catholic Church and Priory, the buildings stood empty and forlorn. The priory had been home to the Benedictine priests and brothers serving at St. Mary's, as well as a former temporary haven for monks stopping on their way to St. Vincent's Abbey in Latrobe. The buildings escaped the wrecking ball by a re-routing of the nearby expressway but were still owned by the Pennsylvania Department of Transportation. The Grafs, ardent preservationists, purchased the church and priory without a definite plan for their use. They just couldn't bear to see another historic building demolished. A friend suggested rehabbing the parish house into a European-style hotel; thus the Priory—a City Inn was born.

The renovation and restoration process, according to Mary Ann, "was like seeing a decrepit, badly dressed old lady fall in the street, and you go pick her up, brush her off, and restore her dignity." They faced poor conditions inside the building, such as a boiler encased in four feet

of ice, burst pipes that had caused a tin ceiling to fall, and hallways covered with pigeon droppings. The only usable features inside the brick walls were woodwork, doors, some hardware, windows, and three original light fixtures. But, the "lady's" dignity was restored, and a jewel of a city hotel emerged. As in the days when Benedictine monks were welcomed, the Priory once again opened its doors to travelers seeking a place to stay in the city. The Grafs received an award of merit from the Pennsylvania Historical and Museum Commission, and the Priory was selected for inclusion in *America Restored*, published in 1994 by the Preservation Press of the National Trust for Historic Preservation.

There's a reserved European elegance to the 24 guests rooms, including three two-room suites, furnished with American and English antiques and reproductions. I stayed in a two-room suite that looked down onto the courtyard and across to the church. In the morning, sunlight streamed in through the bay windows of the sitting room; at night, the trees were outlined in tiny white lights. Pale beige and florals covered the sofa and wing chair, and antiques included an armoire and writing desk. Maze-like corridors lead to a parlor on the first floor where sherry is set out in the evening. I settled in the adjoining library with French lace curtains covering the tall windows, and portraits of five conductors of the Pittsburgh Symphony lining the walls. As a solo midweek traveler, I came down late the next morning and found a good selection of breads and fresh fruits on the antique buffet along with the morning paper. It was a contemplative time, listening to Beethoven with my coffee in the room where monks once dined.

The Priory has a reputation for personal service, including staff that is available 24 hours and weekday-morning limousine service to the city center. It is also one of the cleanest accommodations I have ever visited. Mary Ann says she guarantees that the inn is kept "fiercely clean" and admits to checking under the beds for stray dust bunnies; she also praises her staff, who seem to have a special commitment to making guests feel welcome. One guest described the inn as a world apart from impersonal hotels.

Once the work on the Priory was completed, the Grafs turned their attention to St. Mary's Church next door, unused since 1981. After the church was desanctified, the Grafs removed the religious artifacts and rolled up their sleeves for yet another big project. Along with attending to the expected repairs and revamping of the facility, they brought in artisans to refurbish the decorative painting and gold leaf and to restore the extant stained glass windows. The 141-year-old church was renamed the Grand Hall at the Priory and has become the site of many Pittsburgh celebratory occasions. Wedding parties often stay at the Priory when they have their reception at the Grand Hall.

THINGS TO DO: You can walk to Max's Allegheny Tavern to sample some German-style cooking or to the James Street Inn for jazz and a wide selection of seafood. The Priory is located in the historic Deutschtown community, just a half mile from the Pittsburgh Golden Triangle and the David L. Lawrence Convention Center. Guests of the Priory find themselves near a number of cultural attractions, including the Carnegie Science Center, Andy Warhol Museum, the Mattress Factory (art gallery), and the Photo Antiquities Museum. Three Rivers Stadium is a short drive.

DIRECTIONS: I-80 east to exit 42 for I-76; east on I-76 to exit 3 for US 19; US 19 to I-79; south on I-79 to exit 21 for I-279; south on I-279 to exit 15 for East St.; right on East Ohio St.; left on Cedar Ave..; left on Pressley St.; on left

NEARBY ATTRACTIONS: Carnegie Science Center, National Aviary, Pittsburgh Children's Museum, Andy Warhol Museum, Mattress Factory Museum, football and baseball stadiums

Hiram D. Ellis Inn

Watch the world go by on charming Adrian Street from the comfortable front porch.

Christine Webster
and Frank Seely, Innkeepers
415 W. Adrian St.
Blissfield, MI
(517) 486-3155
www.cass.net/~ellisinn/welcome.html

RATES & RESERVATIONS:
Hours: 8 a.m.–9 p.m.;
Season: Year round;
Rates: $$$;
Specials: AAA, weekly specials;
Reservations recommended;
Check, Visa, MC, Amex accepted

ACCOMMODATIONS: 4 rooms w/bath

AMENITIES: Cable TV,
phone in room, air cond.

MEALS: Full breakfast

SPECIAL CONSIDERATIONS:
Not fully handicapped accessible;
Parking available: Lot

W hen friends suggested that we try their favorite restaurant in Michigan, the Hathaway House Restaurant in Blissfield, 12 miles from Toledo, we not only found a gourmet dining experience but also discovered a historic bed and breakfast across the street, the H. D. Ellis Inn. Built in 1883 by Hiram D. Ellis, a banker who also served as postmaster and township supervisor, the house is set back from Blissfield's West Adrian Street. Of brick Italianate design, with bracketed cornice, hip roof, and bay window, the porch didn't seem to fit the Victorian style of the rest of the house; innkeeper Christine Webster explained it had been added in 1920. Furnished with floral-cushioned wicker, it provides a good place to watch the world go by on busy Adrian Street.

The entrance to the inn is directly from the porch into a parlor typical of the era, with a light rose settee filling the bay window area, lace curtains, and the original three-quarter-inch white oak floors. Four guest rooms named for family or community leaders are furnished with a mix of period antiques and reproductions. On the main floor, a guest room that once served as a formal parlor for the Ellis family features flowered wallpaper, velvet chairs, and a matching sleigh bed and dresser. At the top of the stairs, a big old floor-model Philco radio, games, books, and comfy furniture fill a second common room.

Breakfast is served in the parlor, and Christine likes to use the apples and peaches from trees on her property for some of her breakfast specials. This experienced innkeeper laughs when she recounts the time she decided to change the menu and a returning guest asked, like a child who'd been looking forward to a favorite food, "Where's the peach cobbler?" Other oft-requested entrees are baked French toast and sausage-and-egg strata.

THINGS TO DO: Christine has been welcoming guests to the H. D. Ellis Inn for seven years. She finds that some come from urban areas and all they want to do is to spend some time in this small village. Others come as we did to sample the classic cuisine across the street at the Hathaway House. Blissfield is one of those places where you can walk to "town" to shop at gift and antique stores. Christine has many repeat guests who come for the Murder Mystery Train trips. The Old Road Dinner Train picks up folks at the Blissfield East Depot for a two-hour trip. Along the way, a four-course meal, prepared by the Hathaway House Restaurant, is served in the dining-car style of yesteryear while a mystery unfolds. Then there's the Romantic Dinner Train on selected weekends and Santa Trains in December.

Business travelers like the H. D. Ellis Inn because it's a short 20-minute drive from Toledo. This northwest Ohio city has an absolute jewel in the internationally known Toledo Museum of Art, with its outstanding permanent collection as well as traveling exhibitions. The museum also houses an extensive collection of glass. A historic walking tour can give you an in-depth look at the city; for a self-guided walking tour, pick up a brochure at the main library. Drive or walk Toledo's historic Old West End, which will take you past some prime examples of late Victorian architecture including Georgian, Italianate, and Queen Anne homes. For those who search out church architecture, stop to see Our Lady Queen of the Most Holy Rosary Cathedral, the only church in North America built in the Spanish-Plateresque style.

There's upscale dining at the Hathaway House Restaurant. Built in 1851 by David Carpenter, this Greek Revival-style mansion, which has been named both a state and national historic site, is surrounded by expansive lawns and gardens. Casual meals are served at the Stables, directly behind the Hathaway House, where we enjoyed a traditional Sunday brunch. Along with the items usually found on a bountiful brunch buffet, there were also offerings like salmon patties, vegetable lasagna, and beef tips Burgundy. Fresh salads and fruit along with pastries baked in-house completed the selections and made the meal a very good value.

DIRECTIONS: I-80 to exit 4 for US 23; north on US 23; left (east) on US 223 (Adrian St.); on left

NEARBY ATTRACTIONS: Shopping, antiques, Murder Mystery Dinner Train, fine dining

Mill House Bed and Breakfast

A charming getaway near Toledo in a restored flour mill overlooking a canal

Jim and Karen Herzberg, Innkeepers
24070 Front St.
Grand Rapids, OH
(419) 832-6455
www.themillhouse.com

RATES & RESERVATIONS:
Hours: 8 a.m.–11 p.m.;
Season: Year round;
Rates: $$–$$$;
Reservations recommended;
Check, Visa, MC, Disc, Amex accepted

ACCOMMODATIONS: 4 rooms w/bath

AMENITIES: Cable TV, air cond., jet tub

MEALS: Full breakfast

SPECIAL CONSIDERATIONS:
Not fully handicapped accessible;
Parking available: Lot

A chance to stay in a restored flour mill brought us to the Mill House in Grand Rapids, Ohio, only 30 minutes from Toledo. Built in 1899 as Stump's Mill, the property was purchased by Don and Audrey Entenman in 1977. In renovating the old mill, the Entenmans were careful not to make structural changes in this historically significant building; the original hand-hewn beams and exposed brick interior remain. Blue shutters and flower boxes complement this century-old brick house, now partially covered with ivy. It was converted to a bed and breakfast in 1993. Current owners Karen and Jim Herzberg credit the second owners, Dave and Marsha Frost, with the interior decorating and landscaping.

We stayed in the Garden Room, on the lower level of the two-story addition built by the Frosts. With seven windows, this room offers a sweeping view of the canal and the Maumee River. Perhaps best of all, it overlooks the old-fashioned garden; on our May visit, purple irises, white daisies, and peonies about to bloom contrasted with the lush green of trees lining the canal. Weathered wood, brick paths, a lattice-work fence, and a deck that extends over the water add to the garden's appeal. A city park abuts the property, where concerts are held in the summer months. Our room mirrored the garden view with cottage decor including a white picket-fence headboard, birdhouses, and a garland of flowers on a high shelf. White painted woodwork, yellow wainscoting, and a bright quilt of alternating checks and flowers lend a summery feel to the space. A generous-size bath with jet tub adjoins the Garden Room.

The Edward Howard Room, named for an early settler, is a spacious front room with a massive wardrobe and marble-top dresser. Predominant colors in Marcia Frost's stenciling, featuring sunflowers and blue cornflowers, are repeated in the blue and white quilt and contrasting yellow pillows on the queen bed. A table and pair of blue velvet chairs provide a sitting area in front of the tall windows looking out to Front Street. Karen said she likes to book guests who are staying for several days in this spacious room, where a twin bed and a rollaway sleeper allow for four guests. I asked about the honey-toned wood floor and learned from Jim that the wood came from a bowling alley. Lace curtains contrast with the exposed brick wall, on which hangs an early map of the Maumee Valley. On the other side of the entry hall, the Jacob Kundert Room, a cozy room with morning glories stenciled on the wall and a spool bed, awaits the solo traveler. The Ruth Thomas Room honors an early milliner, and includes a white iron-and-brass bed, an antique armoire, and geraniums as a decorative accent on the wall. A nice touch are the prints of turn-of-the-century gowns in the bathroom.

Guests find a welcoming common room with a television, VCR, and a selection of soft drinks and snacks. Breakfast is served upstairs in the family quarters; the setting reminded me of bed and breakfast stays in

Europe. An open kitchen and photographs of the Herzberg children create a homey atmosphere. The dining table is centered under wide windows offering an even more expansive view of the canal and river that we enjoyed in the Garden Room downstairs. Some of Karen's breakfast specialties include cinnamon raisin French toast, German apple puff pancakes, and pumpkin muffins.

The Herzbergs are enthusiastic about their new venture as innkeepers. Karen always wanted to run a bed and breakfast and left full-time employment to be able to concentrate on the

guests' needs. I had an evening of work ahead of me and requested a few extra items—they were delivered promptly to my room on a pretty tray. Jim, who continues to work as a food inspector in Toledo, is the resident historian. He'll be happy to sit down and talk with you about the history of the mill, the community, and the area.

THINGS TO DO: The Mill House, located on the main street of this old canal town, is a short walk from the antique and gift shops alternating with eateries along Front Street. We enjoyed a late Sunday evening meal of large fresh salads at La Roe's on Front Street. The interior, with an oak bar, brass rail, and paddle fans, is reminiscent of earlier times. Portraits of old-time Grand Rapids citizens line the walls. Guests who come to the Mill House in December can make reservations for a popular dinner theater at La Roe's. The Apple Butter Fest brings crowds to Grand Rapids the second weekend of October.

DIRECTIONS: I-80 to exit 4 for US 20; south on US 20; right (west) on US 24; left (east) on SR 64/65; right (south) SR 65 to Grand Rapids; straight to Front St.; on right

NEARBY ATTRACTIONS: Canal boat ride, Ludwig Mill, passenger train, antiques, hiking

Chapter 7

COLLEGE TOWN STAYS

*Drive in any direction in the Buckeye state and you'll come upon
a college town. Here you'll find an annual ritual—the campus
visit by prospective students and their parents. For some, it's an
autumn event and for others, spring brings them to campus.*

Parents and their college-bound students aren't the only ones visiting. The beauty of the campus, splendid architecture, and the youthful dynamic of a student body bring vacationers who simply want to enjoy the charms of these communities. Add to that a myriad of cultural events and you have the ticket for an eventful stay. During the semester, you'll find concerts, recitals, lectures, plays, and art exhibits. Summertime brings Gilbert and Sullivan performances to the College of Wooster campus, and Christmas means madrigals and Christmas concerts on other campuses. Retirees are discovering that college towns offer a viable vacation because of these opportunities for enrichment. Alumni return to sit in the bleachers once again to cheer the home team or to stroll the campus and revisit the library or the chapel of their undergraduate years.

When planning a visit to one of the accommodations listed in this chapter, reserve ahead as rooms are scarce on many weekends during the school year. After spending some time on campus, break away to look over the town. In some of the communities, fine old homes line the street, and the bed and breakfast occupies an early dwelling. An interesting mix of retail shops can be found, from bookstores and art galleries to contemporary clothing stores and coffee shops. Keep in mind that on weekends when parents and alumni inundate the campus, restaurants will be booked, so reserve in advance.

The bed and breakfasts listed in this chapter are all historic dwellings. The newest of the country inns is the Hiram Inn built in 1996. Both the Wooster Inn and the Zelcova Country Manor are full-service inns.

Black Squirrel Inn Bed and Breakfast

In the spring, more than 1,000 crocuses fill the gorgeous English garden.

Ed Schrader and Dan Rider,
Innkeepers
636 College Ave.
Wooster, OH
(800) 760-1710

RATES & RESERVATIONS:
Season: Year round;
Rates: $$;
Reservations required;
Check, Visa, MC, Disc, Amex accepted

ACCOMMODATIONS: 4 rooms w/bath

AMENITIES: Spa, cable TV,
phone in room, air cond.

MEALS: Full breakfast

SPECIAL CONSIDERATIONS:
Guest pets allowed;
Not fully handicapped accessible;
Parking available: Lot, on street

The Black Squirrel Inn, an 1880 Victorian, was renovated by Ed Schrader and Dan Rider, retired university professors. This genteel "Painted Lady" of 120 years now sports a pleasing sage exterior with cream and burgundy trim outlining the double-bracket roofline and bay windows.

You can also find Ed and Dan at their antique shop, Harbor Hill Heirlooms, on Liberty Street in downtown Wooster. They have filled their bed and breakfast with quality pieces and reproductions. The foyer provides a dramatic entrance with gold and green wallpaper in a peacock design. A fireplace with walnut mantel and Chinese slate surround and hearth graces the front parlor. Pocket doors open to a second parlor with comfortable seating and a country cherry secretary. Breakfast is served in an elegant dining room with an English cherry table, an ornamented walnut sideboard, and a French buffet.

Ed and Dan named the rooms in their bed and breakfast for friends and those who helped with the renovation. The Brothers Schwartz Room recognizes the work done by two brothers who assisted with many house projects. It's a spacious room with a Jenny Lind four-poster queen bed, a chaise lounge, an antique slant-top desk, and a luxurious bath with a two-person Jacuzzi. Another guest room, the Yarnell Room, is named for the electrician who brought the house up to code. The McIlvaine Room, a bay-windowed room at the front of the house, honors good friends, while the downstairs room furnished with antiques remembers Miss Ruth Bartel, a longtime teacher who lived in the house for 52 years.

A black Victorian fence borders an English country garden at the front of the house. Dan says they kept the nucleus of Miss Bartel's garden and are slowly adding plants. In the spring, more than 1,000 crocuses fill the space, and passers-by stop their cars to gawk at this colorful display. The wooded backyard with luminaria, a three-tiered birdbath, and a walkway provides a friendly garden experience. The old garage has been restored and is now the garden house.

THINGS TO DO: Fans of the Ohio Light Opera, prospective students, and parents come to stay at the Black Squirrel. The innkeepers are happy to suggest local points of interest. I followed a scenic route recommended by Dan, which was a lovely drive through some of the nearby Amish country. I learned from Ed that the Secrest Arboretum at the Ohio Agricultural Research and Development Center has the largest collection of azaleas and rhododendrons in the world. Another popular garden at OARDC is the Roses of Legend and Romance Garden, with old-fashioned rose plants that have been grown for centuries. Gardeners like to stop at Quailcrest Farm to pick up herbs, perennials, trees, and shrubs, as well as gift items and pottery. Quailcrest also offers display gardens. Dine in an old jail at the Olde Jaol Brewing Company or enjoy gourmet burgers at C. W. Burgersteins on the lower level of TJ's Restaurant. This popular Wooster dining spot also offers an extensive menu featuring prime rib, steaks, and seafood on the main level.

DIRECTIONS: I-71 to exit 209 for I-76; east on I-76 to exit 2 for SR 3; right on SR 3; becomes Cleveland Rd.; becomes Beall Ave..; left (south) on Bever St.; left (east) on Spring St.; right (south) on College Ave..; on right

NEARBY ATTRACTIONS: downtown Wooster shops, Wayne Center for the Arts, Lehman's Hardware

Wooster Inn

The dining room overlooks a golf course in this Georgian Colonial at the edge of campus.

The Wooster Inn, a fine example of Georgian Colonial architecture, stands at the edge of the College of Wooster's campus. Robert E. Wilson, a 1914 alumnus, donated the inn to the college; the inn is patterned after his home in White Plains, New York. The Wooster Inn is a member of the Independent Innkeepers Association and has been featured in *Country Inns* and *Back Roads, North America*.

It's a classic country inn with traditional decor, from the lobby's comfortable sitting-room to the guest rooms with flowered wallpaper, reproduction furniture, and views over the grounds. The college is in the process of redecorating the 13 guest rooms and two suites. A second-floor suite includes a spacious sitting room with mahogany furniture including an armoire and secretary. Bookshelves line one wall, and a sofa and wing chairs provide a sitting area for business or family groups. A bath connects the sitting room to a bedroom with double beds. On the main floor is an inviting suite done up in blue and white with yellow accents. Blue Willow china displayed in a corner cabinet sets the tone with the colors repeated in the comforter and bed-

The College of Wooster
Dining Services, Innkeepers
801 E. Wayne Ave.
Wooster, OH
(330) 264-2341
www.innbook.com

RATES & RESERVATIONS:
Hours: 24 hours;
Season: Year round;
Rates: $$;
Reservations recommended;
Check, Visa, MC, Disc, Amex accepted

ACCOMMODATIONS:
15 rooms w/bath; 2 suites w/bath

AMENITIES: Internet, cable TV, phone in room, air cond.

MEALS: Continental breakfast, lunch, dinner, brunch

SPECIAL CONSIDERATIONS:
Guest pets allowed;
Handicapped accessible;
Parking available: Lot

skirt. Yellow walls and blue-and-yellow plaid club chairs add a cheery note. In the adjoining bath, a sink is set into a mahogany cabinet. A sitting room with comfortable seating and television completes the suite.

The Colonial-style dining room looks out over the college golf course. It's a formal room with white linen and quietly efficient service. Chef Ken Edwards holds fort in the kitchen, where he prepares American-style cuisine. Favorite entrees include cornmeal-crusted walleye with pecan butter, steaks, and chicken Marsala. Dinner salads have recently been added to the menu, with sesame seared tuna a popular dish. Folks come to the Wooster Inn for dinner before performances of the Ohio Light Opera. Others stop for lunch during a drive to Amish country. Inn guests find a continental breakfast in the lobby.

THINGS TO DO: Those who stay at the Wooster Inn find it an easy walk to cultural events on campus. The billiard room on the lower level of the inn features a vintage pool table with matching console and chairs. Guests have access to the nine-hole golf course and driving range. Tennis courts and an outdoor track are nearby.

In 1993, a streetscape project was completed in downtown Wooster; historic lighting, brick walkways, and a gazebo make it an appealing shopping destination. Shop the four floors of Everything Rubbermaid, browse the selection at Heirloom Antiques, and check out the fine art and gifts at Gallery in the Vault. Book collectors will love both Books in Stock Used and Rare and the Wooster Book Company.

A visit to nearby Shreve takes you past Killbuck Marsh Wildlife Area with 5,000 acres of marshland. A five-mile-long observation trail is pop-

ular with bird watchers. It's fun to poke around the specialty shops on Shreve's Market Street. Queen Anne's Lace carries curtains, doilies, runners, and tablecloths as well as Victorian gifts. Across the street, Village Bears and More offers a wide selection of huggable teddies and collectible bears. We stopped for lunch on the return trip at the Pine Tree Barn, where the Granary serves gourmet lunches. It's easy to spend an afternoon browsing the gift shops at this historic landmark barn (circa 1868), which include a Christmas shop and a licensed Colonial Williamsburg shop.

DIRECTIONS: I-71 to exit 204 for SR 83; south on SR 83; right on SR 585 (Akron Rd.); right on Wayne Ave..; on left

NEARBY ATTRACTIONS: Amish country, Everything Rubbermaid store

Porch House

A wraparound porch lined with rocking chairs invites idleness.

The Porch House, at the corner of East Maple and South Pearle streets in Granville, has the kind of porch you would expect to see on a house built in 1903—a generous, wraparound affair that invites you to settle down with lemonade and a book to while away a summer afternoon. Hanging flower baskets, wicker furniture, and a row of green rocking chairs set the stage for chatting, reading, or even napping. Bruce and Lisa Westall have been in business for 10 years and host many returning guests who come back for special events, as well as students and parents visiting Denison University. Some ask to take a book home they have started reading; they also return the books.

Lisa and Bruce Westall, Innkeepers
241 E. Maple St.
Granville, OH
(800) 587-1995
www.porchhouse.com

RATES & RESERVATIONS:
Season: Year round; Rates: $$;
Specials: Children;
Reservations recommended;
Check, Visa, MC, Amex accepted

ACCOMMODATIONS: 5 rooms w/bath

MEALS: Full breakfast

SPECIAL CONSIDERATIONS:
Dog and cat living at inn;
Not fully handicapped accessible;
Parking available: On street

Step into the parlor to a turn-of-the-century scene—matching wing chairs in front of a gas log fireplace fronted with a Victorian copper cover original to the house. Innkeeper Lisa Westall says guests like the downstairs room, which features a library corner, an antique acorn queen bed, and a wing chair. The Westalls added a new bath adjoining this room that looks like it was lifted from an earlier time, with a claw-foot tub and black-and-white patterned floor. We followed the staircase in the parlor to a guest room on the second floor furnished with reminders of Grandma's day—a chenille spread on an iron bed, an antique wardrobe, and a wicker rocker.

The Westalls own a second house next door. This sweet cottage reminded me of similar dwellings in England. The front garden is an English cottage garden with pink climbing fairy roses, hollyhocks, blue salvia, Russian sage, and ferns leading to a porch with a trellis at one end. Couples traveling in groups and business travelers find this house, with its living room, dining room, kitchen, and three bedrooms an ideal accommodation. Its homey interior is furnished with antiques and country accents. Lisa collects colorful old tablecloths and sets the table with Fiestaware and juice glasses known as "Swanky Swigs"—those little Kraft cheese glasses many of us threw away. Samplers are arranged on one wall of the dining room, while Lisa's collection of doorstops line the stairway. The kitchen can be used to fix meals, but most use it only for snacks, as the Westhalls serve a full breakfast every morning with apple French toast, home baked goods, and rhubarb crisp—all favorites of returning guests.

A spacious room on the second level of the cottage is done up in chintz, flowered wallpaper, quilts, and an oversize comfy chair. Lisa used a color scheme of yellow and blue in another guest room that is furnished with her grandparents' 1930s bedroom set.

THINGS TO DO: The Porch House is adjacent to a bike path and within walking distance of Denison University and the village shops; the choices are endless when trying to decide what to do on a visit to this New England-style town. At the top of my list would be walking the shady streets to see the remarkable architectural styles represented in Granville, which claims 119 structures on the National Register of Historic Places. Visitors to Granville also find two historic houses to tour. The Granville Lifestyle Museum, H. D. Robinson House, with nine rooms of the Robinson's family possessions; and the Robbins Hunter Museum, a classic Greek Revival mansion furnished with eighteenth- and nineteenth-century antiques.

It's fun to meander along Broadway with its interesting collection of shops showcasing antiques, books, home furnishings, and upscale clothing. For a casual meal, stop at Victoria's Olde Tyme Deli and Cafe where the tables spill out to the sidewalk in warm weather. You can settle into the oak-paneled dining room at the Granville Inn for fine traditional fare at lunchtime or dinner.

DIRECTIONS: I-71 to exit 140 for SR 61; left on SR 61; right on SR 3; left on SR 37; right (east) on Elm St.; right (south) on Prospect St.; left (east) on Maple St.

NEARBY ATTRACTIONS: Village shops, museums, golf

Zelcova Country Manor

An elegant country inn with a magnificent view of Honey Creek

Michael Pinkston, Innkeeper
2348 S. Country Rd. 19
Tiffin, OH
(419) 447-4043
www.tiffinohio.com/zelcova

RATES & RESERVATIONS:
Hours: 9 a.m.–5 p.m.;
Season: Year round;
Rates: $$$; Specials: AAA;
Reservations required;
Check, Visa, MC, Amex, Disc accepted

ACCOMMODATIONS: 8 rooms w/bath

AMENITIES: Cable TV, pool,
phone in room, Internet, air cond.

MEALS: Full breakfast, lunch,
dinner, snacks;
Beer, wine, and liquor served

SPECIAL CONSIDERATIONS:
Dog living at inn;
Handicapped accessible;
Parking available: Lot

A lovely lane lined with cone-shaped trees leads guests to Zelcova Country Manor in Tiffin. The inn takes its name from the trees, a Japanese hybrid known as Zelcova. This classic Georgian Revival house is set high above Honey Creek, which eventually feeds into the Sandusky River. The house, built in 1952 for a physician, Dr. William Funderburg, was established as a bed and breakfast in 1988 by a group of local businessmen including Michael Pinkston, the innkeeper today. Michael met us as we arrived and invited us to join him for afternoon tea, a tradition at the inn.

The Zelcova Country Manor offers a relaxing and romantic setting for a country weekend; the view from the common room is of the natural beauty of the creek and woodland setting and is spectacular in any season. The color palette for the graciously appointed rooms was taken from the Oriental rugs in the common room. Jewel tones are found in fabrics and window treatments throughout the house, counterpointed by plaids, stripes and crewel designs. On the first floor, the library offers a spot to curl up with a book from the inn's collection of more than 2,000 volumes. Zelcova Country Manor was designed by architect Ned Porter, and the guest rooms carry the family names of other houses he built in Tiffin. The Stacy, a corner room with views to the manicured lawn and herb garden, features striped wallpaper in greens, cream, and rusty rose contrasted with cream-colored drapes and light carpet. Rich mahogany furniture and pineapple lamps make for a classic, traditional look. The Reed Room's king-size bed is draped with French toile in navy tones and offers a view of Honey Creek, the woodlands, and the pool. In 1997, the inn was renovated and three suite-size rooms were added in space that was previously the garage, making a total of eight in all. As I toured the inn, I marveled at the exceptional views from every room.

This bed and breakfast also attracts corporate groups, who find this inn, in its pastoral setting, a good spot for retreats and workshops. The Terrace Room on the lower level can be utilized for meetings, and smaller rooms provide space for break-out sessions.

The Zelcova Country Manor is known for its award-winning dining service. Following the wonderful aromas emanating from the kitchen, where Michael prepares dinner each evening, I stopped in to visit and learned that although he doesn't call himself a chef he did train under professional chefs. The inn offers a full beverage service, and guests gather in the common room between 5:00 and 7:00 p.m. for a reception with hors d'oeuvres. Our candlelight dinner was a memorable meal starting with cream of cauliflower soup, continuing with a main course of salmon with dill, browned potatoes, and julienned vegetables, and

ending with crème brûlée. A full English breakfast is served either in the sunny corner Wine Room, or the more formal dining room.

When you stay at this inn, you can pretend you are lord or lady of an English country manor as you enjoy being spoiled by the classic cuisine, the down comforters, all cotton sheets, and goose-down pillows. Follow the pathways in the woods to take a picnic down by the creek or lounge by the pool. This is the place to relax and refresh before returning to your everyday life. You're in good company—other guests who have enjoyed this inn include Elizabeth Dole, the Princess of Nepal, and Bill Cosby.

The Zelcova Country Manor has been a member of the Independent Innkeepers' Association since 1998.

THINGS TO DO: Tiffin is justifiably proud of the Ritz Theatre, built in 1928 and reopened in 1998 after a 14-month renovation. It's fun to tour this Italian Renaissance theater, with its stucco walls, marble staircases, 30-foot murals, and mammoth chandelier made of 20,000 pieces of Czechoslovakian crystal. The Ritz offers a series of performances, and on our visit we were able to catch an outstanding show with a New York cast. Across the street from the theater, the Tiffin Glass Museum, showcasing glass from the Tiffin Glass Company (1889–1980), is worth a stop. Tiffin, home to Heidelberg College and Tiffin University, brings prospective students and their parents to town.

DIRECTIONS: I-80 to exit 6 for SR 53; south on SR 53; left (east) on SR 224; right on CR 19; on right

NEARBY ATTRACTIONS: Tiffin University, Heidelberg College, Tiffin Glass Museum

Hiram Inn

A New England-style inn on the Hiram College campus

When he served on Hiram College's Board of Trustees, Robert Merwin often lamented the fact that visitors to the college had to drive to Aurora to find an overnight accommodation. In 1995, Mr. Merwin, a 1936 Hiram graduate, and his wife, Betty, gave a $1.2 million gift to the college to build an inn at the corner of state routes 700 and 82, site of the Young House. Built in 1824 by Thomas Finch Young and his wife, Lydia, the Young House served as a tavern and stagecoach stop on the Warren-Cleveland route and was also the local post office. Renovated and expanded in 1996 into the Hiram Inn, it remains a fine example of New England-style architecture. Innkeeper Nancy LeBlanc came from a computer and hospitality background and provides a warm welcome to business travelers and those seeking a getaway in this quiet college town. Nancy and her staff take care of all the little details that make for a memorable stay.

Nancy LeBlanc, Innkeeper
6867 Wakefield Rd.
Hiram, OH
(800) 447-2646
www.hiraminn.com

RATES & RESERVATIONS:
Hours: 6:30 a.m.–10:30 p.m.;
Season: Year round;
Rates: $$$;
Specials: Corporate rate $99/$115;
Reservations recommended;
Visa, MC, Disc, Amex,
direct billing accepted

ACCOMMODATIONS: 12 rooms w/bath

AMENITIES: Whirlpool tubs,
cable TV, phone in room,
Internet, air cond.

MEALS: Expanded
continental breakfast;
May not accommodate
all special diets;
Beer, wine, and liquor served

SPECIAL CONSIDERATIONS:
Handicapped accessible;
Parking available: Lot

The inn is decorated in the style of the Western Reserve, and each of the 12 rooms carries the name of a person of importance in the history

of the college and the village. The large front portion of the Young House was incorporated into the inn. There you'll find the Young Suite, a cozy room with original floors and a four-poster bed. At the end of the hall a small sitting area includes a Regina music box and the original staircase, with a buttery-soft tiger maple banister. The Jessie Brown Pounds Suite recognizes a famous member of the Disciples of Christ congregation who wrote sacred songs and hymns, such as "Beautiful Isle of Some-where." It seems like a room a woman of that time would have liked, with a crocheted coverlet, pink flowered wallpaper, and an antique library table. Almeda Booth, who served as the first female faculty member of the Western Reserve Eclectic Institute (which became Hiram College in 1867), is honored with a generous-sized room featuring two four-poster mahogany rice beds and scenic wallpaper. Visiting prospective students and parents often book this room. It's rare to find truly handicapped-accessible rooms in small inns, but the Hiram Inn offers two first-floor rooms that are wheelchair accessible.

Business travelers will find laptop connections and a multipurpose meeting room for corporate retreats. Inn guests have access to the athletic facilities at the college, which include an indoor pool, a weight room, and racquetball and tennis courts. Those who come for a romantic weekend are treated to a dozen roses, chilled champagne, and a voucher for dinner at a local restaurant. Four rooms with fireplaces and two with whirlpool tubs are available. After enjoying an evening out for dinner or attending a cultural event at the college, relax in the Merwin Parlor in front of the fireplace with a cup of tea or a nightcap. Bob Merwin made sure that there would be a spot like the parlor where guests could gather to socialize. The next morning, serve yourself from the breakfast buffet of fresh-baked cinnamon rolls, muffins, cereals, fruit, and juices.

THINGS TO DO: If you're exploring the Hiram College campus, walk across the street to lunch at the Squire Hill Dining Room in the Kennedy Center. Lighter meals featuring gourmet pizza, pasta, and subs can be found at CJ's Down Under, behind the inn.

Antique lovers will want to check out Auntie's Antique Mall in Parkman. With 105 dealers, you can idle away a few hours browsing the vintage collectibles in this well-run mall. Within a five minute drive, the Historic John Johnson Farm Home remains much as it was in the 1830s, when Mormon leader Joseph Smith lived here. Free guided tours are offered daily. Special events bring visitors back to Hiram—during the holiday season it's the Yuletide Revels. Be sure to plan ahead and reserve your favorite room for this popular event.

DIRECTIONS: WEST: I-480 to exit 26 for US 422; east on US 422; right (south) on SR 44; left (east) on SR 82; on left
EAST: I-271 to exit 27A for US 422; east on US 422; right (south) on SR 44; left (east) on SR 82; on left

NEARBY ATTRACTIONS: Sea World, Six Flags of Ohio, Punderson State Park, Hiram College, Amish country, Aurora Premium Outlets

Gambier House Bed and Breakfast

A classic inn in a quintessential college town

Jacques and Elizabeth Lavoie,
Innkeepers
107 E. Wiggin St.
Gambier, OH
(740) 427-2668
www.gambierhouse.com

RATES & RESERVATIONS:
Hours: 24 hours; Season: Year round;
Rates: $$;
Reservations recommended;
Check, Visa, MC, Disc, Amex accepted

ACCOMMODATIONS:
5 rooms w/bath; 1 suite w/bath

AMENITIES: Cable TV, air cond.

MEALS: Full breakfast, snacks

SPECIAL CONSIDERATIONS:
Not fully handicapped accessible;
Parking available: Lot

The Gambier House, an 1845 white clapboard dwelling trimmed in green across from the Kenyon College campus, fits this historic college-town setting like a glove. A cast iron fence surrounds the rambling farmhouse. Inside I found the architectural details endless and fascinating—trap doors, two hidden staircases, and little unexpected nooks and crannies. I asked the innkeepers/owners, Jacques and Liz Lavoie, about one of the trap doors on the second floor and learned it was used to light the gas chandelier in the dining room below. Another room intrigued me when I found a wall made up entirely of drawers. A former owner, Dr. Emanuel Adams Daneman, admired Shaker style and had 56 drawers built into the room.

The Lavoies say it was a turnkey operation when they took over the inn in 1995. They give credit to Dr. Daneman for saving the structure and to Patsy Brenneman for opening it as a bed and breakfast. Patsy decorated the interior in a pleasant mix of English country and Victoriana. On a recent visit, I found the Lavoies adding their own thoughtful touches—guests find either an overstuffed chair or a small settee, down comforters, luxurious damask bed linens, and fresh flowers in each room. Liz is fine-tuning the decorative objects in individual rooms as well, and the couple has made the courtyard an inviting place to spend time.

Kenyon students and their parents can spread out in this old house with two common rooms. One is a comfortable family room with TV, VCR (check out the Lavoies' extensive classic-film collection), wood-burning fireplace, and games. A second parlor, a designated quiet room, is the spot where visiting academics can meet or, as Liz related, those serious parent/student discussions can take place. Crimson wallpaper in an Oriental pattern sets off the antiques and china pieces brought back from China by Liz in this formal parlor. A three-course breakfast is offered in the formal dining room, where Liz likes to serve Belgian waffles with pure maple syrup, homemade granola, and freshly baked muffins and coffeecakes. In the evening, guests find desserts under a domed cake server in the kitchen along with coffee and tea.

On the main floor, the Old Library features a double bed as well as a settee that pulls out to a single bed. An exposed brick wall, fireplace, and hardwood floors give a sense of the age of the house. The adjoining bath has a large corner-tiled shower. On the second floor, the Green Room, with sloping ceiling, offers a cozy space for four guests. And the whimsical Drawer Room opens to a large bath with a claw-foot tub. Romantics find a queen bed and spacious bath in the Master Bedroom, with a pink marble tub and shower, bidet, and separate dressing room. We stayed in the Victorian Room, which has interesting architectural details—an overstuffed chair fits in an alcove under a window, and a sink is built into another recessed space. The Carriage House Suite, connected to the house by a plant-filled breezeway, is a two-story unit that can sleep five.

Liz and Jacques Lavoie left high-powered jobs to run their own bed and breakfast. They are very sensitive to the wide range of guests who come to the Gambier House and manage to be warm and welcoming but never intrusive. The Lavoies love living in this college community and enjoy sharing their knowledge of the place.

THINGS TO DO: We found everything a visitor might want to do in a college town within walking distance. The Kenyon Bookstore, just around the corner, of-

fers a wide selection of books, academic and otherwise, and welcomes those who want to sit and read or have a cup of coffee. Cross the street to the alley next to the post office to find the Weather Vane, a boutique of unusual women's clothing and jewelry.

The first weekend in December brings guests to the inn for two events: the Advent, a fine choral program at the college chapel; and the Gambier Craft Show. During our stay at the inn, we met a couple who came to this area to bike the nearby Kokosing Gap Trail. Others come to bird watch, roller blade, or walk the trail.

For light fare and delicious baked goods along with a great cup of java, stop at the Red Door Cafe. The Kenyon Inn Restaurant dining room is an intimate space looking out over a brick patio and gardens. Our meal was outstanding—sesame seared yellowfin tuna with basmati rice cakes and a spring roll, and rosemary pork chops with house mashed potatoes. We also enjoyed salads of baby field greens with fresh fennel, orange sections, and chevre cheese.

DIRECTIONS: I-71 to exit 169 for SR 13; south on SR 13; east on SR 229; left on Wiggin St.

NEARBY ATTRACTIONS: restaurants, bike trail, Kenyon College

Zang House

A historic house transformed into an elegant getaway

Michael and Rosemary Burke, Innkeepers
1350 S. Sawburg Rd.
Alliance, OH
(330) 823-9750
www.zanghouse.com

RATES & RESERVATIONS:
Hours: 3 p.m.–11 p.m.;
Season: Year round;
Rates: $$$$;
Reservations recommended;
Check, Visa, MC, Disc, Amex accepted

ACCOMMODATIONS: 2 suites w/bath

AMENITIES: Spa, cable TV, pool, phone in room, air cond.

MEALS: Full breakfast, snacks

SPECIAL CONSIDERATIONS:
Not fully handicapped accessible;
Parking available: Lot

The Zang House is the oldest house in Alliance. Built in 1797 and set back a bit from South Sawburg Road, the white house with green shutters has a rich history of entertaining dignitaries, including presidents Ulysses S. Grant and William McKinley. McKinley's visit has special significance; while a guest in 1867, he was presented with a scarlet carnation by Dr. Levi L. Lamborn, a politician and developer of the hybrid carnation. McKinley considered it a good luck flower and continued to wear a carnation in his lapel throughout his presidency. Ultimately, the scarlet carnation was adopted as the official Ohio state flower, and in 1959 Alliance was named the Carnation City.

Rosemary and Michael Burke purchased the property from the Zang family in 1999 and spent six months updating the place. Its luxurious interior is filled with classic furniture, rich fabrics, and art. The dining room, the site of the famous presentation of the Lamborn carnation to McKinley, is a light-filled room with a glass table centered under a white-washed iron and crystal chandelier. A floral area rug with a lily design against a dark background contrasts with the pickled flooring. There's a Neoclassical air to the parlor, with its corner pillars, fireplace, Oriental rug, and a game table set up for chess. The pub on the lower level provides a place for guests to unwind with a bar, refrigerator, and television. The Burkes travel widely, and their collectibles add interest to this room, which looks out to a stone veranda.

The suite-like guest rooms, named for Presidents McKinley and Grant, show Rosemary's decorating talents (she's also a bridal consultant). The McKinley Suite is an enchanting space, from the ceiling filled with fluffy white clouds and stars against a bronze background, to the Michael Waite wall covering, to the queen sleigh bed made up with sumptuous fabrics. The adjoining bath gives a sense of the history of the house, with white woodwork, glass knobs on the linen closet, and tiny flowers inserted in the tile wall. A bit of Rosemary's decorating whimsy in this traditional bath is a crossbuck bar chair with lion-head arms. Across the hall in the Grant Suite; its king-size, hand-carved, rococo-style bed is covered with a purple and gold damask comforter, and the original toile wallpaper remains. Features of the oversize executive bath are an orchid whirlpool spa tub surrounded by tall candles and a two-person marble shower.

Breakfast is an elegant affair served on Wedgwood china in the sunny dining room. Some of Rosemary's specialties are crepes, eggs Benedict, and eggs Florentine. Homemade breads include sticky buns and oversize muffins.

Alliance is home to Mount Union College, and guests of the college are beginning to discover this new bed and breakfast. Rosemary excitedly told me that Tobias Wolfe, the American writer and professor at Stanford, stayed with them while presenting some lectures at Mount Union. Former New York governor Mario Cuomo and two Japanese dignitaries were also recent guests. Those who come to stay at the Zang House find a relaxing and pampering stay in this early Alliance house.

THINGS TO DO: The Zang House is a mile west of the Mount Union College campus, site of cultural and athletic events. Tours can be arranged of the Marble Hartzell Historic Home, a fully restored 1867 Italianate residence with original furniture, mementos, and Italian marble fireplaces from the Victorian era. Another historically significant site is Glamorgan Castle, which is open for tours weekdays from 2 to 4 p.m. Golf devotees can choose among seven golf courses nearby.

DIRECTIONS: I-77 south to exit 107B for SR 62; east on SR 62; east on State St.; north on S. Sawburg Rd., on right

NEARBY ATTRACTIONS: Pro Football Hall of Fame, Blossom Music Center, Mount Union College, Amish country, McKinley Monument

Mount Vernon House

*An 1870s farmhouse and
carriage house near
Mount Vernon College*

Theresa Onizchak, Innkeeper
304 Martinsburg Rd.
Mount Vernon, OH
(740) 397-1914
www.ecr.net/mvhouse

RATES & RESERVATIONS:
Season: Year round; Rates: $$;
Specials: Children, seniors, singles,
AAA, discounted extended home
stays for business or leisure travel;
Reservations recommended;
Check, Visa, MC, Disc accepted

ACCOMMODATIONS:
4 rooms w/bath; 3 suites w/bath

AMENITIES: Cable TV, phone in room,
air cond., whirlpool tub, garden tubs

MEALS: Full breakfast, snacks

SPECIAL CONSIDERATIONS:
Not fully handicapped accessible;
Parking available: Driveway off road

The Mount Vernon House, situated on two acres at the edge of Mount Vernon, Ohio, is an 1870s farmhouse with Southern-plantation touches. A circular drive brings you to the front of the house. Wicker furniture fills a screened-in porch that looks out to 100-year-old maples in the side yard.

Built in 1873 by Morgan Rinehart, the house was owned in the 1930s by Major Lanning Parsons, a West Point graduate. When Parsons retired from military service in 1931, he came back to Mount Vernon and built a barn and racetrack on the property where he raised and raced harness horses.

The Mount Vernon House offers four guest rooms and three suites. In the rambling farmhouse, take your choice of the Garden Room, with adjoining bath with a garden tub and separate shower; the Country Victorian Room with a beautiful, rare, glass-tiled bath; or a contemporary room with a king water bed and private entrance. Guests in the house have use of the living room, TV room, dining room, and kitchen. Behind the house, the Carriage House—a rustic, 6,000-square-foot, barn-like structure—offers suites of various sizes.

All the suites share the great room with its brick, wood-burning fireplace, comfortable seating areas, cable TV with VCR, and books and magazines. The great room opens to a deck with a grill. Owner/innkeeper Theresa Onizchak finds that business guests and those seeking an extended stay like the Carriage House. It offers flexible space depending on the number in the group as well as room for visiting family members and a kitchen stocked with breakfast makings and snacks. Well-behaved children are welcome at Mount Vernon House.

THINGS TO DO: Theresa provides bicycles for those who want to ride the Kokosing Gap Trail, a 14-mile paved recreational trail between Mount Vernon and Danville that also attracts joggers, walkers, and roller bladers.

Mount Vernon House is an easy walk from Mount Vernon Nazarene College and a few miles from Kenyon College. Visiting parents and prospective students come to stay at the bed and breakfast. Others come for big band concerts in the R. R. Hodges Chapel on the Mount Vernon campus. The weekend after Thanksgiving, the annual Christmas Parade brings visitors to town.

The first time I came to Mount Vernon and drove down East Gambier Street, I was so taken with the variety of architecture that I turned around and made a second trip to see it again—this street offers 21 magnificent structures. I suggest a walking tour; check with the Knox County Convention and Visitors Bureau for a map and photographs of the homes.

Stop for a meal downtown at the Alcove Restaurant and Lounge on South Main Street, an eatery that has been around since 1911, or another favorite with the locals, Jody's, which is across the street from the Alcove. Pick up gifts and candles at the Woolson Company, another longtime Mount Vernon retail establishment.

DIRECTIONS: I-71 to exit 169 for SR 13; left (south) on SR 13; left on SR 586 (Martinsburg Rd.); on left.

NEARBY ATTRACTIONS: Kokosing Gap Bike Trail, horse back riding, antiques, cultural arts

Friendship House Bed and Breakfast

*This Federal-style home
guards the gates
of Muskingum College.*

Diane and Dan Troendly, Innkeepers
62 W. Main St.
New Concord, OH
877-968-5501
www.bedandbreakfastohio.com

RATES & RESERVATIONS:
Hours: Arrival by appointment;
Season: Year round; Rates: $$;
Reservations recommended;
Visa, MC, checks, cash accepted

ACCOMMODATIONS: 4 rooms w/bath

AMENITIES: Cable TV, air cond.,
screened-in porch

MEALS: Expanded
continental breakfast, snacks

SPECIAL CONSIDERATIONS:
Dog living at inn; Guest pets allowed;
Not fully handicapped accessible;
Parking available: Lot, on street

A brick path leads to the front door of Friendship House, an 1830s home across the street from Muskingum College. This restored Federal-style house with dark green exterior and tan trim is popular with guests of the college, prospective students, and visiting moms and dads. Diane and Dan Troendly have carefully furnished the Friendship House with quality antiques.

Although the house has been a private home, an apartment building, and a doctor's office, former owners (the Bogarts), kept it as true to its history and architecture as possible. Entering the house, I admired the winding cherry stairway and wide poplar floors. To the right of the foyer, the parlor retains the patina of its 170 years, and the flowered wallpaper, grand piano, and family antiques seemed just right for the room. Breakfast is served in the dining room furnished with Diane's great-grandparents' mahogany dining set. A snack is set out in the evening, and guests can take a cup of coffee or dessert out to the 70-foot wraparound screened-in porch. One of Diane's specialities is spice cake with peanut butter frosting.

This inn is set up for parent/student stays; extra beds are placed in some of the rooms, which are named for former owners. Mrs. Maggie Smith's Room, on the main floor, features a marble-top dresser and double and twin beds. The dark wood is lovely against the cameo floral wallpaper and the eggshell-colored comforters and lace curtains. The room has a private entrance from the screened-in porch. Judge David Finley built the house in 1830; his room, across the hall from the sitting room, has an air of stateliness with a queen brass bed and English armoire from the 1860s. Upstairs, the Dr. George Washington Pringle Room is a bright spot with sunflower-splashed comforters and curtains. A king-size bed, extra day bed, oak washstand, and serpentine oak dresser complete the room. Finally, the Dr. Isaac Curtis Room honors the doctor who used the house for his office as well as his home. It's an inviting space with an violet-sprigged bedspread and curtains, white iron bed, and rocking chair. The adjoining bath continues the theme with violet wallpaper and a pedestal seashell sink. Business or longer-term guests like this room with a microwave, sink, and refrigerator.

THINGS TO DO: Returning alumni and parents of current students can walk to all the Muskingum College buildings and McConagha Stadium. Turn right out the front door of Friendship House and you'll find the shops and restaurants on Main Street in the village of New Concord.

There are a variety of shops in the area, including Bogart's Antiques, four miles west on Route 40. Other nearby attractions are the National Road–Zane Grey Museum and Salt Fork State Park. There is a golf course 20 minutes away.

DIRECTIONS: I-77 to exit 47 for US 22; right (west) on US 22; on left

NEARBY ATTRACTIONS: The Wilds, Salt Fork State Park, Longaberger basket factory, golf courses, antiques

Ivy Tree Inn and Garden

Enjoy the garden with 200 varieties of perennials

Steve Coughlin & Ron Kelly,
Innkeepers
195 S. Professor St.
Oberlin, OH
(440) 774-4510

RATES & RESERVATIONS:
Hours: 8 a.m.–10 p.m.;
Season: Year round;
Rates: $$–$$$;
Minimum stay required on
certain weekends, inquire; Reservations required;
Check, Visa, MC accepted

ACCOMMODATIONS:
4 rooms, 2 w/bath

AMENITIES: Cable TV, air cond.,
meeting facility

MEALS: Full breakfast,
afternoon tea (seasonal)

SPECIAL CONSIDERATIONS:
Cat living at inn;
Not fully handicapped accessible;
Parking available: Lot

The Ivy Tree Inn and Garden stands on a knoll overlooking Plum Creek on South Professor Street in Oberlin. Built in 1870 and known as the Finley-Dick House, this white frame house with black shutters is a combination of Colonial revival and Victorian architecture. Steve Coughlin and Ron Kelly have furnished this comfortable bed and breakfast with a mixture of traditional furniture, antiques, Oriental rugs, and the work of local artists. Steve, a landscape designer, planned the garden, which in season has 200 varieties of perennials in bloom. Near the curved brick patio, a huge oak encircled with ivy explains the inn's name. Guests can relax in the living room, which looks out to the garden through French doors and wide windows, or seek out the front parlor, where the owners have placed a Charles X-style sleigh bed piled high with pillows, providing a comfortable place to read, watch television, or take a nap.

Irish breakfasts are served in a cheerful breakfast room to the left of the entrance hall. Specialties that bring raves include scones, muffins,

and bread puddings as well as breakfast cobblers and lemon cheese pancakes. A painted corner cupboard from the 1860s and a deep window with a variety of green and blooming plants make for a pleasant spot to start the day. In warm weather, guests can move to the patio for an alfresco breakfast in the garden.

The largest guest room, the Allie Findley room, named for the son of early owner Captain Findley, is on the main floor. On the windowpane to the right as you enter is Allie Findley's signature and the date, 1879, etched in the glass. This sunny room is centered by a queen-size French iron canopy bed. Blue-and-white Chinese-design wallpaper in the bath is repeated in the bed coverings. Touches of yellow and a wreath designed by Steve complete the room. An alcove provides a quiet reading corner.

Upstairs, the room known as the Front Guest Room is perfect for traveling twosomes, with both a single and a three-quarter-size bed. It features a color scheme of dusty rose and beige, faux-painted walls, and hardwood floors. Follow the hallway around the corner to the Magnolia Room, named for the huge magnolia tree brushing against the window. Blue and white predominate in this room. A corner wall unit of yew and other decorative pieces are showcased by recessed lights.

Thi is a charming and comfortable bed and breakfast. After a stay at the Ivy Tree Inn and Garden, one grateful guest left a note saying, "If friendship is a sheltering tree, then the Ivy Tree is a special friend to me."

THINGS TO DO: Visitors to Oberlin College make up 90 percent of those who stay at the Ivy Tree; visiting scholars and participants in special programs at the college find rooms at this inn. Some families make the Ivy Tree their home away from home throughout their child's college career and book graduation weekend years in advance. Another popular weekend, the Gardening Gathering Weekend, brings gardeners to glean gardening secrets from Steve, the resident horticulturist, share gourmet meals prepared by Ron, and tour nearby gardens at the college as well as the Schoefle Arboretum in Birmingham.

One of the joys of staying at the Ivy Tree is its proximity to the campus, where an unending series of concerts is offered during the school year. The Allen Memorial Art Museum, known for having one of the finest college/university art collections in the country, also offers special exhibitions. If time permits, tour three historic buildings on South Professor Street: the Monroe House, an 1866 Italianate-style house; the Little Red Schoolhouse, the first public school in Oberlin; and the Jewett House, a Victorian built in 1884. When dinnertime rolls around, walk down to the village center, where you can choose from excellent global cuisine at Weia Teia or veggie entrees and seasonal specials at the Black River Street Cafe.

DIRECTIONS: I-480 to SR 10; west on SR 10; becomes US 20; continue west on US 20; left (south) on SR 58; right (east) on Morgan St.; left (south) on Professor St.; on right

NEARBY ATTRACTIONS: Oberlin College, Schoefle Arboretum, Cedar Point, shops and restaurants

College Inn

A bit of the West Indies right here in Ohio

Becky Rohrer, Innkeeper
63 W. College Ave.
Westerville, OH
(888) 794-3090)

RATES & RESERVATIONS:
Hours: 8 a.m.–10 p.m.;
Season: Year round;
Rates: $$–$$$;
Specials: Seniors, singles, corporate;
Reservations required;
Check, Visa, MC, Disc accepted

ACCOMMODATIONS: 3 rooms w/bath

AMENITIES: Cable TV,
phone in room, Internet, air cond.

MEALS: Full breakfast, snacks

SPECIAL CONSIDERATIONS:
Not fully handicapped accessible;
Parking available: Lot, on street

Here's an 1870s brick Italianate bed and breakfast near the Otterbein College campus that's a fooler. Step inside The College Inn in this neighborhood of fine old homes and you'll discover a West Indies–style interior throughout. Owner/innkeeper Becky Rohrer has created a refreshing space for her lodgings opened in 1996. White painted walls and woodwork in the common and guest rooms provide the backdrop for carefully selected art and eclectic decorative pieces. Windows are hung with simple, white wood blinds, while ceiling fans, sisal rugs, and the lush green of plants reinforce the tropical feeling.

Becky showed me her book of photographs and clippings that tells the story of this house. Built in 1878 by J. A. Weinland, a Westerville attorney, it had stood vacant for four years when the Rohrers purchased it in 1996. They gutted the place and managed, with an intensive seven months of work, to produce the sparkling accommodation guests visit today. The walnut and tiger maple staircase was not in place but rather in pieces, and they were able to reconstruct the missing spindles. Three new bathrooms were added on the second level, allowing a private bath for each guest room. The dwelling's history came full circle when Becky hosted a celebration in 1999 for the last family who owned the house. Three generations of the Elberfeld family came back to 63 West College Street for Christmas.

The dining room is stunning with a simple wrought-iron chandelier, an Oriental rug from Becky's family, and an oval table with chairs painted the claret color of the kitchen walls. This young innkeeper said she wanted her dining room to be a cheerful spot on the darkest day of an Ohio winter. Bay windows (one of six sets in the house) bring in the light; a colorful print by Jean Claude Picot on one wall and a Tarkay over the fireplace have brought positive comments from guests. A library and a sitting room complete this floor.

Three guest rooms continue the fresh, uncluttered look upstairs. In a house with 14-foot ceilings, the room at the end of the hall seems especially welcoming with mere 9^1/$_2$-foot ceilings. Botanical prints repeat the pale green of a wing chair in this room known as the "Step-Down Room." The remaining rooms are furnished with a pencil-post pineapple bed, a sleigh bed, and comfortable chairs with good reading lights. A small common room with TV and VCR offers a place to relax.

On our summer stay at the College Inn, we joined other guests and neighbors on the flagstone patio in the side yard. A market umbrella, a grouping of padded wrought-iron chairs, and blooming gardens make it a lovely spot. Becky planted Maiden grasses around the perimeter of the patio that by August are full-grown, providing a grassy privacy wall.

Becky Rohrer is one of the new wave of innkeepers who left professional positions to run bed and breakfasts full time. She lives in a separate section of the house with her young son, Jerrod. Becky has an easy rapport with her guests. Many of those who return to stay at her inn are business travelers who like the rooms equipped with modem ports and telephones with separate guest lines. Guests of Otterbein College make their home here while in Westerville. A couple of favorite breakfast items are Monte Cristo sandwiches, apricot almond couscous, and a variety of homemade breads and muffins.

THINGS TO DO: Westerville is a walking town, and it's an easy stroll to "Uptown Westerville's" nineteenth-century shopping district with its wide range of specialty and antique shops. Head the other direction on West Main and after half a block you'll find the Otterbein College campus. The chimes from Otterbein's College Towers sing out a recital at 6:00 p.m.

Throughout the year, prospective students and their parents come to stay at The College Inn. Special weekends like Commencement are booked in advance. Otterbein College serves as an off-Broadway venue for new works, and this series brings guests to the bed and breakfast. The second week of July brings visitors for the Westerville Arts Festival.

There are numerous dining options in this college town. The Westerville Grille, a popular spot with the locals, is within walking distance of the inn. You'll also find the Persnickety Cottage and Tea Room, serving light meals and tea in a 90-year-old, Gothic-style former church. It's a short drive to the Table of Contents Cafe where we found gourmet offerings including vegetarian entrees.

DIRECTIONS: I-71 to exit 119B for I-270; east on I-270; north on Westerville-State St.; left on College Ave..; on right

NEARBY ATTRACTIONS: Hoover Reservoir, Alum Creek Reservoir, Polaris Amphitheater, Columbus Zoo, The Ohio State University, Otterbein College, downtown Columbus

Chapter 8

THEME INNS

Inveterate inngoers are finding a new kind of accommodation—an inn with a theme. The setting and the interior decor help set the theme, but it's the innkeepers we can thank for coming up with the ideas.

Imagine finding an inn with a bookstore in the basement where you're free to browse in the wee hours and pay for your purchase the next morning at breakfast. How about sleeping in a room dedicated to a favorite composer and then hearing his music in a concert by a major orchestra that evening? Pick a favorite artist and revel in a setting featuring the artist's work lining the walls. Or select an author you admire and find a stack of his books in a room with an interior reflecting the time of the author's life. Nationality theme inns include one with a Scandinavian decor in Michigan and a Scottish inn set in southwestern Ohio that makes you think you might be in the hills of Scotland. An antique lover's dream exists in another inn, while a chance to live with fine Mexican and southwestern U.S. art and artifacts awaits in a bed and breakfast in the countryside. Step back to the eighteenth century in an early mill setting.

These themed accommodations are scattered around Ohio, and a few take you over the state line. All offer a similar stay to those we usually find at a bed and breakfast but are flavored with a twist of imagination and fun.

John Foos Manor

Antique Gallery/ Bed and Breakfast

This bed and breakfast is also an antique gallery—and everything is for sale.

John Glaze, Innkeeper
810 E. High St.
Springfield, OH
(937) 323-3444

RATES & RESERVATIONS:
Season: Year round;
Rates: $$$;
Reservations required;
Check, Visa, MC, Disc, Amex accepted

ACCOMMODATIONS: 7 rooms,
4 w/bath; 3 suites w/bath

AMENITIES: Hot tub, cable TV,
phone in room, air cond.,
copy and fax machines available

MEALS: Full breakfast

SPECIAL CONSIDERATIONS:
Not fully handicapped accessible;
Parking available: Lot

Have you ever stayed in a country inn or bed and breakfast and wished you could take the cherry four-poster bed or marble-top table in your room home with you? Guests of the John Foos Manor can do just that: this bed and breakfast is also an antique gallery, and everything is for sale. Casual shoppers can pick up small items; serious collectors can browse four floors of antiques as well as the coach house. Those who love old houses will revel in the 19,800 square feet of this Italian Renaissance manor.

John Foos built his elegant mansion at 810 High Street atop a high ridge overlooking Springfield in 1860. By 1871, three of the most important men in Springfield connected with the agricultural implement business lived on this block on High Street known as "Industrialists' Row."

Built of solid limestone masonry, the house is ornamented with restrained carving and pilaster decoration. The roofline has a centrally placed, broken pediment and bracketed cornice with paneled frieze. Stepping inside the side entrance hall of this Victorian home, a warren of rooms awaits. A kitchen to the right, a small room of collectibles to the left, and beyond, a central hallway of Italian mosaic tile leads to parlors, music room, dining room, and library. The woodwork is walnut and burled walnut; the hardwood floors are oak, laid in the old log cabin style. Mirrored Victorian carved mantels reach to the ceiling, adding to the feeling of soaring space. One of the eye-catching installations is the center hall chandelier, an amazing configuration of grape clusters, gilded pheasants, and Minerva heads of solid bronze. We learned that the three-story, winding walnut staircase took two workers three years to complete.

When former owners and Springfield natives Dick and Patty Brown purchased the John Foos Manor in 1985, they had to remove dropped ceilings and non-supporting dividing walls that had been added by a former tenant. They stripped paint and refinished doors, floors, and woodwork. Extensive work was done on the exterior as well, including cleaning and retucking. In renovating one of the most prestigious properties in Springfield, the Browns were given the Award of Merit for an outstanding preservation and rehabilitation of the building by the Ohio Historical Society. The John Foos Manor is also listed on the National Historical Registry.

We started the tour of this grand house on the main floor. The library, with floor-to-ceiling bookcases, is centered by a massive cherry conference table. This room served as John Foos' office with a separate door from the residence. The parlor, extending from the front of the house to the back, allowed enough space for after-dinner conversation in an era when men gathered in one area and women in another. A music room and dining room complete this wing. Breakfast is served in the dining room unless guests request it be delivered to their rooms or to the gazebo.

Rooms on the second floor are named for Foos family members and reflect period room settings with antiques and exact reproductions of seventeenth- and eighteenth-century formal and country furniture. Some of the craftsman represented include David T. Smith, John Spicer, and the Riverbend Windsor Chair Company. The wide hallway, lined with antiques, is brightened by a large skylight on the third floor.

The ballroom on this floor was a labor of love for the Browns. They added an oak dance floor and had the bracketed support columns refinished and gilded. You can imagine an evening in the early days of this mansion when Victorian ball gowns swept the floor to the strains of a small orchestra. This is being investigated for reuse because of the area's interest in ballroom dancing; current innkeeper John Glaze is also a professional ballroom dancer.

THINGS TO DO: Visitors to Springfield find two antique malls at exit 59 of Interstate 70 and another at exit 62. In town, the Pennsylvania House Museum, an early inn on the National Road, has been preserved by the Lagonda Chapter of the Daughters of the American Revolution, and nearby on High Street, the Saint Raphael Church is a beautiful example of modified Gothic style. Hikers and bikers can access the Little Miami Scenic Trail in Springfield. The Cedar Street Restaurant was recommended to us and we enjoyed this cozy eatery with oversize salads—try the Cobb and the tarragon chicken—and the baked-on-the-premises desserts including a Black Forest cheesecake and four berry cobbler.

DIRECTIONS: I-71 to exit 119B for I-270; west on I-270 to exit 8 for I-70; west on I-70 to exit for SR 72; north on SR 72; right (east) on E. High St.; on left

NEARBY ATTRACTIONS: Brown Reservoir, Wittenberg University, Russ Performing Arts Center, Springfield Art Museum, antique malls, Clifton Mill, Air Force Museum, Mac O Cheek castles, Ohio Caverns

50 Lincoln Inn

Stay in the artsy part of town in
rooms themed to artists.

A discreet sign and an iron fence distinguish 50 Lincoln Inn from its Victorian brick neighbors in the Short North area of Columbus, a block from High Street with its buzzing galleries, restaurants, jazz clubs, and pubs. It's an easy walk to the Convention Center and to downtown Columbus. Visitors to The Ohio State University, business guests and locals looking for a city getaway make this inn their destination. Stepping through the front door of this turn-of-the-century house, visitors find a bright contemporary interior.

50 Lincoln Inn fits this artsy neighborhood, with its artist-themed rooms—Van Gogh, Picasso, Degas, Monet, Toulouse-Lautrec,—and suites featuring Norman Rockwell, Frank Lloyd Wright, and Ansel Adams.

Patricia Livingston, Innkeeper
50 E. Lincoln Ave.
Columbus, OH
(614) 299-5050
www.50lincoln.com

RATES & RESERVATIONS:
Season: Year round;
Rates: $$$;
Reservations required;
Check, Visa, MC, Disc, Amex accepted

ACCOMMODATIONS:
5 rooms w/bath; 3 suites w/bath

AMENITIES: Cable TV, phone in room,
Internet (data port), air cond.

MEALS: Expanded
continental breakfast

SPECIAL CONSIDERATIONS:
Not fully handicapped accessible;
Parking available: Lot

The Monet room provides a romantic retreat with familiar Monet prints, and the palest of pink, green, and violet floral wallpaper contrasted with green and white stripes. The verdigris canopied bed is made up with white eyelet bedding, and sheers hang at the front windows. Decorative fire screens front, fireplaces that are just for show throughout the house. Down the hall, it's a taste of New England in the Norman Rockwell Suite furnished with a cherry four-poster bed and a comfy sofa. Blue-and-white plaid wallpaper bordered with a small-town scene, and mattress-ticking drapes, make for a very Rockwell-esque feel to the suite. Decorative accents include Rockwell prints and teddy bears on the mantel.

Business guests like the top floor of the house, with its two large suites tucked under the eaves. The Frank Lloyd Wright Suite has no-nonsense arts and crafts bed, desk, and Wright-design linens in blacks and tans, and is brightened by a skylight. The Ansel Adams Suite has a black-and-white treatment in linens and towels, and framed Adams photography on the walls.

A spacious dining room does double duty as a gallery, with local artists' work displayed on white walls. It's a cheerful place for breakfast, with round tables set with black-and-white china, fresh flowers, and colorful napkins. Pat serves a delicious breakfast with freshly baked croissants, a hot entree, and fruit from the nearby city market. She keeps a cookie jar on the buffet supplied with homebaked treats, and teas and coffees are available around the clock. Guests can settle down in the front parlor to read or chat, or seek out the compact English garden at the back of the inn.

THINGS TO DO: Fine restaurants abound in this area. At the corner of Lincoln and High streets, award-winning R. J. Snappers Bar and Grill features the freshest of fish with popular starters of coconut fried shrimp and oysters Rockefeller. We ordered the chef's evening special and found the potato crusted grouper paired with fresh vegetables, garlic potatoes, and a house salad outstanding. Other dining options offered along High Street include several coffeehouses, some of the best coney dogs in the city, fusion cuisine, and neighborhood bars.

The first Saturday night of every month there's a happening on Short North: the Gallery Hop. Folks descend upon the area to wander in and out of galleries and shops which cater to the crowd with late hours.

DIRECTIONS: I-71 to exit 110A for 5th Ave..; west on 5th Ave..; south on High St.; left on E. Lincoln St.; on left

NEARBY ATTRACTIONS: Convention Center, COSI, State Capitol Building, Short North art gallery district, fine dining, jazz clubs, park

Symphony Hotel and Restaurant

Adjacent to Cincinnati's Music Hall, this inn dedicates rooms to favorite composers.

Patricia Robb, Innkeeper
210 W. 14th St.
Cincinnati, OH
(513) 721-3353
symphonyhotel.com

RATES & RESERVATIONS:
Hours: 7:30 a.m.–midnight;
Season: Year round;
Rates: $$;
Specials: Children, seniors, singles;
Reservations required;
Check, Visa, MC, Disc, Amex accepted

ACCOMMODATIONS: 4 rooms w/bath

AMENITIES: Cable TV,
phone in room, Internet, air cond.

MEALS: Expanded continental
breakfast, dinner, brunch, snacks;
Beer, wine, and liquor served

SPECIAL CONSIDERATIONS:
Guest pets allowed;
Parking available: Lot, on street

Take your pick: Beethoven, Bach, Mozart, or Schubert. At the Symphony Hotel, a European-style bed and breakfast hotel in Cincinnati, four guest rooms have been dedicated to these composers. In the Mozart Room, I found a bust of the composer on the mantel, along with paintings, and sheet music. It all seemed to fit the Old World feeling of this hotel in Cincinnati's Over-the-Rhine district. There's an elegant dining room with a prix fixe dinner, and the Cincinnati Music Hall is across the street. You can purchase a package for dinner at the hotel, a ticket for a concert by the Cincinnati Symphony Orchestra or the Cincinnati Pops, and a night's stay in your favorite composer's room.

Built in 1871 by Peter Ehrgott, a German lithographer, it was known as the Ehrgott "mansion." Over the years it became a neglected city property until it was purchased at auction by Eber Associates in 1995, rehabbed, and opened as the Symphony Hotel in 1997. The hotel won the Restoration Award from the Cincinnati Preservation Association in the same year. And a fine hotel it is. The original gas light hangs at the doorway, the first of several such remnants from the original building that also include cast iron fireplaces, raised central ivory ceiling medallions, and black walnut stairs. A large 1870s painting of Venus hangs over the dining room fireplace. The bar is an eclectic room with dark green walls, marble floor in a mosaic pattern, and louvered shutters. The raised wood front of the bar was saved from the original built-in buffet in the mansion. The Mozart Room is furnished with Federal-style antiques; the Schubert room features Mission-style furniture. Guests find pedestal sinks, feather ticks on the queen beds, and ceiling fans. The manager, Patricia Robb, fits the musical profile of this accommodation; an organist, she majored in organ and minored in voice.

The Symphony Hotel dining room offers an interesting chapter in the history of the place. Peter Ehrgott's son, Louis, taught piano, voice, and theory in what was then the parlor for 49 years. He also served as conductor of the May Festival in 1887–88 and 1891.

A four-course prix fixe dinner is served by reservation only at six o'-clock, which allows time to get to the eight o'clock Cincinnati Symphony Orchestra performance. The menu changes weekly and you can check the current menu when making dinner reservations. There is an escort service from the parking lot to the hotel.

THINGS TO DO: The Cincinnati Music Hall is across the street from the Symphony Hotel. Another architectural gem in Cincinnati is the art deco-style Union Terminal, which has been described as a giant, old-fashioned cathedral-style radio.

The hilly Mt. Adams Historic District with its galleries, boutiques, and eateries is also close to the hotel. While in Mt. Adams, you can stop for lunch at the building where the famous Rookwood Pottery was once made. The tables are inside large kilns, and there is a display of several periods of Rookwood. Mt. Adams borders Eden Park, home to the Cincinnati Art Museum, one of the leading museums in the country.

For restaurant recommendations, check with the innkeeper. But you might not want to leave Cincinnati without trying this city's trademark chili, served in an oval dish over spaghetti with grated cheese on top.

DIRECTIONS: I-71 to exit 2 for Reading Rd.; left on Central Pkwy.; right on W. 14th; on left

NEARBY ATTRACTIONS: Cincinnati attractions, Union Terminal Museum, Mt. Adams Historic District

Sturgis House

The town's strong connection to Stoke-on-Trent, England, is reflected here.

Old houses often have stories; Sturgis House in East Liverpool has several. This lovingly restored, turn-of-the-century house was originally built by the Erlanger family. It later became the Sturgis Funeral Home. In 1934, thousands came to the house for the viewing of Charles "Pretty Boy Floyd" Arthur, considered public enemy number one. Visitors can view a collection of photographs and memorabilia from Arthur's life in the basement of Sturgis House. Frank A. Dawson was the funeral director at that time, and his son, Frank C. Dawson, purchased the house in 1993. As is often the case with houses of this age, the dwelling had seen a succession of owners and, by the time the Dawson family purchased it, had stood unoccupied for three years; the garage was falling in and

Frank Dawson, owner;
Susan Anderson, manager
122 W. Fifth St.
East Liverpool, OH
(330) 382-0194
www.sturgishouse.com

RATES & RESERVATIONS:
Hours: 6:30 a.m.–9 p.m.;
Season: Year round;
Rates: $$;
Specials: Children;
Reservations recommended;
Check, Visa, MC, Amex accepted

ACCOMMODATIONS:
6 rooms, 4 w/bath

AMENITIES: Cable TV,
phone in room, air cond.

MEALS: Continental breakfast, snacks

SPECIAL CONSIDERATIONS:
Handicapped accessible;
Parking available: On street,
garage ($5)

water damage had taken its toll. The Dawsons gradually restored the building, but it was a community event planned for the weekend of July 4, 1998—the East Liverpool High School All-Class Reunion—that pushed them to complete the project. And that's the second story about this house.

East Liverpool, Ohio, has a strong connection to Stoke-on-Trent, England, as many ancestors of the current citizens of East Liverpool came from the North Staffordshire area to help establish the pottery industry. The first guests to stay at the newly opened Sturgis House that July weekend in 1998 were visitors from Stoke-on-Trent who came for the All-Class Reunion. The six rooms in the bed and breakfast are named for the towns of Stoke-on-Trent: Hanley, Burslem, Longton, Fenton, Tunstall, and Stoke City. Similarities between the two municipalities are many, and there is a friendly exchange of visits between the two. You can find the same family names on both sides of the Atlantic, and when East Liverpool citizens first visited to Stoke-on-Trent, they found buildings very similar to those in their own downtown center.

Fans of Victoriana will adore this home filled with period furniture, Victorian Revival wallpapers, and polished hardwood floors with inlaid parquet borders. Decor is lightly romantic, with roses, cherubs, and angels featured throughout. And trappings of Victorian life are on display—framed collages of greeting cards, lace, old photographs, fine linen, and the fashions of the day for women and children. The Fenton Room, with a cherry four-poster bed and a charming alcove overlooking the West Fifth Street neighborhood, is also known as the Bridal Suite. Another often-requested room is the Longton Room, where renowned college football coach Lou Holtz stays when he comes back to East Liverpool. I found this spacious room, done in a rich burgundy and green and furnished in cherry traditional furniture, to be very comfortable. Business travelers appreciate the Stoke City Room, a guest room with an adjoining kitchenette. Following the stairs to the third floor, you'll find a pink Victorian dollhouse resting on the landing. At the top of the stairs, the Hanley Room is filled with white wicker, a painted iron bed, and Victorian baby books and clothing. A few steps away, the Burslem Room offers an elegant, purple, full-canopied bed and adjoins a room under the eaves with twin beds. A spring-like lavender wall covering, a fan window, and antique rockers complete this suite. Terry cloth robes and fine toiletries can be found in each room.

The manager, Susie Anderson, helped open Sturgis House, and the

household staff keeps everything running smoothly. The kitchen is open
around the clock, with a variety of
snacks and a refrigerator stocked with
juices and soft drinks. A continental
breakfast is available from 7:30 to 9:30
each morning.

This house with a colorful past has
had a number of famous guests: Kareem Abdul-Jabbar, Reggie Jackson,
and Joe Montana stayed at the Sturgis House when they were inducted
into the Lou Holtz Upper Ohio Valley Hall of Fame. Regis Philbin and
Notre Dame legend Daniel "Rudy" Ruettiger have also been guests.

THINGS TO DO: East Liverpool, known as the pottery capital of the United
States, continues to churn out pottery and china. Popular tour stops are
Hall China Company, with a line of Longaberger pottery, Homer Laughlin China Company, maker of the popular Fiestaware, and Pioneer Pottery. The Ohio Historical Society operates a fine museum in East Liverpool, the Museum of Ceramics, with the largest public collection of Lo-
tusware. Additional stops include two antique malls.

A popular spot for lunch or dinner is Yanni's Cafe. The locals recommend grabbing a lighter meal at the Fifth Street Sampler and picking up
some donuts from L and B Donut Shop.

The strong connection between East Liverpool and Stoke-on-Trent
continues. The youth soccer team from the East Liverpool area traveled
to North Staffordshire for the Gordon Banks OBE Millennium Soccer
Tournament. If you are lucky while a guest at Sturgis House, owner
Frank C. Dawson may stop in and share some of the history of the city
as well as some of his down-home East Liverpool hospitality.

DIRECTIONS: I-480 to exit 42 for I-80; east on I-80 to exit 16 for
SR 7; south on SR 7; straight on US 30; left on Jackson St.;
right on W. 6th; right on Broadway; right on W. 5th St.; on left

NEARBY ATTRACTIONS: Homer Laughlin China,
Lou Holtz Hall of Fame, Museum of Ceramics,
Thimpson Historical House, antiques

Book Inn

*This inn is all about books—
there's even a bookstore in the
basement.*

Ona business trip to South Bend, Indiana, I planned a stay at this inn out of curiosity—two of my favorite things, books and inns in combination, seemed too good to be true.

Innkeeper Peggy Livingston always wanted to own a bookstore. So when her husband, John, retired, they purchased this French Victorian house in the historic district of downtown South Bend. The inn has a quality used bookstore in the basement! I found a great selection of my favorites—travel, cookbooks, and children's books, along with nonfiction—on my two forays to the bottom of the house. Guests are free to browse the well-organized collection at any hour. It is interesting to note that Albert Cushing, the local businessman who built the house in 1872, also owned a bookstore in South Bend.

John and Peggy Livingston, Innkeepers
508 W. Washington St.
South Bend, IN
(219) 288-1990
www.book-inn.com

RATES & RESERVATIONS:
Season: Year round;
Rates: $$$–$$$$;
Two-night minimum stay
required some weekends;
Reservations recommended;
Check, Visa, MC, Amex accepted

ACCOMMODATIONS:
5 rooms w/bath; 2 suites w/bath

MEALS: Full breakfast, snacks

SPECIAL CONSIDERATIONS:
Not fully handicapped accessible;
Parking available: Lot

There are many references to, and decorative accents featuring books throughout the house. In 1991, the Book Inn was included in the designer showcase for the South Bend Symphony, and this group created themes around authors. A corner room, the Louisa May Alcott Room, is done up in flowery chintzes and soft greens with an antique writing desk. I stayed in the Jessie Willcox Smith Suite with prints of that well-known artist's smiling children circling the room. The Cushing

Suite, named for the original owners, offers a spacious bay-windowed room with a sitting area and a king-size four-poster bed. Additional rooms are named for Jane Austen and Charlotte Bronte. On an initial stroll through the house, I kept finding reminders of books and authors—a quote from Emily Dickinson as a border in the spacious entry room, radiator covers and wardrobes painted like bookshelves, and books everywhere. I settled in to read in the cozy library, with its deep leather chairs, a gas log fireplace, and family memorabilia sharing the shelves with the Livingstons' personal collection of books.

An elegant bed and breakfast, the house, with its mansard roof and arched dormer windows, is an outstanding example of Second Empire architecture. There are 12-foot-high ceilings and hand-hewn butternut woodwork. The heavy entry doors with double leaf wood and applied decoration won first place for design at the 1893 Colombian Exposition in Chicago. Three gorgeous stained glass windows sparkle on the staircase landing.

Peggy strives for beauty and comfort in her inn, and the result is a

pleasing mixture of quality antiques, overstuffed furniture, and bouquets of fresh flowers. Breakfast at this inn is a treat for those of us who just grab a quick breakfast at home. Peggy serves breakfast at a table set with 100-year-old Haviland china, sterling silver, and Waterford crystal.

A bookmark from the inn suggests to the guest, "Sit deep and come often. You're one of the folks." In chatting with other guests in the bookstore downstairs and at breakfast the next morning, we agreed that the Book Inn provided one of our most satisfying of bed and breakfast stays. The American Automobile Association (AAA) seems to agree, having designated the Book Inn as a four-diamond accommodation.

THINGS TO DO: Gourmet dining can be found next door to the Book Inn at Tippecanoe Place, a South Bend landmark in this historic West Washington neighborhood. Once Clement Studebaker's home, this Romanesque stone structure, with rounded arches and corner entrance porch, was the setting for parties and weddings in the late 1880s. The massive fireplaces and grand staircase from that era remain, and tours of the 40-room mansion can be arranged. Guests return to Tippecanoe Place for the house specialty: prime rib, slow roasted with an herb crust. A traditional dish, roasted Indiana duckling topped with a tart sauce of raspberries and dried Bing cherries, also brings raves.

If you have an extra day or even an afternoon, South Bend offers a variety of venues worth exploring. A guest we met during our stay at the Inn came to South Bend specifically to visit the Studebaker National Museum, where you can trace the history of transportation from an 1835 Conestoga wagon to the last Studebaker to roll off the line. Another popular stop is the College Football Hall of Fame, with films dating back to the 1920s and interactive displays. Next trip to South Bend, we want to visit Copshaholm, a 38-room Victorian mansion filled with the original furniture of the J. D. Oliver family. The Northern Indiana Center for History has also preserved the small cottage behind the mansion, Dom Robotnika (polish for "worker's home"), a dwelling typical of Eastern European laborers who came to work in the South Bend factories.

DIRECTIONS: I-80 west to exit 77 for US-31; south on US-31; left (west) on West Washington St.; on left

NEARBY ATTRACTIONS: Notre Dame College, Studebaker Museum, College Football Hall of Fame, restaurants, antiques

The Spencer

Find your favorite author in this literary fantasy hotel.

Helen Edgington, owner/innkeeper of the Spencer, was looking for a four-unit apartment building to buy at the Chautauqua Institution when she was shown the old Spencer Hotel. She bought the aging Victorian landmark and entered into a renovation process that she says was "like building a house all over again without having to build the exterior walls." The structure was gutted and 41 box-like rooms became 28 rooms and suites; an elevator, air conditioning, new plumbing, and electrical work were installed. The exterior is now a fresh cream color, and Helen has created a Monet garden in pinks and reds that hugs the porches; a fountain sits amid the English garden alongside the hotel. The dining room's dropped ceiling was removed, and the higher ceiling is accentuated with Victorian peacock chandeliers. English lace curtains at the windows, an Eastlake hall mirror, and tables for four with flowered tablecloths provide a gracious setting for breakfast and after-concert desserts. The dining room opens to the reception area and comfortably furnished parlor. With Boston ferns, Oriental rugs, books, and a selection of current magazines, it's the spot to sit and read or meet a

Helen Edgington, Innkeeper
25 Palestine Ave..
Chautauqua, NY
(800) 398-1306
www.thespencer.com

RATES & RESERVATIONS:
Hours: 8 a.m.–11 p.m.;
Season: Year round; Rates: $$$;
Specials: AAA, groups;
Reservations required;
Check, Visa, MC, Disc, Amex accepted

ACCOMMODATIONS:
22 rooms w/bath; 5 suites w/bath

AMENITIES: Spa, cable TV, phone in room, Internet, air cond., Jacuzzi and whirlpool tubs, 4 floors of porches, elevator, apartment available

MEALS: Continental breakfast, snacks; May not accommodate all special diets

SPECIAL CONSIDERATIONS:
Not fully handicapped accessible;
Parking available: On street

friend. Artist Rita Argen Auerbach's Monet series graces the walls throughout the downstairs public rooms. A Kawai grand piano is used often by guests who come to this summer haven of music and culture.

The guest rooms set the theme for this hotel. Helen calls it a literary fantasy accommodation. I call it sheer bliss to find a room dedicated to a favorite author. The Isak Dinesen suite has a pale green-and-white striped tent painted on the ceiling with tasseled ropes hanging down that are so believable I wanted to touch them. You feel like you're in Africa, with the Serengeti Plain on the wall behind the king bed. A whirlpool tub tucked into a corner, a kitchenette, and a sitting area complete the suite. Return to childhood in the Beatrix Potter room, with Mr. Jeremy Fisher on the headboard of the white double bed, Peter Rabbit in the garden on the bathroom wall, and a floor that is painted to look exactly like a cabbage patch. It's a delightful room done in pastel colors with a wicker settee and chairs. Or take an imaginary trip to C. S. Lewis' *The Lion, The Witch, and the Wardrobe*—open the antique wardrobe and you're on your way to Narnia. There's a light tropical feel to the Agatha Christie suite, with its Prince of Wales wallpaper and light green ferns against a white background. The green and white is repeated in the cotton coverlet and bedskirt, and the fern motif appears again in a high narrow window over the whirlpool tub. Come find your room at the Spencer—Isabel Allende, E. B. White, Jane Austen, and George Eliot are some of the authors honored with rooms of their own.

Helen did her homework in researching the authors, and local artists Nancy Wells and Rita Argen Auerbach captured the scenes in creative murals and decorative touches. Chautauqua is famous for its porches, and some of the rooms have access to a porch that allows a view over the busy Chautauqua grounds or a private box from which to hear the concerts in the amphitheater down the way.

THINGS TO DO: During the Chautauqua season, visitors find not only a resident orchestra but also ballet, opera, and theater. There are gate and parking fees from late June through the end of August. In late August, the Chautauqua season winds down, the summer folks leave, and the resident population dwindles to some four hundred. This is the time to explore the streets of this Victorian village and look closely at cottages with fanciful trim. Walk or jog along sparkling Chautauqua Lake or read on the center green. The library and bookstore stay open all year. The Spencer keeps a list of suggested tours, whether your interests are browsing the countryside for antiques, stopping at wineries, or following Lake Erie's Seaway Trail. It's a short drive to Bemus Point to dine at Ye Hare n' Hounds Inn, a restaurant recommended by friends. Neither the food nor the atmosphere disappointed; we sat in the comfy Old English-style inn and savored the seafood and veal entrees and the view of Chautauqua Lake.

DIRECTIONS: I-90 to exit 60 for SR 394; left (south) on SR 394; left (north) on Elm Ln.; right (east) on Hedding Ave..; right (south) on Prospect Ave..; left (east) on Palestine Ave..

NEARBY ATTRACTIONS: Chautauqua Institution, Lucille Ball's birthplace, Amish country, antiques, art galleries, historic museums, wineries, nature trails, boating, golfing, skiing, dinner yacht cruises, Midway Park, 1891 Fredonia Opera House

Old Northside Inn

Be a star for a night in the Theater Room.

Susan Berry, Innkeeper
1340 N. Alabama St.
Indianapolis, IN
(800) 635-9127
www.oldnorthsideinn.com

RATES & RESERVATIONS:
Hours: Mon–Sat 10 a.m.–5 p.m.;
Season: Year round;
Rates: $$$–$$$$;
Specials: Single corporate;
Reservations required;
Visa, MC, Disc, Amex, cash, checks
2 weeks in advance accepted

ACCOMMODATIONS: 6 rooms w/bath

AMENITIES: Cable TV, phone in room, Internet, air cond., whirlpool tubs in every bath, 2 rooms with fireplaces

MEALS: Full breakfast, snacks

SPECIAL CONSIDERATIONS:
Cat living at inn;
Handicapped accessible;
Parking available: Lot

The Old Northside neighborhood in Indianapolis has witnessed a renaissance in the past 30 years, and one of the dwellings brought back to its former glory is the Old Northside Inn. This elegant Romanesque Revival house was built in 1885 by Herman C. DeWenter, an early Indianapolis industrialist. The DeWenter family lived in the red brick house on North Alabama Street until 1920, when it was made into apartments. An antiques business took over the space in 1975, followed by an architectural firm. When Susan Berry purchased the house in 1994, she spent two and a half years restoring the place. Since the house had seen so many owners, she had to reconfigure the space to bring it back as close as possible to the original floor plan. Each guest room has a framed collage of photos that tells the story of the work involved for that particular room.

Some of the special architectural features of Old Northside Inn are 11-foot-high ceilings, original pocket doors, a hand-tooled mahogany staircase, and Italian tiles. There's an Old World elegance to the place, warmed by Susan's collection of European art and special touches provided by the work of Ukrainian artisans she brought over from the former Soviet Union. These craftsmen stayed for two and a half months painting murals like the one above the dining room fireplace. The music room's gold moire walls and heirloom Oriental rug accompany a 1926 Chickering grand piano. A fretted clock from Denmark and instruments from the Ukraine complete the room. At the front of the house, the formal parlor with marble-top tables and floral settees and chairs provides a gathering place for guests. In pleasant weather, Susan serves breakfast on the side porch, which overlooks an English border garden. Those who stay at the Old Northside Inn find snacks and drinks at any hour in the butler's pantry. We were pleasantly surprised to find an early-morning coffee and juice service waiting outside our door.

Guests at this bed and breakfast have the fun of choosing from themed rooms. In the Literary Room, the king-size bed has a quarter canopy of literary tapestry, and the bookshelf offers Indiana authors like Booth Tarkington and James Whitcomb Riley. Fans of theater can take the stage for a night in the Theater Room, cleverly done in black and white. Large silver stars, signed by previous guests, grace the walls, and the dressing table is outlined with lights. But it's the bed on a raised platform, circled by star-studded sheer curtains, that makes a guest feel like a star. The bath is papered with early sheet music, and a collection of playbills cover one bedroom wall. For a romantic interlude, reserve the Bridal Room with a two-person Jacuzzi, double shower, and gas log fireplace. Susan designed the queen-size bed after finding an antique headboard. She added eight-foot pillars and a canopy intertwined with silk

panels, and covered the bed with a luxurious champagne silk comforter. A corner room named for the builder of the house is a favorite with business guests. It's a cozy retreat with a wall of exposed brick and early photos of the DeWenter family. Corporate amenities include use of a fax and computer access. Business meetings and receptions for small groups can be arranged.

VENTURING OUT: The inn is minutes away from the Circle Centre Mall and Convention Center. Popular destinations while in Indianapolis include the Eiteljorg Museum of American Indians and Western Art and the James Whitcomb Riley Museum Home in the charming neighborhood of Lockerbie Square.

DIRECTIONS: I-71 to exit 119B for I-270; west on I-270 to exit 8 for I-70; west on I-70 to exit 83B for I-65; north on I-65 to exit 113 for Pennsylvania St.; left on Pennsylvania; left on E. 11th; left on N. Delaware; right on E. 13th St.; left on N. Alabama St.; on left

NEARBY ATTRACTIONS: RCA Dome, convention center, Conseco Fieldhouse, Indianapolis Zoo, Indianapolis Children's Museum, Indianapolis Motor Speedway

Benmiller Inn

*A luxurious stay in a
former woolen mill*

The Benmiller Inn is a retreat of unspoiled beauty situated in the rolling hills of Huron County, Ontario, on the banks of the Maitland River. At first glance, we saw a secluded, wooded property intersected by a rushing creek (Sharpes Creek) with a full-service inn. Upon further exploration, we discovered it was all part of a restored mill town. Originally it was a bustling, self-contained pioneer village with a woolen mill powered by Sharpes Creek. A brother and sister duo, Peter and Joanne Ivey, who had spent childhood summers nearby, were interested in historic preservation and saved the buildings. The first building restored was the original woolen mill, a two-and-a-half-story, cast lime structure with dormers, edged by a brick patio, fountain, and baskets of geraniums. Now the woolen mill houses 12 cozy guest rooms, a fireside lounge, and the dining room. During the restoration process, old pieces of mill machinery were saved and transformed into lamps, sconces, chests of drawers, and room dividers. We found a wall sconce that was once a gear, a mirror that was a hayfork, and a chandelier in the dining room that was a large wooden pulley.

Randy Stoddart, Innkeeper
C.R. 1
Goderich, ONT
(800) 265-1711
benmiller.on.ca

RATES & RESERVATIONS:
Hours: Reservations 7 a.m.–11 p.m.;
Season: Year round; Rates: $$$–$$$$;
Specials: Seniors, AAA, midweek;
Two-night minimum stay
required on weekends;
Reservations recommended;
Visa, MC, Amex, Enroute,
Diner's Club accepted

ACCOMMODATIONS:
47 rooms w/bath; 15 suites w/bath

AMENITIES: Hot tub, sauna, spa, indoor pool, phone in room, air cond., hiking/cross-country trails, cycling

MEALS: Full breakfast, lunch, dinner, brunch, snacks;
Beer, wine, and liquor served

SPECIAL CONSIDERATIONS:
Handicapped accessible;
Parking available: Lot

Our stay was in the River Mill, the former gristmill. The Iveys kept the original building in mind during the renovation and put back as much as possible. The result is a soaring rustic structure with the old cedar siding used for the exterior and exposed hand-hewn posts and beams in the interior. Additional accommodations include the turn-of-the-century Gledhill House, where nearly all the rooms include a balcony or patio; the Mill House, with two deluxe suites and two guest rooms; and Cherrydale, a six-bedroom guest house.

The Ivey Dining Room looks out on Sharpes Creek and is known for its international cuisine as well as old-style Canadian fare. Guests find a hearty Huron country breakfast in the solarium.

Relaxation is an essential part of any getaway, and the Benmiller Inn offers an on-site spa with full services as well as a fitness center with pool, whirlpool, and sauna. The swimming pool, in the River Mill building, was particularly delightful as it afforded yet another view of the river. There are eight miles of wooded, hilly hiking trails to explore, as well as groomed cross-country ski trails.

The Benmiller Inn has been a member of the Independent Innkeepers' Association since 1995.

THINGS TO DO: We spent a half-day in the port town of Goderich with its octagonal town square, museums, antique shops, and wonderful examples of nineteenth-century architecture. The Goderich Tourism Office provided us with a guide to an architectural walking tour. Three public beaches are connected by an old-fashioned boardwalk. Goderich is known for its glorious sunsets—they're worth sticking around for. You get to view the sunset twice in one evening by first watching it from the beach and then clambering up the hillside walkway to see it again from the bluff—what a way to end a day!

This is theater country. Visitors have a choice of three theaters—the Stratford Festival, the Blyth Festival, and the Huron Country Playhouse. There are also two 18-hole championship golf courses nearby.

DIRECTIONS: I-80 to exit 5 for I-280; north on I-280; north on I-75; east on I-94 to Blue Water Bridge; east on SR 402; north on Provincial Hwy 21; right (east) on Rt. 8; left (north) on CR 1

NEARBY ATTRACTIONS: Stratford Festival, Blyth Festival, Huron Country Playhouse, beaches of Lake Huron, museums, antiques, specialty shopping

Inn At Willow Pond

A fine collection of Mexican and Southwestern folk art

Bea and Chuck Delpapa, Innkeepers
41932 S.R. 517
Lisbon, OH
(888) 345-2809
www.virtualcities.com/oh/
willowpond.htm

RATES & RESERVATIONS:
Hours: 7 a.m.–10 p.m.;
Season: Year round;
Rates: $$$;
Specials: Singles;
Reservations recommended;
Check, Visa, MC, Disc accepted

ACCOMMODATIONS:
3 rooms w/bath

AMENITIES: Phone in room,
air cond., hot tub

MEALS: Full breakfast, snacks

SPECIAL CONSIDERATIONS:
Cat living at inn;
Not fully handicapped accessible;
Parking available: Lot

Aspiring innkeepers should visit the Inn at Willow Pond and take some notes from owners/innkeepers Bea and Chuck Delpapa. They opened their inn in 1998, and in two short years have seen a steady flow of first-time guests as well as satisfied returnees. What brings them back to this 1860s New England farmhouse in Columbiana County?

For some, it is the joy of finding a different style of accommodation. The weathered brown exterior of this house provides a shell for Southwestern decor and an extensive collection of Mexican folk art that this couple has accumulated in their travels. Transplanted from Colorado to Ohio, the Delpapas have arranged their stunning collection against a simpler backdrop of Shaker and arts and crafts furnishings, resulting in a comfortable home rather than a museum-like setting. Should you wonder about those Mexican dolls on the wall of the great room or the masks lined up over the Jacuzzi in the Santa Fe Room, just ask. Bea, an avid collector, and Chuck, an artist/ designer, will give you a history of the piece as well as background on the artist.

Another reason folks come back to the Inn at Willow Pond is Bea's cooking. This excellent cook previously ran a cooking school in Lakewood and is happy to prepare an authentic Mexican breakfast. I enjoyed huevos Oaxacanos, Mexican hash browns, and refried beans. Bea freezes the chiles and tomatillos she grows in her garden and picks up fresh eggs from her neighbor. An alternate option is the country breakfast featuring homebaked breads, a hot entree, and homemade jams and jellies. I was welcomed to this inn on a frigid winter day with a comforting cup of herbal tea, just-from-the-oven oatmeal cookies, and conversation with Bea. At 6:00 p.m., everyone is invited to a wine and cheese hour in the gathering room for a chance to get to know the other guests. Returning from dinner at a nearby restaurant that night, I found fresh flowers, candlelight, chocolates, and a carafe of ice water in my room. These are the special touches that make this inn one you want to come back to again.

I loved the view from the dining table on my February visit—a winter landscape of snow-flecked trees and birds fighting for a place on the feeders outside the window. I could imagine the same scene in other seasons, when migrating waterfowl stop by Willow Pond or when the gardens are in full bloom. A cozy sitting room with shelves alternating books and folk art provides a quiet spot to read or watch videos.

Three guest rooms showcase the Southwest decor. The Sante Fe Room, largest of the three, is in the oldest part of the house and has a king-size bed with a bent willow headboard, wood carvings from Oaxaca, Mexico, and a Shaker rocker by the fireplace. The generous size bath features a Jacuzzi tub and walk-in shower. The Taos Room contains examples of the Delpapas' varied collections—an antique armoire from Eastern Europe, a Shaker nightstand, and a writing table from the arts and crafts period. Mexican baskets and a display of sun faces from Mexican, Italian, and American ceramists complete this room. Upstairs, the Cordova Room welcomes with wooden shutters, a yellow duvet-topped queen-size bed, a hand-woven wool rug from Oaxaca, and an antique easy chair.

Once you've stayed at the Inn at Willow Pond, Bea will keep you abreast of events and specials at the inn through her newsletter, *Willow Ponderings*.

THINGS TO DO: The Delpapas provide guests with a list of local crafters, and I whiled away a morning touring the back roads of Columbiana County to find these artisans who work out of their homes. Linda Bertanzetti weaves cotton and wool rugs in an interesting collection of small outbuildings at her place. Next stop was Sue Hahn's Old Time Baskets, where Sue invited me to watch her weave a basket. Near Lisbon, artisan and blacksmith Ken Crawford hand-forges designs for decorative and functional pieces for the home and yard. A final stop was at Naomi Shaum's shop filled with Amish quilts and handcrafts. With no set hours, it's important to call ahead to these crafters to make sure you'll find them at home.

Make reservations for dinner at the Spread Eagle Tavern in Hanoverton or Lock 24, an 1830s barn on the Sandy and Beaver Canal in Elkton that has been converted into a restaurant and shops. Devotees of diners will want to stop at the Steel Trolley, a 1950s stainless steel diner where you can get breakfast around the clock.

DIRECTIONS: I-80 to exit 42 for I-76; east on I-76 to exit 16 for SR 7; south on SR 7; right (west) on SR 558; left (south) on SR 517; on right

NEARBY ATTRACTIONS: Fiestaware factory, crafts, antiques, hiking, Beaver Creek State Park, Mennonite farm stands, birding, boating, horseback riding

Glenlaurel, a Scottish Country Inn

Relax to the sound of bagpipes in the Loch Ness Pub.

Michael Daniels, Innkeeper
14940 Mt. Olive Rd.
Rockbridge, OH
(800) 809-7378
www.glenlaurelinn.com

RATES & RESERVATIONS:
Hours: 9 a.m.–7 p.m.;
Season: Year round; Rates: $$$$;
Specials: Anniversary discount;
Two-night minimum stay required on
weekends; Reservations required;
Check, Visa, MC, Disc, Amex accepted

ACCOMMODATIONS:
4 rooms w/bath; 3 suites w/bath

AMENITIES: Hot tub, spa,
phone in room, air cond., fireplaces

MEALS: Full breakfast, dinner,
lunch basket, snacks

SPECIAL CONSIDERATIONS:
Handicapped accessible;
Parking available: Lot

Scotland awaits at Glenlaurel. Owner/innkeeper Michael Daniels had a lifelong dream of building an inn and looked to his Scottish and Welsh ancestral lineage when he developed Glenlaurel. A wide swath of green meadow leads to the stone and stucco Manor House in southern Ohio's Hocking Hills, where we were welcomed into a small sitting room for afternoon tea by the fire.

Guests who want to stroll down to dinner can book one of four luxurious traditional rooms/suites in the Manor House, with queen beds, gas log fireplaces, and two-person whirlpool tubs. We stayed in the Carriage House, a mere hundred feet from the Manor House, and found the Douglas Highlander Suite to be at one with nature. The bedroom/sitting room looks out to the woods in all directions, and the muted color scheme used for the duvet and love seat blends with the view. Decorative accents were simple, natural materials. A corner whirlpool tub for two, a cheery green gas log stove in the corner, a kitchenette, and a deck that extended into the treetops made this suite an exceptional getaway. Upstairs in the Carriage House, two garret rooms off a central sitting room and kitchenette offer the perfect accommodation for two couples. There are four wooded cottages on Thistle Ridge, a 10-minute walk from the Manor House. After checking out the Drummond, a cottage done up in royal blue, cream, and red with a fireplace between the sitting room and bedroom, a screened-in porch, hot tub on the deck, and a kitchenette, I wished I could stay there a week. You soon feel like a pampered guest in the well-appointed rooms in this inn, with Egyptian cotton towels, luxurious suede-like robes, and fine toiletries. Treat yourself to an hour of relaxation in the newly constructed Glenlaurel Grotto, where a certified practitioner on staff offers a session of Watsu, a relatively new form of bodywork, in the Watsu pool.

At Glenlaurel, guests gather downstairs in the Loch Ness Pub before dinner. As we entered the cozy space, friendly banter and the clink of ice against glass greeted us. Darts are the game here, and comfy seating by the fire invites socializing. At seven o'clock sharp, the sound of bagpipes quieted the group and we were piped to dinner to the tune of "Scotland the Brave." Michael brought a piper from Scotland to Hocking Hills to live at Glenlaurel and play daily. The piping prior to dinner isn't the only time you might hear bagpipes during your stay; perhaps while hiking the trails, you'll catch the piper's melancholy wail from the Camusfearna Gorge—you'll have to remind yourself you're not in Scotland.

Our table in the Glasgow Dining Room was marked by a place card with the menu for the evening. The room is elegant and romantic, with a beamed ceiling, diamond windows reflecting the candlelight, and tables spaced far enough apart to allow privacy. Once seated, Michael welcomes guests and recites a poem appropriate for the occasion. The pac-

ing of our dinner service was leisurely but even. The staff at Glenlaurel do an exceptional job of being sensitive not only to the guests' needs but also to Michael's philosophy and reasons for creating this inn. Intimacy is key, and once the first course was served, staff moved quietly about the dining room but never intruded. We savored the culinary offerings, from a roasted red pepper bisque starter to the seared tuna entree served with garlic lemon rice and the freshest of vegetables, finishing with an espresso chocolate crème brûlée. As we were finishing our coffee, Chef Shannon came around to each table to chat—another nice touch indicative of Glenlaurel's style. A five course prix fixe dinner is served Sunday through Friday, and a special seven-course New Zealand rack of lamb on Saturday evening. We returned to the Glasgow Dining Room the next morning for breakfast, with a choice of blueberry griddle cakes or an omelet with red peppers and portabello mushrooms, scones, and freshly squeezed orange juice.

If you arrive in the Hocking Hills a bit of a skeptic, you may leave thinking of yourself as a dreamer and true romantic. Glenlaurel gets to you—the sound of rushing water as you walk the gorge, finding the unexpected (like a swing for two near the waterfall), the quiet of the woods broken only by birdsong. These are some of the magical moments Michael intended for guests to discover. And guests return—for weddings, for special occasions like anniversaries, or for no reason at all other than the chance to spend time once again at this inn called "The Premier Romantic Getaway in the Midwest" by *Country Inns Magazine*. Glenlaurel has been a member of the Independent Innkeepers' Association since 1995.

DIRECTIONS: I-71 to exit 107 for I-70; east on I-70 to exit 105A for US 33; (south) on US 33; right (east) on SR 180; left (south) on Mt. Olive Rd.; on left

NEARBY ATTRACTIONS: Hocking Hills State Park, Logan antique and craft malls, Lake Logan, swimming and fishing

Inn at Union Pier

Enjoy the warmth and beauty of Swedish ceramic cylindrical fireplaces—Kakelugns.

Joyce and Mark Pitts, Innkeepers
9708 Berrien
Union Pier, MI
(616) 469-4700
www.innatunionpier.com

RATES & RESERVATIONS:
Hours: 8 a.m.–11 p.m.;
Season: Year round; Rates: $$$$; Specials: Corporate, off season weekday packages;
Two-night minimum stay required on weekends, 3 nights on holidays;
Reservations recommended;
Visa, Check, MC, Disc accepted

ACCOMMODATIONS:
14 rooms w/bath; 2 suites w/bath

AMENITIES: Hot tub, sauna, spa, cable TV, phone in room, air cond., bicycles, lawn games, beach chairs, antiques Swedish fireplaces.

MEALS: Full breakfast, snacks

SPECIAL CONSIDERATIONS:
Handicapped accessible;
Parking available: Lot, on street

When we arrived in quaint Union Pier in southwestern Michigan's scenic Harbor Country, we felt something familiar about the place. It is one of those summer communities that families return to year after year, with well-kept cottages lined up alongside bed and breakfast inns. Lake Michigan's white sand beaches beckon visitors for summer stays or weekend getaways.

The Inn at Union Pier is an inviting complex of three houses with blue exteriors complemented by white latticework and numerous porches and balconies. We stayed in the largest of the three, the Great House, and found it to be a well-run hostelry.

The inn has an interesting history and is just one of the accommodations in this community that are part of the renaissance of resort properties. It was built in the 1920s as Karonsky's Hotel; Madeleine and Bill Reinke had the vision to buy the building in a dilapidated state in 1983, and spent two years renovating it. Joyce and Mark Pitts purchased the inn in 1993.

An eclectic mix of antiques and painted furniture fills the 16 rooms of the inn. It's a refreshing Scandinavian style, with polished hardwood floors, pristine white curtains, and rooms painted in pastels. The many windows of the inn and white painted woodwork make for a light-filled interior. But it is the antique Swedish ceramic cylindrical fireplaces, the Kakelugns, that distinguish the place. Imported from Sweden, the Kakelugns were disassembled, shipped to the inn, and reconstructed by two Swedish artisans. Each is unique and beautiful. Dainty blue flowers accent the white tile on the Kakelugn in the Larkspur, a large sunny room in the Great House. A queen-size four-poster bed with a floral comforter, and comfy chairs, complete the room. Across the hall in the Chardonnay Room, grape clusters on the Kakelugn are repeated at the footboard of the painted original 1930s beds. The corner fireplace in our room, with a dandelion motif, provided warmth and a pleasant glow on a chilly spring evening.

Across the flagstone courtyard from the Great House is the Pier House with six more rooms (and six more Kakelugns). Madeline's Room opens to a private balcony; the Beachcomber's porch overlooks the English garden.

A final accommodation is the Cottage of the Four Seasons, with four guest rooms. Our favorite was the Spring Room, with lavender walls, a white iron-and-brass bed, and a collection of Swedish artist Carl Larson's prints.

Part of the charm of the Inn at Union Pier are the little touches like hand-painted signs over each doorway identifying rooms, needlepoint "do not disturb" signs, and, in the lobby, a well-organized guide to the area. The spacious great room, anchored by yet another massive Kakel-

ugn, is a natural gathering place where local wine and popcorn are set out each evening. Breakfasts at Union Pier are leisurely affairs served in a dining room with windows looking out on the garden. Favorite entrees include vegetarian eggs Benedict and apple cheddar frittatas.

The Inn at Union Pier was chosen as "One of the Best Small Inns" by *Chicago Magazine* and has also been featured in *Country Living* and on the Travel Channel's "Romantic Inns of America." Joyce and Mark, who left high-stress careers in Chicago to run this inn, have hosted corporate groups, family reunions, and small weddings, as well as many returning guests.

THINGS TO DO: The inn is only 200 steps from the beach (Joyce counted them); it's delightful to return from a day at the shore and soak in the sauna and hot tub. You can take the inn's bicycles on the quiet country roads, play croquet, or browse the antique shops, galleries, and boutiques in the area. Union Pier is in the fruit belt, with many orchards and farm markets, and some of that fruit appears in the next morning's pancakes and muffins. We headed to nearby Miller's for dinner, and the highly recommended restaurant didn't disappoint. Seated at a table looking out to a beautifully landscaped yard with big old trees, we dined on shrimp pesto pasta and grilled Norwegian salmon, and didn't leave until we tasted the signature dessert, an award-winning flourless chocolate cake. A popular casual eatery, the Red Arrow Roadhouse is an easy walk from the inn. You can combine a tour of the Tabor Hill Winery and a meal at their restaurant overlooking the vineyards.

DIRECTIONS: I-80 to exit 72 for US 31; north on US 31 to exit 3 for US 12; west on US 12; right on Lakeside; left on Union Pier; right on Locke; left on Red Arrow; left on Berrien; on left

NEARBY ATTRACTIONS: Warren Dunes State Park, Tabor Mill, Heart of the Vineyard Winery, Prime Outlet Mall, Notre Dame University

ALPHABETICAL INDEX

GEOGRAPHICAL INDEX

IDEA INDEX

Little Inn of Bayfield, Bayfield, ONT, 152
Mill House B&B, Grand Rapids, OH, 183
Mount Vernon House, Mount Vernon, OH, 207
Old Stone House, Marblehead, OH, 120
Outback Inn B&B, McConnelsville, OH, 136
Pitzer-Cooper House, Newark, OH, 87
Red Maple Inn, Burton Village, OH, 29
Spread Eagle Tavern and Inn, Hanoverton, OH, 32
The Spencer, Chautauqua, NY, 231
Wagner's 1844 Inn, Sandusky, OH, 115
Water's Edge Retreat, Kelleys Island, OH, 123
Whispering Pines B&B, Atwood Lake, OH, 91
White Oak Inn, Danville, OH, 94
William Seward Inn, Westfield, NY, 150

Birding
Benmiller Inn, Goderich, ONT, 237
Blackfork Inn, Loudonville, OH, 70
Fitzgerald's Irish B&B, Painesville, OH, 14
Frederick Fitting House, Bellville, OH, 75
Glenlaurel, Rockbridge, OH, 242
Hasseman House Inn, Wilmot, OH, 54
Heartland Country Resort, Fredericktown, OH, 78
Inn at Brandywine Falls, Sagamore Hills, OH, 20
Inn at Cedar Falls, Logan, OH, 130
Inn at Honey Run, Millersburg, OH, 57
Inn at Union Pier, Union Pier, MI, 245
Inn At Willow Pond, Lisbon, OH, 239
Little Inn of Bayfield, Bayfield, ONT, 152
Mill House B&B, Grand Rapids, OH, 183
Miller Haus, Walnut Creek, OH, 60
Oak Ridge Inn, Walnut Creek, OH, 63
Old Stone House, Marblehead, OH, 120
Red Gables B&B, Sandusky, OH, 118
Red Maple Inn, Burton Village, OH, 29
The Spencer, Chautauqua, NY, 231
Vineyard B&B, Put-in-Bay, OH, 126
Wagner's 1844 Inn, Sandusky, OH, 115
Water's Edge Retreat, Kelleys Island, OH, 123
Whispering Pines B&B, Atwood Lake, OH, 91
White Oak Inn, Danville, OH, 94

Boating
Benmiller Inn, Goderich, ONT, 237
Blackfork Inn, Loudonville, OH, 70
Captain Gilchrist Guesthouse, Vermilion, OH, 107
Captain Montague's B&B, Huron, OH, 112
Fitzgerald's Irish B&B, Painesville, OH, 14
Frederick Fitting House, Bellville, OH, 75
Georgian Manor Inn, Norwalk, OH, 109
Inn at Brandywine Falls, Sagamore Hills, OH, 20
Inn at Dresden, Dresden, OH, 81
Inn at Union Pier, Union Pier, MI, 245
Little Inn of Bayfield, Bayfield, ONT, 152
Michael Cahill B&B, Ashtabula, OH, 102
Old Stone House, Marblehead, OH, 120
Outback Inn B&B, McConnelsville, OH, 136
Pitzer-Cooper House, Newark, OH, 87
Red Gables B&B, Sandusky, OH, 118
Searle House, Plymouth, OH, 89
Spread Eagle Tavern and Inn, Hanoverton, OH, 32
The Spencer, Chautauqua, NY, 231
Vineyard B&B, Put-in-Bay, OH, 126

Wagner's 1844 Inn, Sandusky, OH, 115
Warner-Concord Farms, Unionville, OH, 105
Water's Edge Retreat, Kelleys Island, OH, 123
Whispering Pines B&B, Atwood Lake, OH, 91
White Oak Inn, Danville, OH, 94
William Seward Inn, Westfield, NY, 150
Children welcome
Captain Gilchrist Guesthouse, Vermilion, OH, 107
Checkerberry Inn, Goshen, IN, 139
Fitzgerald's Irish B&B, Painesville, OH, 14
Hasseman House Inn, Wilmot, OH, 54
Heartland Country Resort, Fredericktown, OH, 78
Hiram Inn, Hiram, OH, 199
Inn at Brandywine Falls, Sagamore Hills, OH, 20
Inn at Cedar Falls, Logan, OH, 130
Inn at Dresden, Dresden, OH, 81
Inn at Honey Run, Millersburg, OH, 57
John Foos Manor B&B, Springfield, OH, 218
Michael Cahill B&B, Ashtabula, OH, 102
Mount Vernon House, Mount Vernon, OH, 207
Oak Ridge Inn, Walnut Creek, OH, 63
Old Stone House, Marblehead, OH, 120
Red Gables B&B, Sandusky, OH, 118
Red Maple Inn, Burton Village, OH, 29
The Spencer, Chautauqua, NY, 231
William Seward Inn, Westfield, NY, 150

Conference/meeting facilities
50 Lincoln Inn, Columbus, OH, 221
Baricelli Inn, Cleveland, OH, 163
Benmiller Inn, Goderich, ONT, 237
Captain Montague's B&B, Huron, OH, 112
Checkerberry Inn, Goshen, IN, 139
Georgian Manor Inn, Norwalk, OH, 109
Heartland Country Resort, Fredericktown, OH, 78
Hiram Inn, Hiram, OH, 199
Inn at Cedar Falls, Logan, OH, 130
Inn at Georgian Place, Somerset, PA, 144
Inn at Honey Run, Millersburg, OH, 57
Inn at Union Pier, Union Pier, MI, 245
Inn of Chagrin Falls, Chagrin Falls, OH, 26
Little Inn of Bayfield, Bayfield, ONT, 152
Morning Glory Inn, Pittsburgh, PA, 174
O'Neil House B&B, Akron, OH, 160
Oak Ridge Inn, Walnut Creek, OH, 63
Old Northside Inn, Indianapolis, IN, 234
Old Stone House, Marblehead, OH, 120
Red Maple Inn, Burton Village, OH, 29
Spread Eagle Tavern and Inn, Hanoverton, OH, 32
The Spencer, Chautauqua, NY, 231
White Oak Inn, Danville, OH, 94
Wooster Inn, Wooster, OH, 190
Worthington Inn, Worthington, OH, 172
Zelcova Country Manor, Tiffin, OH, 196

Cross-country skiing
Benmiller Inn, Goderich, ONT, 237
Blackfork Inn, Loudonville, OH, 70
Fitzgerald's Irish B&B, Painesville, OH, 14
Heartland Country Resort, Fredericktown, OH, 78
Inn at Brandywine Falls, Sagamore Hills, OH, 20
Inn at Georgian Place, Somerset, PA, 144
Inn at Union Pier, Union Pier, MI, 245

Inn of Chagrin Falls, *Chagrin Falls, OH*, 26
Little Inn of Bayfield, *Bayfield, ONT*, 152
Mount Vernon House, *Mount Vernon, OH*, 207
Red Maple Inn, *Burton Village, OH*, 29
The Spencer, *Chautauqua, NY*, 231
Warner-Concord Farms, *Unionville, OH*, 105
William Seward Inn, *Westfield, NY*, 150
Winfield B&B, *Ashland, OH*, 97
Downhill skiing
Fitzgerald's Irish B&B, *Painesville, OH*, 14
Frederick Fitting House, *Bellville, OH*, 75
Heartland Country Resort, *Fredericktown, OH*, 78
Inn at Brandywine Falls, *Sagamore Hills, OH*, 20
Inn at Georgian Place, *Somerset, PA*, 144
Warner-Concord Farms, *Unionville, OH*, 105
William Seward Inn, *Westfield, NY*, 150

Farm destination
Felicity Farms B&B, *Beaver, PA*, 147
Heartland Country Resort, *Fredericktown, OH*, 78
Inn at Brandywine Falls, *Sagamore Hills, OH*, 20
Vineyard B&B, *Put-in-Bay, OH*, 126

Fishing
Benmiller Inn, *Goderich, ONT*, 237
Blackfork Inn, *Loudonville, OH*, 70
Captain Gilchrist Guesthouse, *Vermilion, OH*, 107
Captain Montague's B&B, *Huron, OH*, 112
Fitzgerald's Irish B&B, *Painesville, OH*, 14
Frederick Fitting House, *Bellville, OH*, 75
Gambier House B&B, *Gambier, OH*, 202
Georgian Manor Inn, *Norwalk , OH*, 109
Heartland Country Resort, *Fredericktown, OH*, 78
Hiram Inn, *Hiram, OH*, 199
Inn at Brandywine Falls, *Sagamore Hills, OH*, 20
Inn at Dresden, *Dresden, OH*, 81
Michael Cahill B&B, *Ashtabula, OH*, 102
Mount Vernon House, *Mount Vernon, OH*, 207
Old Stone House, *Marblehead, OH*, 120
Outback Inn B&B, *McConnelsville, OH*, 136
Pitzer-Cooper House, *Newark, OH*, 87
Red Gables B&B, *Sandusky, OH*, 118
Spread Eagle Tavern and Inn, *Hanoverton, OH*, 32
The Spencer, *Chautauqua, NY*, 231
Vineyard B&B, *Put-in-Bay, OH*, 126
Wagner's 1844 Inn, *Sandusky, OH*, 115
Warner-Concord Farms, *Unionville, OH*, 105
Water's Edge Retreat, *Kelleys Island, OH*, 123
Whispering Pines B&B, *Atwood Lake, OH*, 91
White Oak Inn, *Danville, OH*, 94
William Seward Inn, *Westfield, NY*, 150

Fitness center
Benmiller Inn, *Goderich, ONT*, 237
Inn at Dresden, *Dresden, OH*, 81
Red Maple Inn, *Burton Village, OH*, 29

Gardens
Black Squirrel Inn B&B, *Wooster, OH*, 188
Blackfork Inn, *Loudonville, OH*, 70
Burl Manor B&B, *Lebanon, OH*, 133
Captain Montague's B&B, *Huron, OH*, 112
Checkerberry Inn, *Goshen, IN*, 139

College Inn, *Westerville, OH*, 214
Cowger House #9, *Zoar, OH*, 73
Felicity Farms B&B, *Beaver, PA*, 147
Fitzgerald's Irish B&B, *Painesville, OH*, 14
Flannigan's Historic Guest House, *Hudson, OH*, 17
Frederick Fitting House, *Bellville, OH*, 75
Gambier House B&B, *Gambier, OH*, 202
Georgian Manor Inn, *Norwalk , OH*, 109
Harrison House B&B, *Columbus, OH*, 169
Hasseman House Inn, *Wilmot, OH*, 54
Heartland Country Resort, *Fredericktown, OH*, 78
Inn at Brandywine Falls, *Sagamore Hills, OH*, 20
Inn at Cedar Falls, *Logan, OH*, 130
Inn at the Green, *Poland, OH*, 23
Inn at Union Pier, *Union Pier, MI*, 245
Inn At Willow Pond, *Lisbon, OH*, 239
Inn of Chagrin Falls, *Chagrin Falls, OH*, 26
Ivy Tree Inn and Garden, *Oberlin, OH*, 211
Kingswood Inn, *Kingsville, ONT*, 155
Little Inn of Bayfield, *Bayfield, ONT*, 152
Mill House B&B, *Grand Rapids, OH*, 183
Miller Haus, *Walnut Creek, OH*, 60
Morning Glory Inn, *Pittsburgh, PA*, 174
Mount Vernon House, *Mount Vernon, OH*, 207
O'Neil House B&B, *Akron, OH*, 160
Old Northside Inn, *Indianapolis, IN*, 234
Olde World B&B, *Dover, OH*, 66
Pitzer-Cooper House, *Newark, OH*, 87
Porch House, *Granville, OH*, 193
Red Maple Inn, *Burton Village, OH*, 29
Searle House, *Plymouth, OH*, 89
The Spencer, *Chautauqua, NY*, 231
Walker-Johnson Inn, *Middlefield, OH*, 35
Whispering Pines B&B, *Atwood Lake, OH*, 91
William Seward Inn, *Westfield, NY*, 150
Winfield B&B, *Ashland, OH*, 97
Wooster Inn, *Wooster, OH*, 190
Zelcova Country Manor, *Tiffin, OH*, 196

Golf nearby (within 10 miles)
Black Squirrel Inn B&B, *Wooster, OH*, 188
Blackfork Inn, *Loudonville, OH*, 70
Burl Manor B&B, *Lebanon, OH*, 133
Captain Gilchrist Guesthouse, *Vermilion, OH*, 107
Captain Montague's B&B, *Huron, OH*, 112
Checkerberry Inn, *Goshen, IN*, 139
College Inn, *Westerville, OH*, 214
Cowger House #9, *Zoar, OH*, 73
Felicity Farms B&B, *Beaver, PA*, 147
Fitzgerald's Irish B&B, *Painesville, OH*, 14
Flannigan's Historic Guest House, *Hudson, OH*, 17
Frederick Fitting House, *Bellville, OH*, 75
Friendship House B&B, *New Concord, OH*, 209
Gambier House B&B, *Gambier, OH*, 202
Georgian Manor Inn, *Norwalk , OH*, 109
Hasseman House Inn, *Wilmot, OH*, 54
Heartland Country Resort, *Fredericktown, OH*, 78
Hiram D. Ellis Inn, *Blissfield, MI*, 180
Hiram Inn, *Hiram, OH*, 199
Inn at Brandywine Falls, *Sagamore Hills, OH*, 20
Inn at Dresden, *Dresden, OH*, 81
Inn at the Green, *Poland, OH*, 23
Inn at Union Pier, *Union Pier, MI*, 245